THE
GROUPSEX
TAPES

THE GROUPSEX TAPES

*98 Participants in the Newest, Most Revolutionary
Release of Sexual Inhibitions Tell What
They Do, Why They Do It, and What It Reveals
About New Dimensions in Male-Female
Relationships*

by
Paul Rubenstein
and
Herbert Margolis

DAVID McKAY COMPANY, INC.
New York

There is no intent to identify the material in this book with any individual, living or dead. In order to preserve the anonymity of those who were kind enough to talk with us, as well as the anonymity of others to whom they referred in conversation, we have used fictional names for all individuals and have also fictionalized occupations (except that of Dr. X), geographical locations and other data which might be thought to identify any individual.

Table of Contents

FATHERS, MOTHERS, AND
THEIR CHILDREN

THE GROUPSEX PHENOMENON

Foreword by Martin Grotjahn, M.D.

There is no doubt in my mind that this is an important book and a significant, original contribution to man's knowledge of sex.

It is also a useful book that can have, for many readers, the same liberating effect that was gained by some of the participants of the parties described in this volume.

I may add that I read it with great fascination, and in no place did I find obscenity described, which may be taken as praise or condemnation. The book is well written, with restraint and yet full of relevant details. Some of the taped interviews will, I think, become classics.

In sum, this book proves again that the average person is capable of learning more than we thought he could learn—that he is capable of reaching great heights of sexual fulfillment, which can be an ego-strengthening experience. It also seems to show that the average person is well gifted to accept, to tolerate and to enjoy the highest degree of freedom.

Acknowledgments

We doubt very much whether this book would ever have been completed had it not been for the trust and generosity of the people we interviewed. They accommodated our schedule, sometimes at no little inconvenience, opened their homes and their feelings with but one stipulation—that we allow them to speak freely.

The unselfishness, good humor, and tireless energy of our secretaries were of enormous importance. They worked under sometimes almost impossible pressures, transcribing information and helping meet the deadlines of preparing a manuscript—which kept growing and growing.

Last, but hardly least, we thank our wives for letting us get into this project—but not too deeply.

THE GROUPSEX TAPES

PART I

Making The Scene

1

Swinging Is Here to Stay

In the spring of 1969 one of us, Paul Rubenstein, working as a television news writer in Los Angeles, came across rumors of a sizable group of people in the San Fernando Valley who were said to be engaged in group sexual activities on a considerable scale. The reports were so detailed that they seemed certain to contain at least some truth.

A few weeks later at lunch with Herbert Margolis, a long-time friend who was developing film properties, the conversation turned to these reports of groupsex. We agreed that anyone who would swing was either a deviate or on drugs or determined to get a divorce. Nevertheless, the novel (to us) idea that respectable married couples were swinging and that some of them might even be our next-door neighbors, piqued our curiosity.

We decided to investigate, but our initial contact with the swinging scene came about quite by accident. Herb was flying North on business and became involved in a casual conversation with the passenger next to him. The talk moved from the weather to politics, from there on to morality and then to married couples who swing. The man and his wife happened to be swingers. They knew a number of swinging husbands and wives in Los Angeles and after a relaxed atmosphere was established, they disclosed one possible source of substantial information about groupsex in our area.

Meanwhile, Paul had found a friend of a friend who was a swinger. When we got together we discovered that we had come up with the same name: a man who had been swinging for more years than he cared to recall. He was considered something of a pioneer and had also traveled extensively to other parts of the country to do what evidently came naturally to him.

We arranged to meet this informant and, almost as an afterthought, took along a tape recorder, just on the off-chance that the conversation might turn out to be extended.

We suspected that we would meet a super-muscular physical specimen. Instead, he was middle-aged, middle-sized, middle everything, except that he talked for four hours about swinging. And everything was said with feeling and with an honesty that came through. He also agreed to introduce us to some of his close friends who were swingers. After that we would have to make our own contacts. It would all depend on whether the first few married couples would respond favorably to us.

As we went over our first tape, we realized that the recorder seemed to be a stimulating conduit. As the reels turned, the thoughts flowed. Sometimes scattered, sometimes fragmented, but always living. We seemed to be encouraging a confessional, a "souling out." That's what we wanted. When consenting adults participate in plural sexuality, their reasons and their emotions go much deeper than the act itself. We were after the totality of the groupsex experience: how it affects value systems, ethical standards and life priorities.

Our sampling was quite random and grew largely out of an accidental accommodation to time and availability of swingers. Nevertheless, the vast majority of those people we interviewed were upper middle class, most of them were married, and we gather that this seems to constitute the majority now involved in the groupsex phenomenon.

Occupations also reflect a cross-section of the upper middle-class scene: medicine, engineering, law, education, the natural and social sciences, arts, and politics. Clearly, the life styles of the swingers in our sampling are traditional.

Dr. L. James Grold, a Los Angeles psychiatrist who has also made inquiries into swinging, found that ". . . respectable middle-class people who a few years back would have been horrified at the thought [of swinging] are now indulging in activities historically coveted only by the wealthy leisure class . . . Our mode of total sexual freedom, the tremendous growth of nude encounter and sensitivity groups, and a lessened fear of pregnancy and venereal disease have all contributed to people's willingness to experiment with different forms of sexual behavior."[1]

The "punch-card, feed out" quality of life within our modern technology may also encourage swinging. A Midwestern college psychologist who is also an ordained minister, Dr. James McHolland, says, "I would predict that 'swinging' as a phenomenon and 'Group Sex' as a subclass of swinging will continue to thrive in the next few years. The social upheavals of our time have resulted in a questioning and temporary overthrow of traditional restraints in many areas." Dr. McHolland concludes: "The growth of this phenomenon does not necessarily establish it as either healthy or morally sound," but he agrees it "may represent a counterthrust to an unconscious societal puritanic emphasis that pleasure is evil."

Exactly where is the swinging subculture? Field studies in Philadelphia, New York, the Southwest, Chicago and other areas in the Midwest indicate that a considerable variety of swinging subcultures exist all over the United States today. Two researchers at the University of California in Berkeley, James R. Smith and his wife, Lynn, said in their study on swinging among marrieds and singles in California: "Generally speaking, our data and our observations indicate that this subculture, at least in California, is composed of relatively mobile, educated, affluent, mostly Caucasian, upper middle-class persons trying, sometimes desperately, to be free of sexual taboos and restrictions upon their sexual lives."[2]

[1] Grold, James L., M.D., "Swinging: Sexual Freedom or Neurotic Escapism." *American Journal of Psychiatry*, October 1970.
[2] Smith, James and Lynn G., "Co-marital Sex and the Sexual Freedom Movement." *Journal of Sex Research*, vol. 6, no. 2., pp. 131–42, May 1970.

What about the mental health of the majority of those who swing? Dr. Gilbert D. Bartell, an anthropologist at Northern Illinois University, suggests in his study of 280 middle-class swingers in the Midwest and southwest: "If one means that swingers are doing something that other people are not doing, and that the others are a majority and the swingers are a minority, then obviously swingers are deviant. The same could be said for any special interest group: parachute jumpers, salt water tropical fish enthusiasts, and other hobbyists. But obviously people think that swingers are deviant and/or sick because their sexual morals are unconventional. It is our position that swinging is absolutely not deviant behavior in terms of American cultural patterns."[3]

Some critics of groupsex dismiss swingers as degenerate sexual demagogues who foster the notion of communal copulation when they really just want to satisfy their sexual appetites. A well-known psychologist, Dr. Albert Ellis, argues differently: "Many people find that they are freer, more labile, and more truly themselves (as distinct from well-behaved conformists) when having promiscuous rather than when having conventional mating relationships . . . Although some sexual varietists . . . believe they *need* plural sex-love affairs for neurotic reasons, almost all healthy individuals, at some time during their lives, strongly *want* such affairs for normal biological and social reasons. When such individuals manage to have their varietist inclinations fulfilled without seriously defeating their other goals and desires and without coming into great conflict with other members of the community, they may well be enhancing their own existence (as well as those of their chosen partners) in a quite harmless manner . . . Promiscuous sex participations enable many males and females to discover exactly what they want, sexually and non-sexually, and to know many other people quite intimately."[4]

While it appears certain that groupsex is on the increase, the subscription lists of swinger magazines, our interviews with owners of swinging clubs, resorts, retreats, and our discussions with many

[3] Bartell, Gilbert D., Ph.D., *GROUP SEX: A Scientist's Eyewitness Report on the American Way of Swinging.* New York: Peter H. Wyden, Inc., 1971.
[4] Ellis, Albert, Ph.D., "Sexual Promiscuity in America," *The Annals of the American Academy of Political & Social Science,* Vol. 378, July 1968.

psychiatrists and social scientists permit no more than the admittedly vague estimate that several million Americans are actively exploring the groupsex phenomenon. Specialized magazines and underground newspapers cater to the swinging crowd via classified ads placed by "modern marrieds" or singles, inviting other interested couples to exchange phone numbers, addresses, and even pictures.

Moreover, the majority of people whom we interviewed had already advanced to a point where answering ads was passé. The stream of "new faces" at swinging parties is so constant that within a month a married couple can accumulate as many new relationships as they want without bothering to place ads.

While large groupsex parties may be attended by twenty-five to one hundred couples, the majority of swingers to whom we talked feel that such orgies tend to become dehumanizing. Most groupsex activities occur at informal, selective parties, involving anywhere from two to fifteen couples, and on any weekend in Los Angeles alone, several hundred swinging parties go on. Our informants report that the pattern is the same in all other major cities across the country and in a surprising number of more sparsely-populated towns.

The use of marijuana appears to be moderate among swingers, and only two couples whom we interviewed had encounters with venereal disease. Swingers are not only almost obsessed with personal cleanliness; they also live by an unwritten rule that the first person who notices a V.D. problem must phone all his recent sexual contacts so that they can seek out medical treatment. Sometimes doctors are among the infected group and can administer antidotes quickly, but the true incidence of V.D. caused by groupsex is unknown.

As to the problem of divorce among swingers, James and Lynn Smith conclude: "The myth is that sexual permissiveness and sexual plurality inevitably cause marital instability and divorce, and that view is just about as true to fact as the now antiquated belief that viewed masturbation as leading to insanity and debility. Both are cases of self-fulfilling prophecies."[5]

Indeed, some studies suggest that swinging supports monog-

[5] Smith, James R. and Lynn, "Co-marital Sex and the Sexual Freedom Movement," *Journal of Sex Research*, vol. 6, no. 2, pp. 131–42, May 1970.

amous marriage. "It keeps the couple together, or at least in the same house," note two assistant professors of sociology, Duane Denfeld and Michael Gordon, at the University of Connecticut. As these researchers point out: "It is an activity which involves common planning and preparation, and provides subject matter for conversation before and after. Thus it could further consolidate the marriage. Finally, the sexual activity that takes place is, to a greater or lesser extent, under the surveillance of each; this means that each exercises control over the extramarital activity of the other, and the danger that the sexual relationship will become a romantic relationship is minimized."[6]

Much of the sexual experimentation that is practiced and preached by swingers is still technically against the law in most (but not all) states, even when practiced by consenting adults in private. The threat of exposure and censure implies a jeopardy to status in the neighborhood, in the family, with one's employer, and at church. Approval is one of the most important needs of swingers, and its absence causes frustration as well as self-defensive attitudes.

We had presumed that the permissiveness of swinging would have a corollary effect on swingers' political views. In our sampling this appears not to be the case. Sex clearly crosses party lines. The politics of the people we interviewed ran from the far right to the far left. If anything, swinging couples seem to be more conservative in terms of political views than one would believe at first examination.

Swingers tend not to be devout practitioners of any religious denomination. We interviewed Catholics, Protestants, and Jews. Some indicated they were agnostics. A few said they were atheists. The largest majority did say they believed in God, and almost all exhibited something of a religious fervor about their groupsex experience.

Their feelings about nudity were particularly fervent because public display of one's body is feared by most newcomers; indeed, it may be the principal barrier to swinging. In recognition of this fear, it is not mandatory at any swinging party for the

[6] Denfeld, Duane, and Gordon, Michael, "The Sociology of Mate Swapping," *ibid.*, pp. 85–99.

participants to be totally naked at all times. Some walk around in the nude while others maintain partial dress. Still others put their clothes back on between sex sessions, although this is relatively rare. Once the clothing barrier drops, other inhibitions seem to fall by the wayside, and this includes anxieties about the comparative dimensions of penises, breasts, and buttocks. We had presumed that the swinging society consists mainly of superior physical specimens. And while the swingers' concern about keeping in good physical shape usually rules out obesity and deformity, the vast majority are just average American types.

What happens to swingers once they become integrated into the sexgroup scene? Dr. James Grold, writing in *The American Journal of Psychiatry*, reflected: ". . . Some swingers awake one morning to discover that they have neglected all of their square friends and limited their activities exclusively to swinging. For some, swinging may become an addiction that is increasingly compelling but less and less satisfying.

"For others the dire consequences predicted by the moralizers do not develop. Instead, swinging becomes an integral part of their lives, not a total preoccupation. For these individuals, sensitive to each other's needs, swinging develops into a highly pleasurable sharing experience adding variety to their lives. They discover not only heightened desire and love for each other but also that their ability to give and receive sexual satisfaction increases with greater experience."

Is swinging really a viable alternative to the Puritan morality? For all troubled marriages? For some? For none?

Among those who read sections of this manuscript before publication, one observer refined these questions further. He was Rabbi Allen Secher, former dean of the National Leadership Institute of the National Federation of Temple Youth. He told us:

"The central issue is: how many swinging married couples have the honest and deep capacity to handle the situation? How many have an understanding of the psychology of groupsex? The majority of those interviewed for this book claim they have. I must admit that I remain skeptical."

The rabbi also felt that some swingers treat their partners as mere sex objects. "In Buberian terms," he said, "the shift is from an I-Thou relationship to and I-It relationship."

7

Yet for all his skepticism, Rabbi Secher conceded that mental hangups of married couples may be reduced by the swinging experience and that it "may have a continual therapeutic value for a woman's sexual life." Above all, the rabbi would make no ultimate judgment. "Far be it from me," he said, "to point a finger and shout, 'Sinner!' "

We are not qualified to judge, either. We are convinced, however, that the groupsex phenomenon is genuine, that it is expanding and will continue to grow. We hope that qualified researchers will find enough merit in our study to undertake more scientific evaluations of the groupsex experience: the emotions that it generates and inhibits; the perceptions that it changes; and the common sense plausibilities that it seems, at times, to challenge. Meanwhile, we feel that much light can be shed just by listening.

2

For the Record

For the record, we met and talked at length with 628 swinging people across the country—in large metropolitan cities and smaller communities. Almost half of them lived in the western half of America, and a majority of those were in California. Our sampling consisted of:

176 married couples	—ages 23 to 56
64 couples living together	—ages 22 to 37
120 singles (65 women and 54 men)	—ages 18 to 35
28 children of swinging parents	—ages 11 to 20

Ninety-three percent of our sample were upper middle-class white people. The remaining seven percent were blacks, Mexican-Americans and Orientals.

Our in-depth interviews involved ninety-eight people from our total sample:

40 married
16 people living together
27 singles (14 women and 13 men)
15 children

The approximate length of each taping session was three and a half hours, which adds up to a total of 343 tape-recorded hours. This does not include additional calls and meetings with many people for follow-up questions and, in some instances, additional taping.

We did edit the tapes to screen out repetitions, change names, occupations, locations, and other identifying information to assure the privacy of all concerned. And considering some of the questions we asked, we sometimes feel we should have provided ourselves with the same anonymity.

3

ALAN:

An Old-Timer Speaks

Alan is forty-eight years old, a musician and composer, widower and the father of three children. He started swinging twenty years ago in California, and continued to swing when he moved to the Midwest. Alan likes to think of himself as one of the pioneers of groupsex parties and is considered by many swingers to be their resident philosopher.

Long ago his hair turned gray. He keeps it cut short but thick, styled every two weeks by the same barber who has cut it for the last ten years. "I call it my Cassius look," he says.

Alan talks with a smile that wrinkles his face into an expression of almost constant satisfaction. He is of average height, around five-foot-nine, broad shoulders, well-trimmed waist. "Let's say I know how to keep in shape," he says. "Most of my exercising comes on weekends."

Alan played for a number of the big bands and then toured with them until he decided that family life and traveling could not be reconciled. He claimed permanent residence in the Midwest in the early fifties and has remained there ever since, composing and working as a musician.

Alan is an early riser. Six o'clock every morning. By seven, he is finished showering, eating and now he is outside enjoying a casual walk. "If it's warm enough, I'll walk to my office. It's only a couple of miles from my apartment. I walked a lot when I was a kid in California. When I had some money I bought a car and then a bigger car. I think sometimes I walk long blocks to remind me of what it was like before all this. Maybe I keep my legs in shape—just in case.

His day is planned so that the first interruption leads to the second and third and fourth. Then he ad-libs the rest of the day, and it can last as long as sixteen hours, nonstop, when he is pressed to complete a composition: "Some people can't function under pressure. I guess I'm a lucky soul. Maybe really I'm not so lucky, but I manage to outlast the clock."

This pace goes on for six days. The weekends are usually limited to making business decisions during the morning and early afternoon, with enough time in the late afternoon to relax before swinging in the evening. Alan says: "Don't shake your head like that. I could work eighteen hours a day knowing the kind of time I'm going to have on my weekends. Swinging is good therapy."

Alan was always used to working. In high school he worked in a shoe store, sold encyclopedias during the summer months, worked as a lifeguard, a camp counselor. He married at twenty and spent the next twenty-three years with one woman. She was a swinger: "We had some great times. If I had it to do all over again, I would not change any of it, any of it, except when my wife died. It was hard . . ."

Alan remembers his early interest in music. He took university courses when he could: music theory, composition. His first job with a band was playing one-nighters all over California. And it all started because his uncle owned a clarinet and gave it to Alan on his tenth birthday.

He considers himself lucky. He made it as a musician, and a lot of talented people don't. He was helped by breaks, timing, and just plain sweat, no secret formula.

His children are not living with him anymore. The oldest son, twenty-three, is in his last year of law school. The younger son, who is twenty-one, is teaching. His daughter, nineteen, is studying abroad.

Alan lives in a high-rise apartment overlooking a lake, with a view of private white yachts that shimmer in the sunlight, and the sleek sailboats, inboards and outboards. From the fifteenth floor, these luxuries look like expensive toys bobbing in a pool of water. Alan likes his six-room apartment for the extra space he can use when his children come to visit him ("It's still their home").

A number of men like Alan are still part of the swinging scene, men who were among the first few who dared depart from normal "partying" to turn to something different, something new. Those who are left, like Alan, have found swinging to be a formula for keeping their bodies and minds young. Since Alan is a veteran and a spokesman for swinging, we decided he would be the logical choice to speak first.

INTERVIEWER: *When did you first become interested in swinging?*

ALAN: Almost twenty years ago. . . . There were four of five of us who used to get together at a nightclub for drinks and we'd put swinging parties together. We'd take dates that we met at the club and go to somebody's house. There we'd have sex together, exchanging girlfriends all through the evening. Just have a ball . . . We continued doing this on and off, with steady girlfriends, and some of us with our wives. In those early days, we were really pioneers, so to speak. It wasn't easy to get your girlfriend or your wife into a swinging relationship . . . We used to get together and discuss why we were swinging, what we were getting out of it . . . And a lot of strange questions came up that really made everybody dig deeper into themselves: "Why am I doing this?" "Is it right?" Lots of soul searching.

INT.: *What about the law and swinging when you started out?*

ALAN: It was very touch and go. We had to swing on the sly, hide, and make sure that we didn't talk too much about it. Most of the time, when we had parties, people took turns watching at the windows and doors. And still there were several parties that the police busted. Oh, we had lots of problems at first . . . But now, it's no sweat.

13

INT.: *After all these years, have there been any significant changes in the swinging scene?*

ALAN: There are more people doing it, it's become an accepted middle-class leisure activity. Maybe the biggest single change is that married couples have taken over. And this has put a new direction on the scene.

INT.: *In what way?*

ALAN: The emphasis now, more than ever before, is on finding new couples . . . Say you start swinging with four of five of your personal friends that you like to be with. If you see those people too often, the sexual excitement wears off as it does in almost any marriage and then the honeymoon is over. This creates one of the big problems in swinging: the need to find enough men to take care of the women. I mean, a man can go to bed with almost any woman because of the animalistic nature of the male, but with a woman it's different. She is still the dreamer; she needs an image of a lover whom she must confront and accept before she can be turned on and have sex. I'd say this is true with most of the women swingers I know.

INT.: *Is this difference cultural or psychological?*

ALAN: It's not cultural, it's psychological . . . Most women are basically romantics. They think that just because a man is six feet two, has shoulders like a football player, muscles and everything else, that he's going to be a fantastic lover. In most cases they're wrong. The big hero type is too busy worrying about his profile ever to take enough time to learn about a woman's sensitivities.

INT.: *Do you think that this knowledge is a key to making a good lover?*

ALAN: You can't be one without it. Of course, I can only comment on my own experiences. I've always tried to find out what makes the woman I'm with tick, and what it's going to take to make me the big man in her eyes . . . Most straight men come on fast, jump on, put it in, start moving up and down and they think that's all there is to making love. Sure, it's great for the man if he's only interested in getting it off. He doesn't stop to realize that the woman is not going to come as fast as he does; or that some women will climax

14

ten, fifteen, twenty times in the course of a very short period while others will come once and they're satisfied and won't need any more . . . No two women are alike. Therefore, a man's ability as a lover depends on his technique, his finesse, and, more than for a woman, it's a matter of control.

INT.: *What do you mean by that in terms of swinging?*

ALAN: To keep the woman climaxing and avoid climaxing myself. In order to be a real success at swinging parties, a man has to be able to sustain himself. He can't just take a ride—wham, bam, thank you ma'am. If he does it and he's through after that, if he's unable to have another erection in a half hour or so, he's not going to be very popular. That's why I study control to sustain a hard-on.

INT.: *Half the male population of America joins me in asking you how you do it.*

ALAN: (laughing) Practice . . . Like anything else, it's mind over matter. It's difficult at first. Sometimes I think of what I have to do the next day at work. If I'm close to the edge of the bed, I'll grab the frame of the bed and pull as if to lift it up. This will stop me from coming although I'll lose a little of my erection . . . I keep this up until I can get a woman to climax several times. When she's really satisfied, then I finally let myself go.

INT.: *Do you think that swinging women have more orgasms on the average than nonswinging women?*

ALAN: That stands to reason, doesn't it? Most swinging women know how to enjoy the sexual experience and make it work for themselves . . . You don't find that too often among the so-called square women because they don't have much of a chance to learn how to relax psychologically or physically, and most of their bed partners are no help. These women, in their climaxes, are muffled—no sound at all—or stiffening. There's no telegraphing to their mates that they're having a climax—no verbalizing; and, therefore, their climaxes do not reach the fullest potential. There's a whole thing about really letting go, and once a woman learns how to do this, she'll be able to climax again, and again, and again—for hours even. I've seen some women who climax until they pass out . . .

15

INT.: *How does that make the man feel?*

ALAN: Great . . . But that brings up the problem I raised earlier. Women, if they want to, can out-screw men. Men can't hold out as long as they should with a woman who really gets them going. They're tired, their backs give out, their legs give out, they come too often and they are through . . . But if the woman is really loose by now she may want to make love for several hours.

INT.: *What happens then?*

ALAN: Generally, the guy ends up hollering for help. If he's lucky, somebody taps him on the shoulder and takes over—you know, keeps it going.

INT.: *How does a woman feel about switching partners during the act of intercourse?*

ALAN: At first, as I told you, she's a romantic. She would resent it, but at this point she's climaxing. She has moved on to a higher condition—sort of a primitive exhilaration. She doesn't care who's in the saddle as long as "who" can keep the experience going for her.

INT.: *That sounds pretty animalistic.*

ALAN: Do you mean bad, vulgar, dirty?

INT.: *I guess that's the feeling I have.*

ALAN: That's not the feeling we get when we're doing it. If you're going to let society dictate the sounds, the gestures and the movements that you use in making love, then "society" is in the saddle—not you, the individual.

INT.: *I take it you feel the human animal has a great need for sex?*

ALAN: The animal in the human does, yes. But through the ages, churches, governments, all those holier-than-thou institutions have done a pretty good job of stifling these needs and fostering sexual taboos . . . And what's it gotten them? What have all these virtuous restrictions led to? A constant, unending need to violate them.

INT.: *But how do you explain to a nonswinger what seems to be an unending preoccupation with sex in the swinging scene?*

ALAN: (shaking his head) You're not seeing it right. A swinger doesn't have to think about sex. He knows he can have it anytime he wants. When you *don't* swing, the need for sex

16

often becomes too important—a hangup. You think about who you're going to date and whether she'll go to bed with you or not. If one girl won't, then it's another girl, and if that one doesn't work, who's next? No one can tell me that this doesn't drain your energies! It affects so many other parts of your life—the way you handle your business, your family, etc. I'll bet when social scientists get around to documenting the swinging experience—I mean, really doing clinical studies on it with an open mind—they'll find out what a freeing experience it is for most of the people indulging in it. I've seen swingers through the years expand and prosper and change drastically for the better. But I don't want to sound like I'm selling swinging. It doesn't need my endorsement . . . I think I'm a better man for it. My wife said that many times and today my business associates feel that way. I don't mean to sound philosophical, but those societies that have been freer with their sex have, historically, been less violent. Maybe they haven't conquered the world, but maybe we'd have a better world if people were less driven in that direction. There are a lot more casualties on the battlefield than we swingers have in bedrooms and living rooms . . . I'll tell you this—almost twenty years ago I stopped pussyfooting around in search of pussy. Now, I'd rather die than kick the habit.

INT.: *Let's talk a little more about this "habit" of yours.* (Interviewer takes out an article from his briefcase.) *Did you ever read this article by Dr. Albert Ellis?* (He hands it to Alan who scans it.)

ALAN: No, but I've heard of the good doctor . . . written lots of books on sex, hasn't he?

INT.: (Nodding) *Have you read any of them?*

ALAN: (Smiling) No.

INT.: *Why?*

ALAN: Should I say I was too busy doing it?

INT.: (Laughing) *That's what this article is all about—sexual promiscuity in America.*

ALAN: (Returning to the article) Promiscuity—I don't think I like that word.

INT.: *Let me read a section from it: "in the more usual sense of*

17

the term, especially as it is used in the United States, promiscuity refers to an individual's having a good many (say, two dozen or more) *sex partners during his entire lifetime or to his having a few bed mates simultaneously or in fairly rapid succession . . ." Would you care to comment on that?*

ALAN: (Shaking his head) if that were really true—it would be terrible. I wonder what he'd say about my sex life if he knew how many women I've taken to bed in twenty years of swinging.

INT.: (smiling) *Can you come up with an approximate figure?*

ALAN: Let's see. It's really hard to figure it—if you want to be serious. In those first five or seven years, when I was putting together parties or going to parties that my friends arranged I used to swing much more frequently than I do now.

INT.: *Can you estimate an average?*

ALAN: Well, in the formative years . . . (reflecting) I would say I went to parties every weekend, Fridays, Saturdays and Sundays. I don't think there were many weekends when I didn't go to bed with, oh . . . (thinking) at least nine to twelve women . . . You got a pencil?

INT.: (Digs one out of a side pocket of his briefcase) *Here . . .*

ALAN: All right, if we're going to do it, let's do it right . . . (He starts scribbling) I'd figure an average of ten women a week, times fifty-two . . .

INT.: (Starts laughing) *Wait a minute, didn't you ever miss a weekend?*

ALAN: You mean time off for good behavior?

INT.: *Something like that. Weren't you ever sick?*

ALAN: Not often . . . Maybe I was out of commission two weeks every year.

INT.: *What about vacations?*

ALAN: It varied. Say I took an average of three to four weeks a year, but I was only taking off from work. The sex went way up on vacations.

INT.: *All right. Let's just figure on fifty weeks a year.*

ALAN: Okay, so you figure fifty times ten for the first seven years. What does that give you?

INT.: *Convulsions . . .* (They both laugh) *I'm sorry, please keep on figuring.*

18

ALAN: I may need a computer.

INT.: *It doesn't matter. No one will believe this anyway.*

ALAN: It comes to . . . 3500 for the first seven years.

INT.: (After a pause) *What about the last thirteen years—how can we average that out?*

ALAN: Will you settle for that same fifty week average?

INT.: *If you say so.*

ALAN: In those last years we're talking about parties mainly on Friday and Saturdays and an average, say, of seven, eight women on a weekend. (He gives the pencil back to the interviewer) You tote it up. This *is* getting silly.

INT.: (Scribbling) *Well, I come up with a total of around 8700 women in twenty years . . .*

ALAN: (Shakes his head rather soberly, seeming more shocked than elated about the disclosure.) Really, that many?

INT.: *What's the matter?*

ALAN: (He is scratching his chin now, his lean body slouches forward, his legs spread out loosely) I don't know. It sort of makes me feel, well . . . old.

PART II

The Couples

---

4 JOHN AND SANDY:

"Swinging Is the Best of All Possible Worlds"

John is thirty-four years old, a graduate of an excellent Eastern Law School and now a partner in a law firm in California. His wife, Sandy, is thirty, a former dental technician, now a housewife, an "active organizer of things" and mother of two children—Angie who is three and Tommy, five.

"Honey, where'd you put my pipe?"

"I didn't put it anywhere, Tommy has it. He's playing enemy submarine and using it as a periscope."

"C'mon Sandy, that thing's expensive."

"That's what you get for leaving your stem around where anyone can pick it up . . ."

"Thanks . . ."

(Enter John and Sandy.)

John walks in and the first thing we notice is his look of controlled panic. His brown hair falls over his face and is mussed in curls around the neck ("executive long"). He gives the impression of being taller that he really is—five-foot-nine—and looks no different than he did when he graduated from law school: eyes deeply set, eyebrows bushy, and they, too, are raveled. His face is square—thick jaws, firm nose—not long, but fitting the strength of his face. He wears a pair of freshly pressed Levi jeans, a shirt open at the collar, a bulky but well-fitting sweater, and tennis shoes which are scuffed. The first day he bought them, Sandy told us, he went in the backyard and rubbed them in the sand to turn them off-white.

Sandy is a redhead, but her complexion is not as fair as one would expect a redhead to have. Rather, it is a mixture of tan and yesterday's sunburn. Her eyes are green. She has a tiny snip nose, full cheeks and always moist, sparkling lips. She's five-foot-two and, as John says, "well stacked." She, too, was wearing Levis, tennis shoes and a western-style blouse.

John and Sandy first met in the dentist's office. She was cleaning his teeth. And John swears his hand slipped accidentally when it touched her as she bent over.

Sandy's version is somewhat different: "He goosed me, pure and simple, when I bent over to turn the water spray on."

Accident or not, that's how they met, started dating, and six months later were married.

John and Sandy refer to themselves as the "everything-goes-wrong-at-the-same-time" kind of family. When we walked in the door we saw why. Angie was running around the house with her pants loose around her ankles and Sandy was in hot pursuit with a change of clothing. Tommy was crying because their over-stuffed Puli dog, had picked up the pipe and was scampering all over the house, looking for the first open door that led outside. John gave Tommy to us while he chased out of the house after the dog who was playing hide-and-seek.

This was a typical weekend. The typical week was just as frantic. John is an early riser. He's up at six in the morning and tries to get in a round of golf when the weather's right, at least nine holes at the club. He is an art collector and has traveled throughout the country to keep up his own gallery of paintings. One room in the home is a private gallery furnished with leather benches that are placed in the middle for anyone to sit and become immersed.

The home has a Mediterranean and Spanish influence. A wrought-iron fence runs the complete width of the lot and huge

21

cement walls run along the sides. The ten-room house is off-white stucco, and four wooden columns run from the top of the red tile overhanging roof to the long front porch which takes up the entire front of the house.

In the order of her priorities Sandy is: volunteer mother for Tommy's grammar school, two days a week when a girl comes in to take care of Angie. That's Monday and Wednesday. Tuesday and Thursday it's work around the house. Friday is her leisure day, preparing for the weekend of swinging.

John and Sandy have been married for seven years, and swinging for the last five years.

INTERVIEWER: *Is there a difference between love and sex?*

SANDY: Yes. They have nothing to do with each other. Really, I'm not kidding. I've gone to bed with some pretty groovy men since I've been married to John. Sexually, I wouldn't be married to any of them. John's the best in bed.

INT.: *Can you explain the difference?*

SANDY: You don't have to fall in love with a person, have a crush on him, just because you're having intercourse with him. Swinging is physical.

JOHN: That's very true. If I'm pleasuring another woman, that doesn't mean that I love my wife any less.

SANDY: So many people think that if a husband and wife go to a swinging party, why don't they get a divorce? . . . Because, after all, they're having sex with other married couples.

JOHN: I don't know of any people who swing and wind up getting divorced. In fact, we know a lot of swingers who met each other at parties and are now getting married and continue to swing.

SANDY: We're not saying that everyone who swings is going to end up being your close friend. Some swingers we've met we don't like.

INT.: *What happens then?*

SANDY: We don't swing with them. It's like any other social situation. The people you don't like or don't want to be with you simply avoid. But I can tell you one thing: we've met better people, more friendly, honest people in swinging than we have at straight parties . . . People who go to swinging parties know how to handle it if they come up to me and say, "Let's go to bed," and I say, "No, thank you, let's have a drink and talk instead."

INT.: *Did you have any sexual barriers to break down before you started swinging?*

SANDY: No. I had been dating before I was married and going to bed with men I liked. Sex was never a serious problem to me —that is, the enjoyment of it . . . John took me to an orgy the first time out and everything happened at once. I didn't take one step at a time. If you *have* any inhibitions, you lose them fast at an orgy.

JOHN: That's all so true.

SANDY: At that first swinging party, a black girl went down on me, gave me head . . . And I didn't realize what was going on until later.

INT.: *You didn't know she was there?*

SANDY: That's right. There were two or three men kissing me, too. One of them, I believe, was on top of me, so I couldn't see who was pleasuring me at the other end. I couldn't tell who was doing what, but I didn't care because the feeling was beautiful.

INT.: *Did it make any difference when you found that a woman was also pleasuring you?*

SANDY: No. The fact that she was black didn't make any difference either.

INT.: *John, were you close to Sandy when this was happening?*

JOHN: I was across the room with another group of people, but I was thinking about Sandy all the time because every once in a while I'd peek up from the pile of bodies I was under and see Sandy enjoying herself. I could also hear her.

SANDY: Yes, I guess I'm somewhat of a yeller when it comes to sex. I just like to verbalize, show my enjoyment to the other men. And making loud, sighing noises and groaning turns some men on.

INT.: *Do you think about each other when you are both having sex with someone else?*

JOHN: At a party where we don't know most of the people or possibly none of them at all, I prefer that all the doors to all

23

the rooms remain open. Some swingers prefer to start off a party by groups of couples going into different rooms and closing doors. I won't stay in a house if the doors are going to be locked. I want access to where Sandy is, and I don't like the feeling of being shut out unless we're with very close friends, people we've known for a long time. I like to know where Sandy is all the time and I think about that a great deal. I remember once we were at a swinging party up in the hills and I was very upset because for a period of time I didn't know where Sandy was.

SANDY: Which party was that?

JOHN: The one where you came home and said, "That guy was great," and I said, "Who?" and you said, "I don't know his name. He had a short haircut and he was blond." Don't you remember? That was the first time we were ever separated long enough to worry about each other, and after you had sex with him you didn't even remember the guy's name!

SANDY: It happens. Lots of times I'll see a guy who's groovy, really great in bed and then I won't remember who he was . . . What's in a name?

INT.: *Do you prefer swinging at large parties or smaller parties?*

JOHN: A two-couple party commits you and we don't like commitments of that kind. I don't want to feel that I have to have intercourse or go down on every girl at a party and Sandy doesn't want to feel that she has to have sex with every guy. If we've talked about it with each other and Sandy says, "I really like what's her face's husband", and I say, "What's her face is fine with me," then it's predetermined and it's fine. But we both hate being asked for dinner knowing that the couple who's asking us wants to take us to bed afterward. I'd much rather suggest to them that we all go to a party where there are five or six other couples. Then if I want to go to bed, and Sandy wants to go to bed, at least we have more than one couple to go to.

INT.: *What happens at a typical swinging party?*

SANDY: There isn't a typical party.

INT.: *Let's talk about a party that both of you thought was most fulfilling. What happened at it?*

JOHN: The one you gave for me.

SANDY: I gave John a party three years ago for his birthday and I invited just the right people whom we had known for some time. I put together a group that was excellent, I thought.

JOHN: I thought so, too.

SANDY: Most of the couples were married. Two couples weren't. And we had invited an interracially married couple; the fellow is black and the girl he's married to is a beautiful brunette. I hadn't told any of the other guests the couple would be there that night because I really didn't give it a second thought. Everyone who was at the party was an experienced swinger and it was interesting to see their reactions when they met Bernie and his wife. Some of the husbands hemmed and hawed around a bit because, evidently, none of their wives had swung with a black man before. But by the end of the evening, all the girls had had fun with Bernie and all the men enjoyed his wife. Just out of curiosity I asked the girls, "Would you have come if I told you Bernie was going to be here?" A few of them said they weren't too sure. But all of them were glad that he came and each one was delighted with him.

INT.: *What made the party such a success?*

SANDY: Mostly it was the mood, the atmosphere. The way our home was lighted helped a lot. We had different colored light bulbs in each room.

JOHN: It was beautiful, just beautiful.

SANDY: And we had planned a series of surprises.

JOHN: Like those negligees.

SANDY: (Laughing) I knew John's favorite colors and I got the sizes of all the girls whom I had invited. Instead of buying John an obvious birthday gift, I shopped for these lovely negligees and bought John a different kind of experience.

JOHN: It was amazing how well they fit. But the best part was when they started coming off.

SANDY: The negligees were falling around the floor in all the different colors.

JOHN: It was done with taste.

INT.: *How did you pick the people?*

SANDY: They were people we had known and both of us had liked.

JOHN: What you did, if you remember, dear, was to pick out those

25

married wives and single girls whom I had seen and talked to at parties before, girls I had known and liked, but had never had a chance to make it with before . . . Sandy was making an effort to get these people for me, which was physical and fun . . . And very exhausting.

INT.: *What about the men, Sandy, were you attracted to any of them?*

SANDY: Well, after all, they were the husbands of some of my best friends.

INT.: *I have to admit that sounds like a unique birthday party. But this blatant selection of bed partners, do you feel this was being a little aggressive?*

SANDY: Oh, no. It was a desire we all shared, wanted to participate in. Our friends are very gentle, and that's part of what swinging is all about. I don't know why it is, but the nonswinger somehow views sex as rough or aggressive. Well, in swinging you learn how to express your sexuality in a fun, pleasuring way. We *have* been to some semirough parties, but when they become rough, we leave.

JOHN: Swinging parties where most of the people are in the entertainment field and drink a lot tend to become rather boisterous.

SANDY: Maybe that's because many men at those parties don't bring their wives.

JOHN: I don't like that—when a man brings a girl other than his wife to a party.

INT.: *How can you control that sort of thing?*

JOHN: You can't. It's up to the host and hostess to plan the guest list.

SANDY: What we do, usually, is ask the host or hostess whom they're inviting. Sometimes we ask if we can bring another couple along, too. Especially if we're going to a home for the first time, we definitely prefer to have at least one couple we know with us.

INT.: *Sandy, how would you define a successful swinging party? Would you measure it in terms of how many men you went to bed with?*

SANDY: Oh, no! I may only be with one fellow for an hour in a room and not even relate to the other people there. Then after we have our sex together, I could have a long conversa-

26

tion with him about whatever he does for a living, and possibly I may not go to bed with anybody else the rest of the evening. There's a lot of social aspects to a party, too. It's not just going to bed. Swingers are people. We look like human beings . . . We belong to the PTA, we love our children, we pay our taxes, we vote, we even mow the lawn.

JOHN: *You* do.

SANDY: It's good exercise for the body tone, you know. (To John:) You could use a little of that.

JOHN: (To Interviewer) She's full of those gentle reminders. I get my exercise talking.

SANDY: (Smiling) He does—in courtrooms and bedrooms. (She laughs) It's true. You get him started on art and he goes on forever.

JOHN: I remember at one swinging party I met a girl who was having her period. She was crazy about photography and had taken a lot of pictures on a trip to Italy—the Sistine Chapel and so on. Well, we just talked for hours about different styles of painting, the contradictions in the patron system during the Renaissance, how destructive it was to some talents.

INT.: *In the midst of all this sexual activity you two were commiserating about Michelangelo's agonies?*

JOHN: I preferred to talk with this girl instead of going into a room with someone I didn't care about. That particular night there wasn't anyone around that I felt like having sex with.

SANDY: That happens.

JOHN: Other times I'm ambivalent about my feelings. I'm at a party—I may walk into a bedroom and see people having sex for the fun of it . . . I tell you something, seeing three women in the same room reaching their climaxes almost together, getting the feeling that one triggers the other, is really something to see. The expression of complete pleasure and release on their faces. The men exhausted, staying in for a while and softly talking to the women—really, it's a wonderful experience. In that situation I join in, become part of that group orgasm . . You can't be inflexible about what or what doesn't happen at a swinging party. Here is another side of the coin: sometimes Sandy and I arrive at a party

27

where there are more men than women. We resent that. I'll have a drink, thank the host very much and leave. If there isn't an equal distribution of men and women, we just don't stay. I don't like some fellow who walks into a party expecting to have intercourse with my wife without bringing someone along for me and others to enjoy.

INT.: *Does all this open sex minimize marital problems?*

JOHN: Oh, yes . . . I wouldn't dream of cheating on Sandy. It just wouldn't cross my mind. It's ludicrous.

SANDY: You know what's really happening with so many couples when a man says he's going out on a business lunch or the wife says she's going to play tennis in the afternoon . . . A lot of them really are messing around, the husbands as well as the wives. There are very few men—and I think women also —who, since the pill, haven't had the opportunity and taken advantage of it with someone other than their spouse.

INT.: *Are your political beliefs and religious beliefs equally liberal?*

SANDY: Very liberal in politics. Religion? I guess we're not that religious. We were married in the Presbyterian Church in a candlelight service and by a minister, but we're not in the throes of religion.

INT.: *Have you met swingers whom you would consider very religious?*

SANDY: Yes, we know some that are. We know one married couple where the wife, after a Saturday night swinging party, has to get up early the next morning and teach Sunday school.

INT.: *Don't you think that causes conflicts, if not on the surface then at least subconsciously?*

SANDY: You're being too vague. I had gone to bed with men before I married John and I don't think I felt disturbed about it . . . Funny, your asking that question reminds me of the time I was dating a psychiatrist. He thought if a girl went down on a man or the man went down on her, they were perverted.

JOHN: He ought to see what Sandy's doing now.

INT.: *We've been told there are many categories in swinging. How would you describe your activities? Do you consider your-selves hard-core swingers?*

JOHN: Oh, no. A hard-core swinger is a husband or wife who'll sit down on Monday morning, after partying Friday, Saturday and Sunday night, and start planning the next weekend . . . Before we had our children, we did do a lot more partying. We had somehow fallen into the "jet set" of swinging, with luminaries, stars, important people in the movie industry.

SANDY: We know one couple where the husband is an executive in the film industry. Both he and his wife swing. They hold small parties, most of the time inviting over only one other couple. They're very careful swingers.

INT.: *But if they're true swingers, why should they be concerned with their position?*

SANDY: I suppose because he's so important at the studio.

INT.: *Does the fear of being exposed as swingers bother you?*

SANDY: Not at all. Some people, just a few, I'm sure it does.

INT.: *Have you ever encountered any serious problems as swingers?*

SANDY: Problems, no. Funny situations, yes.

INT.: *Like what?*

JOHN: There's a couple who lives near us. They have a massive apartment . . . One evening the bedroom was packed and the lights were very low . . . People on the bed, on the floor. One girl finished whatever she was doing and was making her way to the bathroom to douche. She was at the head of the bed, walking over people to get to the other end, not knowing that our host was lying on the floor nude, with his legs spread, down on some girl who was sitting with her back against the wall. Well, as the girl stepped off the bed, she landed right on his balls. He let out a yelp and at the same time bit down on his girl. She went up the wall four feet; it looked like something out of a Rube Goldberg cartoon. It was step–spring–bite–jump. The girl who was bitten started to cry and we were all trying not to laugh as we were comforting her.

SANDY: We know one swinger who's got trouble because every time he has an erection, his joint somehow turns a little to the right which, needless to say, makes it quite difficult for him to get it into a woman.

JOHN: I remember an orgy we held for a celebrity from New York who asked us if we'd put together a swinging party for him. We had known him from some other swinging parties. He asked us to throw him a "celebrities only" party—just swingers in the motion picture and television industry. He was bringing a friend of his from New York and he was prepared to spend about five hundred dollars for food, maid service, and private guards to protect against gate crashers . . . We planned for almost three weeks and invited people in the industry who had either partied with us before or knew who we were. There were no strangers. I told them that only swinging couples would be invited and that no one inside would be there just to watch. I also said that we would have uniformed men at the gate to check all the invitations before anyone could come in. Inside the house I hired a nude under-cover man who mixed with the crowd, had drinks, but still kept his eye out.

SANDY: You can't really tell this story.

JOHN: Yes, I can.

SANDY: Well, don't use any names.

JOHN: I won't.

SANDY: It won't be any fun that way.

JOHN: It's still funny. The word was to leave jewelry and anything of value inside the house. We made up a list for each person and locked his valuables in the safe . . . After a while it was a mob scene like a Hollywood premiere without spotlights. We had hired a young couple, who were dancers, to do a nude dance. He choreographed the number and brought his own music. After their performance they did an encore which I guess you couldn't call anticlimactic because they wound up screwing each other. It was really wild . . . Meanwhile, at the gate outside there was a big muscular, black young guard.

SANDY: Athletic looking.

JOHN: Really a huge man. And he had on a uniform that was too tight for him. I think the fellow was a bouncer. Well, up drives a well-known actor whose name was left off the list because someone had forgotten to put it on. The actor peered out of the window and gave the guard his name. He checked the list and said, "I'm sorry, Mr. ———, I'll have to call the house and make sure it's okay. I'm sure it is." Well, the actor in the car apparently was stoned out of his mind and before the guard had a chance to walk to an outside wall telephone, he hurled a full quart of whiskey through the window and hit the guard across the kneecap. The guard came limping into the house, blood pouring down his leg. I saw this poor guy and then went to find Sandy, who was always great in emergencies: Florence Nightingale in the nude . . . Anyway, we brought the young guard into the kitchen and Sandy pulled down his pants and placed a butterfly tape around his knee . . . The lights were on in the kitchen and people were coming in with no clothes on for a drink or some food, and some of them sat down to see what all the trouble was about . . . When Sandy was finishing up, two starlets came waltzing into the kitchen and noticed the poor kid. They both stared at this young man and he got so nervous that he started pulling up his jockey shorts, which made it difficult for Sandy to complete the taping. The girls were saying, "Oh, the poooooor babiiieeee, he's all hurt, we'll take care of him." Before Sandy and I could stop them, they had surrounded him and taken off the rest of his clothes and were leading him into one of the rooms. They placed him on the floor and one girl started going down on his joint . . . The other girl was kissing his chest and then I remember still another girl was running her fingers up and down his good leg. This went on and on . . . The guy was going out of his mind. The girls finally finished and he staggered to his feet, the sweat pouring off him. Sandy was back fussing with the tape that had come loose in the interim. He looked around the room and then said to everyone, "You know, there's one thing I'm sorry about. Who's gonna believe me? I mean, every time I watch these people's television series and tell my friends what they did to me, I know nobody's gonna believe it!"

INT.: *How many people were at the party?*

SANDY: There must have been close to a hundred . . . Sometimes it's difficult to count heads when they're underneath people, but I know we had approximately one hundred names on the guest list.

INT.: *Is there any difference between a swinging party and an orgy in terms of atmosphere or attitude?*

JOHN: An orgy is very physical, nothing barred.

SANDY: Everybody's doing everything to everybody else. It's just one big groupsex scene. An orgy is many things. It's the atmosphere, it's the people and, of course, you don't want to drink too much, at least we don't, so we won't miss out on anything. People are rubbing against each other and they're having sex. You've got to be turned on to all this, you can't lie there like a brick.

JOHN: You walk in and it always seems that an orgy has begun before you get there. Some swingers take an orgy seriously, others humorously. It becomes a little desperate after a while. I mean, desperate in a physical sense. There's an abundance of bodies, a cornucopia of sex. You have smells, bath oils on bodies, various kinds of douches, vaginal odors and sometimes a practical joker sprinkles everyone on the pile with Wesson oil. Literally, it's wall-to-wall bodies. There's nothing individual about it, nothing emotional. It's purely physical— hands, tongues, arms, legs, vaginas, penises, you see fragments of bodies, pubic hairs. You're so close to bodies that all you see are bits and pieces of the anatomy, almost never a full body. You see orifices all over the place. Here an opening, there an opening, everywhere an opening. It's really wild. What I dig at orgies is watching two girls who are lying side by side on their backs with their heads on the bed and their legs dangling over the edge, and two of us men are on the floor, each giving the girls head, sometimes taking turns with each girl. All of a sudden, I'll look up and see the girls kissing each other while we're giving them head, They may not even know each other, but they reach for the nearest thing next to them, which is a real wild sight to see . . . I can honestly say an orgy is something every swinger should experience at least once or twice a year. I admit that after participating in one, I feel a little unclean. It's very dehumanizing, but still it's an experience and one you don't forget the next day.

INT.: *As you look back on your years of swinging, is there one moment that stands out above all others?*

(They look at each other and break out laughing.)

JOHN: Yeah! There sure was one rather long moment . . . but you won't believe it.

SANDY: (giggling) You'll think we're putting you on.

32

INT.: *All right, put me on.*

SANDY: I guess I'd call Mary our "Most Unforgettable Character."

JOHN: But it's not the kind of story that would make the *Reader's Digest.*

SANDY: Mary was a nun.

JOHN: No she wasn't.

SANDY: Okay, but she looks like one, I mean a beautiful nun. She has the same soft innocent features.

JOHN: I know what you mean, but don't give him the idea that we've ever swung with a nun.

SANDY: We were asked to help her out.

JOHN: Okay, tell the story, but remember: she's a friend of a friend of yours, not mine.

SANDY: Anyway, my friend called me and told me that one of her closest girl friends was getting married, that she was deeply in love with her husband-to-be but she was honestly afraid that she couldn't satisfy him sexually, and could I help her out? I said, "Sure!"

JOHN: It was a crash program in sex.

SANDY: I talked to John about it and I suggested that he give her a few pointers in sex. So we invited her over on a Thursday evening for dinner.

JOHN: Sandy always calls upon me in a pinch.

SANDY: Anyway, we bundled up the kids, and John drove them over to my mother's for the Labor Day weekend. When he got back he noticed a girl walking in and out of front yards looking for . . .

JOHN: The right address. She was really something. I mean she was a beautiful girl and everything about her was in place. She looked like the kind of girl who got up in the morning with everything ironed and went to sleep at night without any wrinkles. She was carrying a huge bag slung over one shoulder. I watched her for a while and then she turned and walked into our driveway and I thought maybe Sandy had called the Avon lady or something. I was about to tell her we didn't want any when Sandy opened the door and yelled, "Mary."

SANDY: Before she did anything else, even sit down, she took out all kinds of books on sex from her bag and charts on positions.

JOHN: Those charts were wild. They looked like blueprints on how to take over the world. I had never seen anything like it. She was really serious. There must have been fifty dollars worth of books and charts on sex and she didn't look like she knew what any of them meant. She had one book, I don't know where in the world she ever found it, with the most erotic-looking sexual positions I had ever see in my life, and I thought I had seen them all. At one point she slumped back in her chair with the most distraught look on her face and said, "You know, a picture is worth a thousand words, but I don't even understand some of these pictures." I told her, "Don't try to."

SANDY: I made John's favorite dish that evening, roast duck. Mary talked about her fiancé all through dinner, how much she wanted to please him—and how little she knew. Mary was very very worried about her brother-in-law who got a divorce and her aunt who wasn't married. We talked to her for about three hours and I finally convinced her that it wouldn't bother me in the least if she went to bed with my husband, that I would be in the bedroom with them, looking over his shoulder to make sure she would be all right.

JOHN: So, off we tripped to the bedroom, my wife behind me to make sure I didn't turn into another room and lock the door; not because the girl wasn't attractive—she was really a very beautiful girl—but I had been working on a case in court that whole day and I was very tired and a little weak.

SANDY: The first thing I told her was how to get undressed in a sexy way.

JOHN: That took the first hour and fifteen minutes. Sandy kept telling her, "No, no, that isn't the way, put your clothes back on and try it again." I finally pulled out a full-length door mirror from the closet so she could see herself. She kept wriggling her rear end when she got out of her dress, which wasn't sensual.

SANDY: I told her the idea was not to get undressed so fast and not to wiggle around, but to lift one foot out and then the other, slowly. She finally did it. Then I pulled back the covers and told her to lie down with one leg crossed over the other.

JOHN: That's when she got the cramp in her leg.

SANDY: I don't know what happened; apparently she pulled a muscle.

JOHN: Probably from taking off her clothes so many times.

SANDY: Then John got into bed. She looked at him and he looked at her and she kept right on looking until I pushed and pulled them closer together. Then I said that most men like to have their genitals caressed, rubbed, licked, you know, the whole works. So I held up John's penis, which was limp at the time, and rubbed it a little to get it up and then told her to hold onto it.

JOHN: For a few minutes I swear she thought it was coated with poison or something.

SANDY: She started stroking it and then she would pull her fingers away and kept up this advance and retreat until she finally decided to hold onto it. Then I told her to press her lips on the head and sip down at it as if she was drinking something out of a straw.

JOHN: That's when she got even more nervous and left a red mark on me.

SANDY: I guess she was a bit too rough because she still didn't know how quite to do it, and John came in her mouth.

JOHN: It was an accident.

SANDY: The next morning John had to be in the office early to finish up working on a brief. John is very conscientious, I mean incredibly conscientious in everything he does. I remember when we got dressed and walked into the kitchen, Mary was already up and dressed and waiting for us. She got a little anxious when I told her that John had to leave and wouldn't be back until the evening. It was the worst thing I could have said because she looked as if she'd go into withdrawal symptoms. The poor kid really felt she would be unable to be sexually responsive to her husband and would fail as a wife. But the more we talked and the more I listened, the more she relaxed. I called up some of my friends, and by four in the afternoon I had a party arranged and a catering service to bring the food in. Everybody who met Mary just couldn't believe that such a sweet person could have so many anxieties when it came to sex. They did everything they could to calm her down and help her out.

35

JOHN: I walked in about six and I was hit with a sea of humanity, faces and boobs and women I had swung with and hadn't seen in years. And there was Sandy, walking around in just that college sweatshirt of mine that came down to her knees, carrying a tray full of hors d'oeuvres, and here was Mary, that beautiful, innocent young girl, in my home, in my bed, using my friends. She had taken over the house completely . . . I tell you, it looked like a scene from "Guess Who's Dining the Comer."

SANDY: The party lasted all night and into the next morning . . . Everybody was pitching in, showing Mary different positions. It was a very warm, extremely funny situation, if you can imagine being clinical about sex while you're doing it.

JOHN: Sort of on-the-job training, marathon style. And the place was quite a mess by the next morning.

SANDY: (Laughing) Half the time, I didn't know what was going on upstairs because I was downstairs cleaning up as best I could because it was the maid's day off.

JOHN: Day off, my foot! She left to bring her boyfriend back. She was upstairs with the rest of them.

SANDY: Really I didn't see her . . .

JOHN: I'm telling you she was *there*.

SANDY: All right, I won't argue . . . Anyway, I ran out of food and somebody suggested we move the party over to his house, and we did. It looked like one big parade of cars heading down this street. This went on through Sunday morning, and then some of the people washed up and went to church long enough to pray for Mary.

JOHN: By Monday afternoon, Mary had learned enough about sex not only to last for her first marriage, but to get her through the next fifteen. I'm not exaggerating. One fellow walked up to me and asked if I knew where to find a chandelier. I looked at him and said, "What do you need a chandelier for? You've got enough light," and my friend said, "It's not for me, it's for Mary because that's one position she hasn't tried yet—swinging from a chandelier." That did it! I got bombed, I mean, really stone drunk. All I can remember after that is someone putting a pillow under my head and the next morning when I got up, I was back in my own home, in my own bed, and Sandy was waking me up to have breakfast.

36

SANDY: About a half hour later, Mary walked into the kitchen with not a hair out of place. Her dress was pressed and clean. She was the nun all over again.

JOHN: She quietly walked up to us carrying her overnight bag and said in a soft and gracious voice, "All of you have been so very kind to me, I don't think I'll ever be able to thank you enough. I learned a lot, and I enjoyed every minute of it. Thank you. Goodbye." That was it. She walked out of the door and waved to us.

SANDY: Afterward, we got to talking about Mary, and I figured she must have had sex at least forty times. It was something like ten men a night.

JOHN: That was quite an active Labor Day weekend. This year I promise you—we'll go out of town, take the kids up to the mountains and read them nursery rhymes.

INT.: *I'm almost afraid to ask—did Mary turn into the all-time swinger?*

JOHN: No. As a matter of fact, the only time we saw her was at the wedding, and Sandy cried through the whole service . . .

INT.: *I'd like to wrap things up by asking you, as swinging parents, how you relate this activity to your children.*

JOHN: They're very young.

SANDY: They don't know about it.

INT.: *Would you ever encourage your children to swing?*

SANDY: No. I would not involve them in my swinging parties, of course not. I know people who are pretty sick that way. I would not involve my child in a party whatsoever. I don't think I would ever have a party so they would know what was going on.

INT.: *Do you know any parents whose children have grown up and have joined their parents in their swinging activities?*

SANDY: I would never go to a party where a child was swinging.

INT.: *I'm not talking about a young child, but someone of age.*

SANDY: I know what you're talking about. I still think it's sick.

INT.: *How about the mothers and the fathers who do this?*

SANDY: They're sick, too.

JOHN: I don't know any.

SANDY: Yes, we do.

INT.: *Do you feel that attitudes about raising your children are influenced by the fact that you both swing?*

SANDY: You try to bring your children up as best you can and explain to them the facts of life and what's going to happen if birth-control protection isn't taken. Because they're going to do it. They're going to have sex. For me to say that my child at fourteen or fifteen isn't going to experience sexual gratification is ridiculous, in this day and age. But I would never have children swing with adults. Swinging takes a certain maturity, and children cannot handle all the sex available to them at a swinging party.

INT.: *Why do you swing?*

SANDY: I think swinging is very exciting. It's exciting to go to these parties and meet new people. It's inexpensive. If I feel I want to swing with a certain man, I can, but John has to be with me at all times. We would never think of taking off some weekend, John with another woman and me with another man and go our separate ways. John and I swing together. We're always together in anything we do. We can swing for hours but we're always constantly together.

INT.: *What about you, John? Why do you swing?*

JOHN: You can meet and be with physically the most attractive, good, intelligent people with your wife's consent and be as sexually stimulated as you want to be and still have a great home life—dinner cooked when I get home from work, a beautiful mother for our children, and have my wife as a great bed partner and still have all the variety any man could want when it comes to sex . . . Swinging *is* the best of all possible worlds.

5

MIKE AND KARYN:

For Them, Swinging Didn't Work

Mike is thirty years old and outgoing. He is tall, well built, around six-foot-two. His sandy-colored hair forever drops over his eyes. He has a little-boy look about him: dimples and a slight smile on his face as if he is on to something you are about to know. He talks in carefully phrased sentences, quiet, barely audible at times. He is the kind of friend who would literally give the shirt off his back to anyone who needed help. He's just that way about people.

Karyn, just turned twenty-nine, is also soft-spoken. She is slender and has long milky-blonde hair. Her features are tiny but striking. She is a beautiful girl with clear blue eyes, rounded lips. However, she tries to keep these qualities to herself. Karyn blushes if you compliment her. And she is not excessively modest. Rather, she is sometimes unsure of a person's motives.

Mike and Karyn's two children came ahead of anyone or anything else. Kevin is four and the little one, Becky, is two. Karyn is extremely protective when it comes to her immediate family.

Mike and Karyn tried swinging for one year and then stopped. They have been married for five years.

Mike and Karyn were born and raised in the same Western city and met at the college that both attended in their hometown. Mike was studying finance and Karyn was enrolled as a music major. They met in their junior year at the University, dated for that semester, and everybody thought it would turn out to be the romance of the year. It didn't quite work out that way. Mike married in his senior year. The marriage lasted two years, and then there was a divorce. A year or so later Mike met up with Karyn once more. This time it was "meant to be," but not without problems. The divorce left Mike unsure of himself. And it left Karyn unsure about their relationship. The fear of the past, particularly Mike's first marriage, seemed to stop what was good between them from becoming as close to perfect as possible.

What kept them going in the beginning was the knowledge that they had so much in common. This feeling is even stronger today: their interest in the same kinds of people; their love of skiing; the love of art and music.

Mike and Karyn have one special room which is used as their personal studio. There is a Steinway piano for Karyn to practice on. In one of the far corners is a long table with an assortment of tools which Mike uses for his wood work and sketching. The house, which has seven other rooms, was custom built for them by an architect friend. It has European charm and resembles a ski chalet.

Before Mike married Karyn he was already successful as a partner in an investment counseling firm. It has grown and prospered so that today he has accumulated more than enough to make their life comfortable.

They belong to a country club and Mike owns sizable interests in a number of companies. Mike and Karyn are both busy in politics, too. They are active campaigners and have helped in the election of two legislators. They are involved in moderate peace movements—nothing radical. They are concerned people and happen to have built enough prestige and respect in their community to be able to contribute time and money for causes to which they feel a deep commitment.

Mike and Karyn are still looking for something more in their lives and this search has brought bad breaks. Even though they have fun and have been disillusioned a few times, they'll risk an experience as they did in swinging, hoping to find what they're looking for, something meaningful and deserving of growth. For them swinging clearly didn't work out.

INTERVIEWER: *How did you both become involved in swinging?*
(Karyn smiles and looks at Mike, who starts to laugh.)

MIKE: The reason we're laughing is not because of the question, but the use of the word "involved" as if swinging is some kind of conspiracy. Actually, if anyone had told me before Karyn and I got married that four months after we were married we'd be swinging, I would have said he was nuts. But about three weeks after we were married we sat down and started to talk about cheating on each other; what we honestly felt it would be like if either I or Karyn found out that either of us was cheating on the other.

KARYN: I guess I had the same anxiety that I imagine most women have when, all of a sudden, you realize, "My God, I really am married now, the honeymoon *is* all over. Am I sure of him? Am I sure even of myself?" I must have been nursing these thoughts in the back of my mind for some time. That evening everything seemed to come out, and I'm glad it did.

INT.: *Was this all supposed to lead up to swinging?*

KARYN: Oh, no. That was the last thing on my mind.

INT.: *And you, Mike?*

MIKE: No, I hadn't thought about swinging either. As Karyn was saying, when we had this talk, it probably was some kind of testing. Although we had dated for quite some time and our engagement was fairly long—seven months—I don't think we really got to a point where we openly revealed any anxieties over our commitment to each other.

KARYN: I think we did at times. I remember sneaky talk when we were with other couples; you know, whether Mike ever thought about the other girls in a sexual way.

INT.: *Why was the fear of infidelity on your mind?*

KARYN: I never thought about it as being a fear, but I guess it

41

really was. What I was looking for from Mike was reassurance that he would always be faithful to me. Yes, that's what I really wanted, no matter how Victorian it sounds.

INT.: *I still don't understand why.*

KARYN: Because Mike had been divorced before.

INT.: *Oh?*

KARYN: And, although I knew Mike loved me, I couldn't help but think that if his first marriage ended in a divorce, what would prevent this from happening to us?

INT.: *Was that going through your mind, too, Mike?*

MIKE: In a way, yes. My divorce did pose some kind of threat to the relationship that Karyn and I had before we were married and after. In my first marriage there had been so many restrictions. I didn't want that to happen again.

INT.: *What do you mean by "restrictions"?*

MIKE: Oh, if I was working late, my first wife had to know where I was or what I was doing and what time I thought I would be home, and if I wasn't home at that time, then we had a big hassle over why. It always ended up in a fight. She had fantasies that I was on the make with a secretary in the office or I was with someone else, another woman. It wasn't true, but she wouldn't believe me. (Pause) And I wanted to avoid that kind of hassling with Karyn.

INT.: *I'm somewhat confused. How did all this lead to your involvement—forgive that word—in the swinging scene?*

KARYN: That night when we were talking about our feelings about love and sex, we also talked about the freedom that each one can bring to a marriage if there is enough trust.

MIKE: If you're really in love, we thought, this meant that we trusted each other. If that kind of trust was extended to its logical conclusion, then, hypothetically, we could be free to do whatever we wanted to do as long as it was within a marital framework. It seemed to make sense.

INT.: *How did you feel about it, Karyn?*

KARYN: For the most part, I listened.

MIKE: C'mon, Karyn, you did more than that.

KARYN: Well, we talked about what would happen if we both wanted to have extramarital relationships. What would the

42

other think? I couldn't imagine us really doing that. But Mike kept saying, "Well, if we had this trust, what would be the difference as long as we both knew about it?" After maybe a month or two of talking, the idea of having sex with more than just Mike was, I guess I could say this, exciting in a forbidden, adventurous way.

INT.: *All right. When did this talk leave the fantasy world and become a reality?*

MIKE: I think it was maybe four months after we were married . . . We had some friends whom we knew and we'd go out with them quite a bit. One night we got very deeply into the subject of sex.

KARYN: *You* did, Mike, you always brought the conversation around to that.

MIKE: Because it was difficult to get them to pin down their own feelings. They always had something to say about someone else and what he or she was doing on the sly. When I'd come out and say, "Well, don't you ever have the urge to get it someplace else?" there'd be a lot of tittering and remarks like, "Oh, us? Are you kidding? We'd never even think of . . .", that kind of bullshit. Why did they have to act like a bunch of school kids? I guess that night I blew my stack, and I said, "C'mon, why in the hell are we so afraid to level about sex? I mean, how *we* feel about it? Talking about it won't lead to screwing; I can't rape your wife with words."

KARYN: I remember that Mike was really mad.

MIKE: Sure, because they could talk about acquaintances and *their* sex lives but they considered themselves so damn pure that it became hypocritical. So that night when Karyn and I came home, I decided I was going to find out once and for all if I was wrong.

INT.: *Wrong about what?*

MIKE: My feelings. Because somehow everything always seemed to come back to sex. I was so damn preoccupied with it.

INT.: *Did you think swinging was a way to eliminate these preoccupations?*

MIKE: Swinging was a way to see if there was another way, at least for us. Karyn and I felt that the sexual aspect of a

43

relationship with other couples would, in a sense, be the frosting on the cake, rather than some overriding attempt to make friendships based on my willingness and my wife's willingness to have sex with other people. Unfortunately, at least with those people we swung with, that wasn't the case ninety-nine-and-nine-tenths of the time.

INT.: *Why?*

MIKE: Basically, we were looking for people to form lasting friendships with. And we thought that if a man could say to me, "It's all right, really, you can have sex with my wife," and I could tell him, "Okay, you can have sex with my wife," and if Karyn's love for me and my love for her didn't suffer, then maybe this openness could lead to friendships where everything could be out in the open.

KARYN: Or so we thought—until we got into it.

INT.: *How did you start?*

MIKE: Probably the dumbest possible way—through an ad.

KARYN: We sent our names, ages, and some other general information out. About three weeks later we got a reply and a telephone number to call.

MIKE: I talked to the man and he suggested that we come by his house, that he and his wife preferred meeting this way rather than at a bar or a restaurant for dinner, so we made plans for a Friday night.

KARYN: Meeting them was the biggest shock of my life.

MIKE: I swear, both the husband and wife were in their sixties, at least. He was rather obese and she was very unattractive. I don't mean to be cruel, but it was an experience I didn't expect, not in the least.

KARYN: We were scared to begin with. I know I was, and Mike looked a little pale as we were driving over, too.

MIKE: Yes . . . I think we must have stopped at least at three gas stations to use the washrooms and twice we nearly turned around and came home.

INT.: *What happened?*

MIKE: We talked to them for a while and then we excused ourselves. We said we had to get home because the babysitter couldn't stay out late, even though we didn't have a baby

44

at the time . . . I don't know why we didn't quit after that, but we didn't. We heard about a nightclub not too far from where we lived, a place where a lot of marrieds went to find other marrieds to swing with.

INT.: *Did you go there?*

KARYN: Yes, the following weekend. It looked like any dimly lit restaurant. But it wasn't long before a couple came up to us and introduced themselves and said that we must be new because they had never seen us at the club. We began talking over a few drinks . . .

INT.: *What was the conversation like?*

KARYN: I think it ranged from politics to religion and then to sex and finally to swinging, and they asked whether we would like to come back to their home. Mike looked at me for a moment and then he said, "Yes, why not?"

MIKE: We went back to their house and right off they started telling us what we could and couldn't do. They said that we had to stay dressed until we switched partners and each couple went into a bedroom; that we would only be allowed an hour with each other's partners and that we would have to put our clothes on before we came out of the bedroom again. As I recall, they didn't offer us a drink; they just waited until we said we were ready.

INT.: *Could you tell me how you felt?*

KARYN: It was quite scary—the whole idea of finding yourself making love to another man in the presence of your own husband. I felt his presence even though he wasn't actually in the room, and I was confused. Yes, at first I was definitely frightened. Even though we had both agreed, no matter how many times I convinced myself or talked myself into doing it, when it was actually happening, when this other man started kissing me and touching me, I wanted to scream out for my husband. I didn't belong there, I didn't belong with this other man, I belong with my husband because that was the way it was supposed to be . . . I felt cold and I felt ugly . . . wrong, I guess. And Mike was in another room and things kept running through my mind: What was this woman like in bed? What was she doing to Mike? Was he enjoying

45

it? Was he enjoying his sex with this other man's wife more than he was with me? It was the most insecure, confused, depressed feeling I ever had in my whole life.

INT.: *What about you, Mike?*

MIKE: It all seemed so mechanical. There was no emotion, really. The woman took off her clothes and pulled back the covers and sort of jumped in and waited for me to do the same. When I did get into bed, I waited for her to make the first move, and that didn't take long. She told me what a nice body I had and was there anything in particular I wanted her to do to get me started. I felt like a kid who was getting laid for the first time all over again. I couldn't get an erection, so she started giving me sixty-nine and stopping every once in a while to ask me how I was doing, and, finally, I wound up giving her straight intercourse. I came and she had an orgasm, although I hadn't thought I performed well enough to get her excited. When it was all over she asked me if I wanted to stay in bed with her a little longer. I told her that if it were just the same, we should get dressed and go back into the living room. I guess she understood because she said she had broken in other couples before.

INT.: *What happened with you, Karyn?*

KARYN: I just laid back and closed my eyes, and he got inside me and did all the work, but he did have me reach a climax. During that moment I knew I was feeling pleasured, but after it was over and I opened my eyes, half expecting to see Mike, the other man was on top of me, and it was . . . really, it was an experience. I never thought I could have gone through with it. But I did. I remember when I saw Mike come back into the room after we all had gotten dressed again, he had a "Did we actually do this?" look on his face. And for maybe ten minutes we hardly said anything to each other or to the other couple.

INT.: *What happened then?*

KARYN: The couple made some coffee and we talked a little about what had happened. They told us we acted pretty much the same as other new couples they had swung with, and in time we would get used to it and probably look back and laugh at the uncertainties we both were feeling that night.

I remember she said that, like anything else, swinging takes practice, but that after I got used to it I would never be able to go back to a straight nonswinging life.

MIKE: All the way back home in the car, I don't think Karyn and I said more than two words to each other. We weren't mad at each other. I just don't think we knew how to say anything that would have made any sense.

INT.: *And when you got home?*

KARYN: The same way. We washed up, brushed our teeth and went to bed. No, we kissed each other goodnight and then went to bed. We reacted in a way that I guess blocked out even the thought of sex with each other. We slept or tried to sleep. I don't know about Mike, but I was up for a while and then I fell asleep.

INT.: *The next morning did you talk about what happened the night before?*

KARYN: Yes, I think it was Mike who brought up the subject.

MIKE: I finally felt we had to talk about it, so I called the office to tell them I'd be coming in late. I don't know how I started. I think it was something like, "Well, we went through with it, didn't we?" Karyn nodded. As I remember, I did most of the talking.

KARYN: Mike asked me what I thought of the other man, and I said, "Well, he was a nice guy and all that; I mean, he didn't do anything to hurt me, and I did reach a climax, although I never expected I would. I remember it took some time." Then Mike told me what the woman was like, so we compared notes.

INT.: *It seems as if you both went out of your way to be nice to each other that morning.*

MIKE: Probably because we honestly didn't know how to begin talking about it. As Karyn said, we talked about the other couple, but what was there to say? We only knew them sexually; we had talked about other things when we first met them, but the real reason was to swing. That was why we met them, and that was at first difficult for us to admit.

INT.: *Why?*

MIKE: Well, we both had been talking about the notion that we were doing this to make friendships. Certainly in this first

47

situation it didn't work out that way. We just had sex with someone else other than each other, at the same time and with both of us knowing what was going on. The experience was quite mind-blowing.

INT.: *Did this lead to a statement that you wouldn't swing again?*

MIKE: No. I don't think we ever said that that morning.

KARYN: We had acted out what we had been talking about for some time. We could have said no, and not gone through with it, but the point is that we did it. I think that was what was bothering me the most.

INT.: *Was your conscience bothering you?*

KARYN: Yes, I'm sure it was.

MIKE: I think it was a combination of things. We didn't consciously feel what we had done was wrong, or I don't think we would have ever gone to bed with the couple. It was a matter of the subconscious—our upbringing, perhaps. All the labeling and the taboos against what we had done.

INT.: *Did you swing again?*

MIKE: Yes, about a month later.

INT.: *What led you to reach this decision?*

MIKE: We just *had* to try again. This time the party was larger. We had gotten a call from the couple we had swung with and they invited us over to a party. This was something new all over again: there were going to be more than one couple swinging. We had a preconceived notion that we'd walk in and everyone would just take off their clothes and start swinging. I think this was one of the things that scared the hell out of Karyn at first. Any more than one couple we thought would mean a mass orgy.

INT.: *But you went anyway.*

MIKE: Yes, and we found that most of the people really didn't care about making any attempts to get to know each other outside of the fact that they were there to have sex. That was all.

INT.: *Did you participate?*

MIKE: No, not that night. There were two other couples who also remained fully dressed that evening, so Karyn and I spent most of our time with them.

48

INT.: *What about the couple that invited you over? Were they upset because you didn't swing?*

MIKE: The man was. He was the host and took it personally. When he came over and asked if anything was wrong, I said that Karyn and I just didn't feel in the mood. A few minutes later his wife came over. She put her arms around me and sat in my lap and tried, in a gentle way, to change my mind and kid me into it. I kept saying we just didn't want to do anything, and finally she got the hint. She pulled back and went to chat with some other people. We stayed for a while and then went home. We did, however, give our number to one of the other couples we had met. They were part of the group that didn't swing that evening, at least not while we were around.

INT.: *Were the people who were swinging in the same room with you?*

MIKE: Two couples, I think.

INT.: *How did you feel about that?*

KARYN: It bothered me a lot. Here we were talking about having children and raising them, and not more than five feet away a man and a woman were going at it. I felt it was out of place, but it didn't seem to bother the other couple we were talking to.

INT.: *Did you see this other couple again?*

MIKE: Yes, they called about two weeks later. They seemed very nice over the phone, and we accepted their invitation to another party.

INT.: *What was that like?*

MIKE: Reserved, very reserved.

INT.: *In what way?*

MIKE: It took a long time before the party started.

INT.: *Why?*

MIKE: Because I think there were other couples there who were new to swinging, too.

INT.: *Did you two swing that evening?*

MIKE: Yes, with the couple who had asked us over.

INT.: *Did you want to or did you feel you were forced?*

MIKE: No, we seemed to like each other. The girl was attractive

49

and her husband was appealing to Karyn . . . At least we felt we knew these people a little bit. They didn't seem as aggressive as the others we had met. I think that helped ease us a little. So, after that, we always went to swinging parties with this couple who, in turn, introduced us to other couples.

INT.: *Were you beginning to feel better about swinging?*

MIKE: Not really. We still found that most of the people at the parties had nothing more on their minds than sex. If they did talk about anything else, the conversations were not very meaningful. We *did* find other couples whom we thought we'd like as friends, but somehow, much as we tried, it was difficult for us to see them on a nonswinging basis.

INT.: *Why was that?*

MIKE: Well, they considered swinging to be the best way of socializing. So it was rare for us to go out for dinner and an evening at a show without it winding up a swinging party.

KARYN: We continued swinging, though, for about six months.

MIKE: We wanted to give it time, but it just didn't work out.

INT.: *Was there any particular reason why you finally decided to drop out of swinging?*

MIKE: Yes, the large number of women who found it rather enjoyable to please other women. They kept telling us that they weren't lesbians. Maybe they weren't, but I was convinced they were at least bisexual, and I just didn't go for that.

INT.: *Why not?*

MIKE: If you had never seen this kind of sexuality expressed before, you had no way of relating it to your own sexual experiences. I mean, seeing two women pleasuring each other, married women, was something that quite frankly shook me up. Because, as a man with a male ego, seeing a woman pleasure another woman as well as a man could or better, well, for me at least, it led to a negative effect. I assumed that it's the man's role to pleasure a woman, and I was seeing those roles changing quite a bit.

KARYN: I found this very, for want of a better word, unfeminine. If swinging is supposed to provide a setting for married couples to have sex in a normal way, and those swingers I talked to considered it to be so, then why was it necessary for women to need other women in a sense as male substitutes? Some swingers said it was because a man can only perform so much and then he has literally had it. Well, if swinging is a mutual thing, why weren't the wives of these swingers ready to stop when their husbands couldn't perform any longer? This, to me, was a very important point. Maybe what they really wanted out of all this swinging was a form of exhibition, and if that was the case then certainly, no matter what these women told me, their sex life at home couldn't have been all that good if they had to think of sex as performing all the time.

INT.: *Were you ever approached by a woman?*

KARYN: Yes, on a number of occasions. But I told them as politely as I could that I was sorry, this was something I just didn't want to do.

INT.: *How did the other women feel about your attitude?*

KARYN: Some understood and I know some were insulted.

MIKE: Another thing that bothered me a lot was the constant need to go after new couples as if this was a way to make sure that real friendships would never grow out of these relationships—just the exchange of sexual partners. I didn't feel like wandering around to meet new people for the sake of sex alone. I think I'm a fairly gregarious guy, but this thought of compulsion or obsession to meet new people turned me off.

INT.: *I've heard that many swingers feel that this search for new couples is very meaningful to them.*

MIKE: I feel it's really an expression of boredom. If these swingers need to go out and find new people all the time, then sex must have had very little meaning to them. I'm sure what I'm saying might be attacked by other swingers, but that's how I feel.

KARYN: And there's something else, too. Swingers who met us for the first time would go out of their way to tell us how good swinging is. It seems they never stop telling you how good it is. Half the time, I think they're trying to convince themselves.

INT.: *Do you think this applied to all the swingers you met?*

KARYN: No. Not all, just some.

INT.: *It seems that for both of you, at least, the swinging experience was somber and serious.*

KARYN: I guess that's what we're emphasizing. But there were some light moments.

MIKE: Yes, especially at the larger parties, what some people might call orgies.

INT.: *What was so funny?*

MIKE: Because there are so many people all over, I always got the feeling Karyn and I had arrived at the start of a great big bargain sale. When we went to these affairs—we didn't really attend that many—there were never enough bedrooms.

INT.: *I guess those homes weren't built with this kind of activity in mind.*

KARYN: (Giggling) I remember once the host and hostess had one of those little cardboard squares that they give you when you go to a busy grocery—you know, where you take a number and wait for your turn. That's what we had to do before we could use one of the bedrooms. Really. I had a number in my hand and I waited until the room was available.

INT.: *I don't quite understand—were you waiting alone or had you already picked out a partner?*

KARYN: (By now she's laughing) Yes, I had a partner, but I still felt I was waiting alone. Finally I just said the hell with it, and went back into the living room without my partner. I gave my number to someone else who had a higher number than I did . . . It was like walking into a crowded delicatessen on a Sunday morning and waiting until you would be called for your bagels and lox.

MIKE: At these big parties it was really very impersonal. As new swingers and then, after six months I suppose as "seasoned swingers," we expected to meet new people and strike up a rapport with them, but we didn't get to know any of these people. They were all strangers.

INT.: *In what way?*

MIKE: They had their own little cliques. They were very clannish, much like people at straight parties. There were "in" groups, and somehow Karyn and I could never get into the "in"

52

groups. We came to the conclusion, and I can't pin down just where in all this process it happened, that there's more to this world than just screwing your neighbor's wife . . . We didn't find swinging to be liberating in any way.

INT.: *Did you find that swinging eliminated hangups or fantasies?*

MIKE: Not at all. It often led to very frustrating experiences. There were times when I couldn't reach a climax or I felt that I was only going through the motions of sex. All the woman wanted to do was screw. If I couldn't please her, then there was someone else who could roll over and do the job. One of the things swinging eliminates is the challenge of seduction. Everybody knows what's going to happen at a swinging party. You know, when you're single and taking a girl out and you want to go to bed with her, there is certainly a distinct challenge there. Will she do it? Is she giving me hints or am I imagining things? When do I make the move? There's none of that in swinging, and that takes the fun out of sex. For me, it's not just a case of falling into the sack and balling.

INT.: *Do you share that feeling, Karyn?*

KARYN: I guess I agree with most of what Mike is saying, but there's something that bothered me much more: jealousy.

INT.: *At the parties?*

KARYN: In most of our swinging encounters—not always, mind you, but at those times when I felt a woman was spending too much time with Mike, I felt threatened. I don't know how a woman who loves her man could feel any other way.

MIKE: I agree. If a man was with Karyn and maybe I didn't see her for a while, I couldn't help but wonder and worry about what was happening. You simply cannot eliminate these jealousies whether they're petty or not. For us, at least, they existed.

INT.: *Then what did you discover about yourselves through swinging, if anything?*

MIKE: We discovered a lot. We had the courage to try a new kind of sexual relationship to see if it could work. We found that, for us, it didn't. We found that if we were truly honest with ourselves and if we couldn't satisfy each other, then there was something wrong.

KARYN: For us, swinging was not a way of life. For others, it is. Maybe I'm old-fashioned, I don't know. I know that I consider sex a private expression of love and mutuality. I don't consider sex, true sex where love is shared, to be a form of exhibitionism. For me, at least, swinging was a contest of performance and exhibitionism rather than an act of honest communication between people on a sexual level. That's how I felt and that's how I still feel. For some, swinging probably fills a need. For me, it didn't.

INT.: *Mike?*

MIKE: I'm happy with Karyn. Maybe out of all this I found out that no one could ever please me more than my wife.

6

MARTY AND LISA:

"It's a Constant Reassurance"

Marty is thirty-nine years old, an engineer and executive with a leading manufacturing company in the Southwest.

Marty finished high school and then was accepted on a scholarship at a Southern university where he was graduated with honors. He married just out of college and had two children, a boy and girl. It didn't work out and there was a divorce. Two years later he met Lisa, and after a short courtship they decided to get married.

Lisa is thirty-seven. She also happens to be a graduate of the same university, although she did not know Marty there. She went on to get her masters degree and taught sociology full time until two years ago.

Marty and Lisa are discreet swingers. They only go to small intimate parties. At times they worry about being discovered as swingers and the possibility of losing their positions. It's taken Marty a long time to reach his executive level and Lisa her academic status.

There also is the nagging fear that they may be discovered

by their neighbors. It has already happened once and Marty and Lisa both decided to move rather than hassle with the problem.

Life for them is not one swinging party after another. It is one of several levels that make up their life and has its meaning. Lisa is also actively involved in an ecological movement.

Marty has a pilot's license. At times he lacks the time to log as many hours as he wants, but flying means that he, Lisa, and his children can take off on vacations and have a wide choice of places to stop in.

Marty and Lisa own a lovely two-story Southern colonial home in a fashionable suburb. He recently added a studio that he designed and built himself. With the help of Lisa and the two children it took a little over six months to complete. There are still a few more things they have to do and Lisa says, "I don't think Marty will ever stop building or adding on to it. He loves to work with his hands. Sometimes he complains how tired he is after he spends a day making some change or another, but he says it with a smile."

Marty looks every bit the executive engineer. Tall, his hair turning grey around the temples, his eyes are set under heavy lids and it often seems that he is looking years ahead while talking of the present. He has a wide face, an instant warm smile and flashes white teeth as the lines on the sides of his eyes draw into webs when he grins.

Lisa is five-foot-six, wears her auburn hair pulled back and then tied. She has a fresh look about her. Brown eyes that seem always to be smiling. "Marty calls me his farm girl, because I do like to run barefooted around the house, and I seem to be getting mussed up every once in a while when I'm gardening. Can I help it if I have my hands into everything?"

INTERVIEWER: *How long have you two been married?*
MARTY: Nine years.
LISA: And three months.
INT.: *Is this your first marriage?*
MARTY: Lisa's first, my second. I have two children from a previous marriage—Leanne who is twelve and Walt going on fourteen.

INT.: *How long have you been swinging?*

LISA: Let's see now, we started about a year after we were married. That makes it almost eight years now.

MARTY: And three months.

INT.: *Why did you start?*

MARTY: (Smiling) I was married before to a very attractive woman with a strong inferiority complex. She blamed me for a lot of her own problems, saying I was unsatisfactory in love and in sex. After my divorce, I had quite some doubt about my sexual ability, and I remember going out with a college girl who was about nineteen—that was great for my ego. I had a rented house near the campus and this young girl, who had such a healthy attitude toward sex, made me feel like a man again. I also learned that I could have a lot of fun in bed with a girl without being in love with her. Swinging has the same virtues. It's a constant reassurance that you're still sexually attractive to other women besides your wife.

LISA: What Marty is saying also applies to a woman; knowing she can be attractive to a number of men is about the best boost to the feminine ego that I know of. Swinging gets rid of many hangups by forcing them out into the open.

INT.: *Like what?*

MARTY: Hypocrisy. It forces you to face reality. You see your wife having sex with someone else, she sees you having sex with someone else . . . It means that the same rules apply to both parties.

INT.: *Isn't sex still a game in swinging?*

LISA: It's a more honest game . . . Before I married, in the dating game, everything was "let's pretend." If I went out with a man, even if I liked him, I had to be the shy one— demure, nonaggressive. He had to win me over and then when we were in bed, half the time I felt I had to pretend everything was perfect, to please the man, the all-important superior being. I used to worry so much about it that I hardly ever enjoyed myself. To this day, I wonder whether he had a good time or was he also just pretending.

INT.: *Don't you think some of your swinging sex partners are also faking it?*

MARTY: (Laughing) Why should they? There's no need to.

INT.: *Suppose a woman or a man wants to convince others at a party that he or she is the greatest. From what I gather, if you groan and gasp and sigh and move around enough, you can be champ.*

MARTY: Sounds to me like you're talking about wrestling . . . The swinger has so much choice that no one has to prove anything to anyone. No one is really watching you, not in the sense that they're evaluating your performance. It's a group feeling. More than anything, it's an encouragement. If things don't work out, there is patience and understanding . . . Look at it this way, it's something like an extended family . . . In our home, at a family gathering, Leanne will sit down and play the piano and some of our relatives may hear the music and come in from another room . . . Everyone is listening, smiling, happy for her if she's playing well . . .

INT.: *Are you comparing the swinging sex act to a piano exercise?*

LISA: In many ways, yes.

INT.: *Don't you think exhibitionistic performances can create new sexual hangups?*

LISA: Perhaps for those swingers who are truly exhibitionistic. If they are motivated by "numbers"; if they have weak egos and over-compensate by trying to "conquer" every girl . . . Yes, in those instances you're probably right. But you have so much more of that outside of swinging: those driving people who must have three cars instead of two or one, who're always reaching for the pinnacle in any given situation. For those poor souls, it's the prize that counts, the status of achieving it. But what have they got when they get it? I wonder if they're ever really satisfied.

MARTY: We are.

INT.: *Has swinging ever led to any problems for you?*

MARTY: When we first started swinging, we were living in the suburbs and some of the neighbors down the block became a little suspicious about our crowded weekend parties. They called the police on several occasions. The officers were very polite, mainly concerned about whether any of the guests were smoking grass or were on hard drugs . . . They were embarrassed, gave us a clean bill of health and left us on our merry way.

LISA: But not those envious neighbors . . . They never forgave us. Pretty soon we found ourselves isolated. People up the street began whispering. I'd walk into stores in the shopping area, places where I traded regularly, and I'd notice a guarded look, a smirk, when I turned away. I didn't like that.

MARTY: The most disturbing aspect related to my children, who were then living with my first wife. They'd spend alternate weekends with Lisa and myself. Well, the other kids on the block ostracized them. Obviously, their parents had put them up to it. That's what finally forced us to move.

INT.: *Did your children know about your swinging then?*

MARTY: (Shaking his head) They were too young at the time.

INT.: *Do they know now?*

MARTY: No. The situation is still delicate. My first wife knows that Lisa and I swing because we told her when we began, and she was and is vehemently opposed.

LISA: We try to respect her feelings; however, we disagree. So to keep the family peace, we've given her our word we would never tell Marty's children without her prior approval.

INT.: *What do you think will happen when your children do find out?*

MARTY: (Reflectively—after a long pause) . . . My daughter is somewhat of a hedonist and a bit of a rebel in her own way. Frankly, when she's old enough, I think she'll embrace the idea.

INT.: *You mean swinging?*

MARTY: That's too speculative. I can't really say. But I don't think she'll be upset with us because *we* do.

LISA: And I'd be surprised if Walt were negative. He's a quiet boy, but open about his feelings. Sensitive, you know . . . We see a lot of the children, and in our own way are already conditioning their response . . . When Marty and I were living together before we were married we had taken Leanne out alone for supper one night. When we returned to Marty's place, I can't remember exactly why, I went up with Leanne to get something out of Marty's bathroom and she saw some of my underthings in his bedroom. She wasn't upset or anything. She came right out and asked if I was having sex with her father. Well, I had never expected that kind of a question, but I chose to answer her honestly . . . Of course we were. We were in love and we were planning to marry soon. Actually, we were waiting for Marty's divorce to become final . . . She smiled and really opened up, asking me questions, things she couldn't discuss with her own mother, she said. (Lisa smiles.) She had a terrible need to know what sixty-nine was. That stopped me, because I didn't know what Marty would think about that degree of frankness.

MARTY: That's about the time I came upstairs and joined the conversation. I was curious about where she'd heard the term. It seems she had picked it up at school. The kids were talking about it and she had heard many different versions about what it actually was. She just wanted to know the truth. Well, Lisa and I both explained it from the male and female points of view. And we used the proper language about how the man kisses the woman's vagina and the woman kisses the man's penis, and that they make love that way because they both want to. You should have seen the look on her face.

LISA: She was so relieved.

INT.: *It's curious that you keep using the word "love." What about all this talk by swingers about separating love from sex?*

MARTY: There are times when one can have sex with little or no feeling, especially at orgies, but when I was explaining it to Leanne, I was telling it to her from our points of view as if we were doing it. Lisa and I are in love and when we have sex, we do make love.

INT.: *You seem to be concerned about your children's approval.*

MARTY: Aren't all parents?

INT.: *I'm talking about wanting their approval for your swinging activities.*

MARTY: Of course we would want them to be sympathetic and understanding.

INT.: *Suppose they weren't; suppose they turned on you the way your neighbors did?*

LISA: I don't think that's possible.

INT.: *But suppose your children did disapprove?*

60

MARTY: It still wouldn't stop us from swinging. Is that what you're getting at?

LISA: Regardless of how they felt, it wouldn't change our devotion to them nor would we allow it to govern our activities.

MARTY: We'll never stop swinging as long as we're physically able. (Lisa nods.)

7

DEBBIE:

A Sense of Belonging

Debbie is twenty-nine years old, divorced, and has no children by her first marriage. She began swinging two years ago.

She has a degree in elementary education from a California college and Debbie is teaching emotionally disturbed children in that state.

She is as big as a minute. But all of her five feet and one inch —and she is proud of that "extra one inch"—are packed into a bundle of boundless energy. Her appearance invites being hugged and held: petite, with jet-black hair in a Peter Pan cut. Her olive eyes never let up for all their mischief and curiosity.

For two years Debbie has lived with a forty-year-old man and his ten-year-old son, Michael. They're the two most important people in her life.

She considers her childhood "typically conventional": a loving mother, a hard-working, loving father, a comfortable home, cheek-pinching aunts and uncles, large family parties, and a Fourth of July party every year where all the cousins would mug in front of the eight-millimeter movie camera. When the film was developed, it always looked like something out of Chekov. Everybody either looked old and chubby, or young and innocent.

Her first marriage was traumatic, especially in bed. Sex was too routine, too quick, too unsatisfying. Until she met Mark. He is a California businessman. Mark is kind, understanding, good-looking, a provider—"and simply great in bed."

Debbie swears by swinging and considers herself a walking endorsement of groupsex. Here, like may other swingers, Debbie for the first time found a sense of belonging, a feeling of freedom. To her, it added up to being able to be herself without worrying about petty jealousies or caustic indifference. She has time now to learn, to think, to teach, to understand. And she attributes this to overcoming a sexual handicap which, she feels, afflicts ninety-nine percent of the nonswinging population.

What we know about Debbie seems to support her view. She is a voracious reader, particularly of philosophy. She can lose herself in Greek mythology and her library occupies two sides of a room from floor to ceiling. She has read all volumes from cover to cover more than once and keeps adding to the collection constantly. Her collection of professional journals is equally impressive.

Her work with emotionally disturbed children is not the world's easiest. Often it leads to exhaustion. But she finds time to donate two nights of her week to help a special class of disturbed children at a nearby hospital.

Debbie's "agreement" with Mark is not as unusual as it would have seemed ten years ago. The concept of a "moving in and sharing" marriage, without benefit of wedding rings, is gaining popularity and receiving serious attention from behavioral scientists. Some have even given moderate endorsement to the idea, especially for young men and women who have agreed not to have children while living together. In Debbie's case, there is the added complexity of Michael and her role as a surrogate parent.

Debbie falls into the category of those swinging couples who live together as a husband/wife unit, and perform as such in the swinging scene.

INTERVIEWER: *Debbie, can you tell me something about your childhood, your family life?*

DEBBIE: I came from a fairly middle-class Jewish family. I have one older brother who is now a dentist, but were you asking about my childhood in relation to sex?

INT.: *We can start with that.*

DEBBIE: Well, my parents insist to this day that I was instructed on all the physiology of sex at the age of five.

INT.: *Do you remember that?*

DEBBIE: No, I don't.

INT.: *But they said they told you.*

DEBBIE: Yes, so I never should have forgotten, should I? But I don't remember anything other than the fact that my parents never tried covering up or hiding their bodies. It's interesting, but I guess when you're a child those are the things you remember—bits and pieces of things rather than words: my father always taking a shower with my brother and me, and my mother never trying to hide her body. It wasn't that I was curious about a naked body, and yet I recall one very upsetting experience when I saw my father playing with my mother's breasts. Their bedroom door was open a crack and I peeked through and was caught looking in. My father stormed out of the room yelling something to my mother. I think it was that she should explain the facts of life to me. *And seeing them that way—*

INT.: *How old were you then?*

DEBBIE: Oh, I was probably around ten. But I didn't really understand any more at that time than I did earlier.

INT.: *Did you feel the same way when you were in high school?*

DEBBIE: Yes, sort of. No matter how many times someone tells you how cute you are you still feel ugly if you can't express yourself. And I know with me this was true. Yet in high school I managed to have a boyfriend all the time. I met a guy just before I was in high school and we went together for about a year. In the course of that year he never once tried petting or any of the other "sex things" that my friends were talking about. One day I decided I had to find out what everybody was talking about, so I had him put his hand on my breast, hold it, fondle it. I sort of forced his hand there, and he became a different person after that.

INT.: *In what way?*

DEBBIE: We would park on dates and it got to the point where he took his pants half-way off. Every time after that I would go home and cry, but I never knew why I was crying. Then I would look forward to seeing him again and park again and make out like that again. Once or twice we got to a point where his penis came in contact with my genital area, but there was no penetration. I think we probably both were scared, although I didn't understand why. Then there were the parties we went to in junior high school. Most of the time the boys would feel the girls' breasts or put a hand inside their pants, and the girls would play with the boys' penises . . . After a while the girls would walk around with big rings of wetness around the vaginal area of their panties . . . How many times I wanted to ask my mother about that! One day I was actually going to, but she told me something which made me feel what I was doing was dirty and shameful. She had been talking to my aunt about my cousin Dorothy who was my age. My cousin had come home from a necking party and told her mother that the boys were feeling the girls up and that the girls were stroking the boys' penises. My mother told me what a bad thing that was and she thought I "wouldn't do anything like that." I wanted to say, "Like what, Mother?", but I couldn't get it out.

INT.: *Did you continue to have these unspoken feelings about sex?*

DEBBIE: For a while. I was fifteen when I started dating another guy I really liked. He was going to become a dentist, and he came from a nice Jewish family who must have stamped him a dentist before he stopped wetting his diapers. Even though he was a lovable dunce, he was a nice-looking boy, sweet and all, and good to me. So I figured that was love. We spent a lot of time together at his house, at my house; even our parents got together and I think that they were already rehearsing how to walk down the aisle. One of the times we decided to leave our parents for a while and drove over to my home. We started petting in my father's den and then we decided to go into one of the bedrooms. First it was my brother's room and we both decided against that. Then it was my parent's bedroom, but somehow the thought of having intercourse in the same bed where my father slept with my mother didn't seem right—although the idea was tempting. Then we went into my bedroom and he didn't want to do it there. I pulled him out of the bathroom when I saw that look in his eye and we finally wound up doing it in the kitchen. Actually, it was the back half of the kitchen which was like a recreation room. It took him a while before he managed to get an erection, and I remember stroking his penis and thinking about my cousin and what my mother had told me a few years before about that party where Dorothy was playing around. I started thinking more and more about that party and how bad my mother thought it was and must have forgotten how hard I was massaging his penis because he told me to slow down. He managed to penetrate me, but he didn't know what he was doing. It kept slipping out and I must not have been ready because I was tight inside and all this made the whole experience very sad.

INT.: *In what way?*

DEBBIE: It was painful. There was no real tenderness and emotion. It was just a very hard, cold thing, and yet I associated love with sex. You loved the person you had sex with. There was no two ways about it. You married him. I thought I loved this fellow, so I figured it was all right. We went with each other for the next six months, and we must have had intercourse a total of maybe five times. But each time it seemed the same—always routine, never that satisfying—and just before school began in the fall we split up. I continued dating a lot through the end of my junior and senior years, but never went to bed with any of the other guys I dated.

INT.: *What about life in general? Did you think about where you were going, what you would be doing?*

DEBBIE: When it came time for me to graduate from high school, all of a sudden I was faced with the idea: "My God! I'm getting out of high school. I've got to do something." I had never thought that much about my future and about going to college. In the middle of the summer I applied to college and was accepted. I was very pleased about that. I still was dating intermittently. Every time I'd go out with a guy, especially someone I liked, I would hold off going to bed

66

with him. After going out five or six times with the same guy, it would always wind up in a fight and I'd feel guilty thinking that maybe I was wrong.

INT.: *About what?*

DEBBIE: When most of my friends dated a guy for any length of time it was almost taken for granted that you would go to bed as if it were some kind of status symbol.

INT.: *Did guilt feelings about sex ever prevent you from enjoying sex or exploring sex with men?*

DEBBIE: Exploring sex, possibly, but not enjoying sex.

INT.: *Did you feel that you could enjoy sex even with those feelings?*

DEBBIE: Oh, yes. I enjoyed it. Not as much as I enjoy sex today, but I enjoyed sex as well as I knew how. Toward the end of my sophomore year, I started dating a fellow I liked. Harry enjoyed sex, too, and he was very well endowed. We'd go hiking in the hills or skiing for a weekend and I would have sex with him. But sometimes, even with him, I felt, well, the best word is "unclean."

INT.: *Physically or mentally?*

DEBBIE: I'm sure that it was a mental process, but I did feel physically unclean . . . You know, if you are not married and you start having as much sex as I was, I had been told so many times that it couldn't be good . . . Also, it dawned on me that I might get pregnant. So every month I would suffer, thinking, "My God! What if I'm pregnant," and I'd suffer through every period.

INT.: *Didn't either of you think of using contraceptives?*

DEBBIE: Harry didn't like using any. It "dimmed" his feelings, I remember he said. So I practiced my version of the rhythm method. I would only allow intercourse right after my period or just before. But I was never quite sure about what the rhythm method was, and I was to ashamed to ask Harry or anyone else, so I was always frightened.

INT.: *And restricting sex to a few days a month?*

DEBBIE: And then making up for the rest of the month in a few days.

INT.: *Were you still having sex with only one fellow?*

DEBBIE: Harry, yes.

INT.: *Is he the one you married?*

DEBBIE: Yes, during the summer of my junior year in college. He had another year left of law school and his parents agreed to support us until he graduated.

INT.: *How did you feel about that?*

DEBBIE: I would have liked to have seen us self-sufficient, but I accepted the fact and got used to it.

INT.: *And your parents . . . ?*

DEBBIE: My mother liked him a lot, but then she wasn't marrying him . . . My dad liked the idea that Harry was going to be a lawyer, but all through the engagement he was noncommittal; turning into what a father-in-law should act like, he thought, but still noncommittal. When the day of the wedding came, Harry's family had never met some of my family. When they walked into the sanctuary, my brother told me, some of them just kept standing not knowing what side of the aisle to sit down in. I suppose that was a harbinger of things to come. The night before the wedding I exhibited, shall we say, twinges of nervousness and asked myself, "What am I getting myself into?" I remember my mother broke down and started to cry. How she wanted that wedding! I announced I was going to call the whole thing off and that's when my father went into a tirade about how much money he had already spent; in my household I was always brought up to figure the dollar was almighty and God forbid you should try to "overspend" that dollar. The arguing and crying finally stopped in time for my mother to make last minute hems in my wedding gown and the big day came. The first night of the honeymoon was spent wiping the slate clean. Harry told me how many girls he had gone to bed with, which started sickening me, so I made up a fantastic number of men that I'd gone to bed with before marrying him, which really pissed him off. It was okay for him but not for me. So for the first night instead of having sex we talked about our past affairs . . . he, mostly, until I finally fell asleep.

INT.: *Did you make any promises about staying faithful?*

DEBBIE: No.

INT.: *Did he ask you?*

68

DEBBIE: No. And I didn't ask him because I never thought about it. We were married, and I honestly felt he would never be untrue to me and I wasn't going to be untrue to him.

INT.: *How was your sexual relationship?*

DEBBIE: It was never spontaneous. It was always sex in bed at night. He would move his leg over me and then his hand would start rubbing up and down my leg and he would start manipulating my clitoris and maybe he'd kiss me. I knew every move he was going to make. I think in all the times we had intercourse together I reached a climax maybe three times. He was a very immature person, and I was very young and immature, too, as I look back on it now. Worst of all, we were both too stubborn to make a go of it. Less than a year later, I think it was eight months after our marriage, we separated and eventually were divorced.

INT.: *What did you do then?*

DEBBIE: I didn't carry my divorce papers around campus . . . I just stayed in school and graduated with a bachelor's degree in education at the ripe old age of twenty-two. Following my graduation I went to Europe and traveled around for two months.

INT.: *Do you think you were escaping?*

DEBBIE: . . . No . . . I just had the bug about going to Europe. I was able to book a flight through a student tour service at college and the first city where I spent a considerable amount of time was Munich. That's where I met Mark. We've been living together for the past two years . . . He was with a group of people when I saw him at the hotel where I was staying. He sort of smiled when I walked by and I smiled back at him. Then I did something without really thinking about it. I walked back to where he was talking to some people, sat down and listened to the conversation for a while until he stood up and asked my name and then introduced me to his other friends. When I started speaking up I guess I told about my four years in college and what I was going to do when I got back to the States, all in thirty seconds. I remember my tongue turning heavy and my mouth pouring out breathless silly things and my lips not helping me shut up either. About an hour later most of the group had left to go outside or back

69

to their rooms and I was alone with him. It turned out that Mark was from my hometown and also on a vacation. I really thought he was a great-looking guy, but more important, he was interested in me and made me feel comfortable.

INT.: *Was he your age?*

DEBBIE: Oh, no. I knew he was at least ten years older than I was. He already had tufts of gray around his sideburns and his hair, and when he smiled he smiled with all his face, everything wrinkled: the sides of his eyes, his nose . . . That night he was to leave for Zermatt. We had dinner before he left and although I wanted to have him ask me to go along to Zermatt, I didn't ask and he didn't.

INT.: *What happened after that?*

DEBBIE: The next day I made arrangements to go to Zermatt. It took about three days, but I found him one early evening at an inn. He was very surprised to see me, but also pleased. I could tell that right away. The next three days we walked around the town, hiked, danced, drank wine. One night he led a group of us through a wild Greek dance at one of the inns . . . I can't remember how it happened because it seemed so natural, but one night we started making love in bed. There was a mutual communication between us.

INT.: *What do you mean?*

DEBBIE: We got to know each other. He told me about his son. How much he loved him and wanted to give him everything he could. His wife had died of cancer two years before and, although he thought about marriage, he wasn't ready for it. We talked about everything. Silly things and beautiful things, about values and why I wanted to teach and how important it was to open up those small minds before society "got to them" and squeezed them shut . . . And most of all he was gentle when we had sex. He knew how to make love to a woman. He wasn't interested in just selfishly getting sex from a woman. He was sensitive to my needs. He was able to stay with me, able to cause me to climax. He created feelings within my body that I had never experienced before. He was the best I had ever had in my entire life. I did things in sex that I never thought I would be able to. I had never gone down on a man before or had a man go down on me . . . I thought that was something terrible. My mother didn't exactly tell me that, but I remember her saying that if a man did that, you know, wanted me to lick him and kiss him down there then he was treating me like a prostitute. Only prostitutes did that.

INT.: *You felt that it wasn't natural?*

DEBBIE: Until I experienced it. I don't know if this makes any sense, but we all live with different hangups, and they feel so real and weigh so heavily on us and then (she snaps her fingers) somehow there is a breakthrough. You do it, whatever it is, what you thought you never would be able to do and then so much of the past, that burden, disappears so quickly . . . Mark was a good teacher . . . The way he worked me up with gentle kisses and caressing, a simple thing like kissing my ear, some parts of my neck, I think, yes, and I was suddenly so excited that when he moved down and started kissing my vagina it all seemed to natural . . . Maybe it was the look on his face or my own desires, but I just wanted to touch his penis, kiss it. You may think what I'm going to say is funny, but it had a salty taste to it. Not bitter or objectionably odored, but it had this taste—plus a sweet perfumed odor from some talcum powder. I had his penis in my mouth and I kept taking it out and asking him, "Is this what you like? Am I doing it the right way?" And he kept saying, "Yes, don't worry, don't ask so many questions." Not in an insulting way, but in an affable way. I must have had his penis in my mouth a long time because he motioned for me to take it out, and he began kissing my vagina again. I was about ready to climax when he stopped and got inside me. I never had an orgasm like that before . . . I can't remember exactly when it was, but I think it was sometime later in the evening when he started talking about swinging couples.

INT.: *Had you ever heard of swingers before?*

DEBBIE: No. Before he brought it up, I didn't know what swinging was about. Mark told me he had the feeling that I could become a good swinger. I laughed at him because the thought of groupsex—having intercourse in the same room with other people—was, at the moment, a little difficult for me to get used to.

INT.: *Did he press the issue?*

DEBBIE: He just asked me to think about it and when we got back to San Francisco he would call me and then see how I felt . . . We talked a great deal about swinging before he left for the States. I wondered if his son knew. He told me he didn't, that he was too young. He wanted me to meet Michael when I came home and see for myself if his son was well-adjusted and if he had been a good father to him . . .

INT.: *Do you think Mark was trying to paint a picture about his son which wasn't true?*

DEBBIE: Actually the two of them had a strong attachment to each other . . . soon after I got home we did many things together, all three of us. Mark even tried to teach me how to play golf and gave up, but Michael kept telling his father not to lose patience with me. That's the way those two were and still are with each other. They talk to each other as equals without Mark having to be condescending. Mark does that with people, even with my mother. The first time I invited him over to my house for dinner (I was still living with my parents at the time), the minute he was inside the home my mother fell in love with him. She thought he was the greatest person in the world, and by then I had the same feeling. And it hasn't changed even after our swinging experiences together.

INT.: *You never did explain why you decided to swing.*

DEBBIE: At first I just wanted to please Mark, that was the main reason. I believed him when he said I would also enjoy it.

INT.: *Do you remember your first party?*

DEBBIE: The initiation—oh, yes, I can't ever forget that. He had called me to tell me that we were going to a couple's home for dinner in two weeks. There would be three other couples there and he was sure that I would get along fine with all of them. Well, the weekend before I went skiing (this was in November), and I broke my ankle. It wasn't bad, but my ankle was in a cast and I was hobbling around on crutches. After the accident I called him, but I didn't tell him what had happened . . . just that I had sprained my ankle. The night when he came over to pick me up and saw me on crutches he was ready to call everything off, but I insisted on going. I had been building myself up for it.

INT.: *Did you think about what was going to happen when you got there?*

DEBBIE: Not really. When we did arrive I met Mark's friends and they seemed to be considerate and quite honest. There was nothing phony about the way they acted . . . After dinner the hostess took my arm and said, "Come on, Debbie," and took me upstairs. She led me into a huge master bedroom, helped me undress and get on to the bed on top of the covers. I was lying on my back wondering what was going to happen next.

INT.: *Were you nervous or scared?*

DEBBIE: I had been through that during dinner. By now I was very relaxed. It felt good getting off my bad leg for a while (she smiles). I remember asking the hostess if she would mind bringing over another pillow so I could prop up my bad leg. I was quite a sight. The white cast was staring at me from my toes, and I was thinking that I hoped I wouldn't ruin anyone's evening because they had invited an invalid for dinner and swinging. But it felt great getting all that attention.

INT.: *How did that night of swinging begin?*

DEBBIE: About half an hour later I heard Mark coming up the stairs with what seemed to be the rest of the party. All of them entered the room and Mark had his hands playfully around one of the girl's breasts, wondering if she had taken silicone shots to make her busts as big as they were. She really had large breasts. And it seemed that everyone started to undress about the same time.

INT.: *Did it bother you seeing so many people undressing in front of you?*

DEBBIE: No. It was interesting to watch. Some of the men had bigger penises than others. One girl had apparently shaved her pubic hair and I kept staring at her vaginal area because I had never seen a woman without hair before . . . Then they started climbing onto the bed, sort of converging all over me. Everyone was careful, though, not to bump my bad ankle . . . I felt someone stroking my good leg and at first I didn't know who it was because all the other people seemed to be attached in one way or another. Then I felt what I thought was a nose rubbing around my vagina like an Eskimo kiss. And then another man started sucking my nipples, not in a rough way, but very lightly. There must have been six people pleasuring me by then. I felt someone's finger inching up to my rectum and moving slightly inside it and every opening in my body seemed to have someone or something inside it, including my mouth because someone had slipped a penis in it when I had my mouth open, laughing . . .

INT.: *Was Mark among the six?*

DEBBIE: Oh, yes.

INT.: *How did you feel about that?*

DEBBIE: I glanced up and noticed that he was smiling and every once in a while he would take hold of my hand and squeeze it. He was watching over me and that made me feel more comfortable . . . That's what swinging is all about for me. In my mind, I don't have to equate love and sex with somebody and enjoy both separately. Mark and I love each other. We understand each other's feelings and we are able to convey our emotions and attitudes about sex to each other and not feel condemned or ridiculed for having them. And I've learned that from swinging. I've learned to be able to say and feel and act and do what pleases me and pleases others and Mark feels the same way. That, to me, is the most important experience of sharing. It's love. It's really the ultimate feeling of love. Mark and I have complete trust in each other.

INT.: *But where does marriage come in on all this?*

DEBBIE: For Mark and me it doesn't.

INT.: *Don't you believe in marriage?*

DEBBIE: No. At this moment, I don't think it's necessary. There's no real reason for marriage as long as two people can live together and be happy and share the good with the bad. Why must I have a slip of paper telling me that the state has validated my love for Mark?

INT.: *What about his son?*

DEBBIE: He says he loves me . . . He sees Mark and me together, sees us having fun. That boy is as much a part of me as if he came from my womb. The fact that Mark and I aren't married and are living together doesn't bother Michael. Why should it? Because society frowns upon unmarried couples living

74

together? What is society but just a term, a word, which some people have to run to and use when they can't justify certain things in their own mind. Then they tell you, "Society says this is wrong" or "That's okay." Mark and I have thought out our relationship very carefully, we want to live *our* way because we have something very meaningful together . . .

INT.: *What happens when you have children?*

DEBBIE: We have a son, Michael. Mark wants to wait to have more children. But giving birth is only the beginning . . . What about kids who have no families? Little babies, days old, who are bundled and wrapped in orphanage bassinets? Are they any less in need of love and care? Mark and I also want to adopt children; they don't have to be ours for us to love them. I teach children from broken homes and if anyone needs attention and a feeling of belonging and being wanted these children certainly do. I know of a number of couples who are unmarried and live together rather happily. They'd love to adopt children, except the law says they can't. We're unfit to raise children because we don't have a legal document that says we're husband and wife. There are a number of psychologists and sociologists who are saying now that the marriage unit, as we think of it today, is changing. I hope so. I hope some day soon any loving couple will have the right to adopt children and provide them with homes and security.

INT.: *Do you really think it makes sense for swinging parents to adopt children?*

DEBBIE: What's so wonderful about the nonswinging background that you or I have come from? Take the subject of sex which is so basic to the way we live and feel and act. Do you think it's any healthier for a growing boy or girl to be brought up in a household where silence surrounds the subject? That's a form of teaching, too. Youngsters learn from their whole environment. A nasty look, a slap, a flash of anger when the "wrong" word is said or a taboo subject is raised . . . That's an indoctrination course in learning how to equate sex with fear and shame and guilt, and I would like you please to explain to me why that's such a valuable asset.

INT.: *I didn't mean to be argumentative.*

75

DEBBIE: I felt more that you were putting me down and Mark as well. What great risks is Mark's son running by living with swinging parents?

INT.: *For one thing, you're not telling him. That's being secretive. I think that indicates some shame or guilt on your part.*

DEBBIE: You may think so, I don't. There's a matter of timing with Mike because of his previous conditioning with his natural mother. If Mike had grown up with us from birth all the conditioning factors would have led to a more natural awareness of sex.

INT.: *How would you have handled it differently?*

DEBBIE: I would start out very young answering whatever questions my children ask. Beyond that, I would take them to nudist camps where they could see other children and other bodies and observe that there wasn't such a terrible need to hide behind clothes all the time. It's a matter of allowing the growing child to understand his growing body, his own maturation process. It's a matter of explaining it to him with a sense of continuity, not forcing it on him—as so many so-called enlightened nonswinging parents do—in one dramatic evening of revelation. In my own opinion, that's just as harmful as years of silence before . . . As a matter of fact, I once suggested to the principal of our school that kids visit nudist camps with their parents, providing, of course, that both parents consent. We had a couple of families who were willing to do it, but the idea never left the principal's office. It died there in some mumbo-jumbo about the idea having great merit in the long run, but in the short run it would meet with too much middle-class resistance.

INT.: *Ironically, we've been finding out that the middle-class "young marrieds" are losing that resistance to the point where they appear to be coming dominant in the swinging scene.*

DEBBIE: (smiling) I still don't believe it, although it appears to be true at the parties we go to. Mostly there are married couples or people who live together. It's quite a change from the old notions of morality.

INT.: *Is it too sudden a revolution? Is the radical change, in this case a sexual change, dehumanizing?*

DEBBIE: How? In what way? Having sex with groups of people is just another aspect of human behavior. It's a natural act, and there's no reason in the world why a woman shouldn't enjoy sex for many hours at a time and in groups. I'm sure every woman has been told that once she reaches a climax she's through, which isn't true at all. She can have as many as five, ten or more orgasms a night, providing that she has a sex mate who can elevate her to these sexual heights . . . Before I was swinging, I never could have multiple orgasms. It used to take a great deal of effort on the man's part, and on my part to get any deep response out of me. Now, it doesn't. I remember at one swinging party, I reached more than twelve orgasms in one evening with nine different men.

INT.: *Nine?*

DEBBIE: In two hours. Mark and I had been invited to a fairly large swinging party . . . I had gone through a rough day at school before I came home. Part of it was caused by a father of one of my students. He kept telling me all his problems and forgetting that his son had some. I was really worn out, and told Mark that maybe we should gracefully bow out of the party that night. He didn't say anything; he just left me alone for a while and ran a bath for me. When I started soaking in it he brought in a chilled bottle of wine, sat down beside me and we sipped and soaked, as he put it. We both recharged our batteries. And the wine, which I usually don't drink, especially on an empty stomach, made me feel light and kind of floaty . . . When we arrived at the party, there must have been fifteen to twenty couples, mostly marrieds . . . One of the men was a doctor who teaches a surgical specialty at ———— University. I was impressed just looking at his hand, because I was told that he was involved in developing new techniques of intricate surgery. I was still responding to the wine I had had before, and that quiet kind of euphoria made everything else that happened happen more naturally. After a while couples started pairing off. I forgot who it was, but one of the men I had been talking to while we were nibbling at canapes walked into a bedroom with me. Nothing was said about, "Do you or don't you?" We both knew we wanted to. I had never seen him at any party before so we started talking about what he did for a living and I (she

77

smiles) started drawing with my fingers the shapes of hearts on his stomach. Then I traced a line from his heart to his penis. It really turned him on. We had a good time, but after he was finished I could tell he was really pooped and I still wanted more sex. I had the feeling that I didn't want to stop. Before I knew it someone else was in bed with me. He was giving me head, and I thought he was going to pass out from not catching his breath. I had never felt a man's tongue move so fast in my life, and, I swear, he wasn't stopping for air. Well, I came twice and I wanted to come a third time, but he was worn out so he went out of the room. I was still riding that fantastic high, not drunk, mind you, but giddy high from the old wine and the new . . . I can remember so much of it. That surprises me a little . . . I was aware of everything—like my skin was rippling all over, up and down. I was aware of every spot on my body . . . And then one of the other men was massaging me. And did he get a response from me! I think it was too much at first. He backed away, and I laughed and asked if there was something I could do for him to help him along. Then he came up with a wild position that I had never tried before. I had one leg over his shoulder and the other leg stretched out, and he started moving up and down and came right away. I reached a climax, how I don't know because my legs were stiffening up, but I did. I wanted to do it that way again, but he was worn out. I had the next three men one right after the other, and none of them could keep up with me. I mean, I was aware of who I was, where I was and who I was with, but the men seemed to lose their identity. I was in control and they weren't. It was as if I was every woman to each man . . . and with each one I became wetter and more excited. Every once in a while I'd glance down and there would be Mark standing near by or lying down next to me, holding my hand or stroking me or coaxing me along. It was the most unbelievable thing that ever happened to me . . . Sometimes instead of seeing a face move down toward me I saw a penis, and you know how it is sometimes when you concentrate just on one subject and it seems to become bigger and bigger until it becomes the whole picture. This is how I was seeing things for a while that night. I think the next man and I reached our climax together. He was getting up, facing me, switching from one position to the next and I saw traces of a man's body, rather than one particular spot. It was like one of those avant-garde underground films where you are hit with an image of a naked body only long enough to know that it must be a hint of sex. And then the next image is flashed across the screen. But I not only felt as if I was in a film, but also that I was a member of the audience because someone had walked in and I heard a crunching noise. When I looked up there was a fellow watching me with his fist raised over his mouth dropping popcorn balls, one at a time, down his mouth. There were other people in the bedroom, some of them standing, others sitting down on the floor watching me. They weren't yelling or anything like that, but sometimes I could hear them making smiling noises, like when a person is happy for you and sort of smiles in a verbal way; that's what my friends were doing . . . None of the men could keep up with me, and it got to a point where the one who finished and the one who was just starting melted together. I was having so many orgasms, one after the other, that there seemed to be a continuity of sensation that heightened and never diminished. Mark told me later on that while I was with one of the men another guy who was waiting for me to finish had already reached a climax with a girl in the hallway. He walked into the bedroom exhausted. Then, as he was watching me, he slowly started raising an erection. As I recall, I think he came in me rather quickly, and before he lifted both feet off the bed the heart surgeon was looking over my shoulders. I said one of the most stupid things I could have said, and it came out not the way I had meant it. I told him I had heard about him, and he thought I meant about how good he was as a lover. It was just a wild feeling that I had about him. Here was a man whose hands had performed critical surgery and now his fingers were inside me. I couldn't help it, but that's what I was thinking. But he knew what he was doing and he caused me to climax twice . . . It felt as if the whole

79

top of my body, my head, my neck, and then my back and my behind were drawing out of me, pushing out of me . . . I guess that was the end of my night of nine.

INT.: *I think the best thing for me is to make no comment.*

DEBBIE: I'd hate to read your mind . . .

INT.: *You think I would disapprove of what you did?*

DEBBIE: I don't think you appreciate it and I don't think you believe it . . . That's the trouble with so many nonswinging men: they can't accept that a woman has the capacity to respond so deeply.

INT.: *It would appear, Debbie, that for you at least, swinging has led to many changes in your life—could you sum them up?*

DEBBIE: I've become more separate and self-sufficient unto myself, but I can live and love and be loved with much more feeling. Swinging has released so much more energy from me (or maybe I have discovered that I have so much more) and it comes out in my teaching, in almost anything—even when I argue with Mark, when we have a yelling, screaming fight. I can get out what's in me so much more honestly. I'm much closer to my feelings . . . When I was married the first time I was nothing but a vegetable. A human body, yes, but just blobs of protoplasm really . . . I had an empty life. I don't have to worry about that ever happening again. I feel like a girl for once. I guess for the first time in my life I do. I truly do feel like a woman.

8

TOM AND MICHELLE:

Swinging In a Mixed Marriage

Tom is thirty-seven, black and grew up in the South. His wife, Michelle, is twenty-five, white and grew up on a ranch in the Midwest. Both learned about life because they saw nature living and doing well. Neither one had it easy in the beginning, but, as Tom says, "So what, it gave us more character."

Tom managed to make the system work for him. To go to college meant to be the best. He was. He went to a Midwestern university where he first studied business administration and then economics. He was graduated four years later a few percentage points under "honors."

He is lean, five-foot-eleven, moves fast, thinks fast, and is not without opinions.

Michelle stays away from anything that will change her looks: "I was born me, I am me, and if I hear praises about my looks, it's because I work with what I have. I don't worry about qualities that belong to someone else, not to me."

She's around five-foot-three, but recently, being pregnant, she feels ten feet tall.

81

She looks devilish. Soft-spoken, but you know she'll bounce into action when she is given room: "Tom's the big black giant, and I'm his little white pixie wife."

Mixed marriages have their problems, and Tom and Michelle's is no different.

Tom's job with a computer corporation requires a considerable amount of traveling, and he takes Michelle along with him as much as he can. They have been swinging together for five years. And add two more years for Tom's swinging before he met Michelle.

"Tom's an organizer and it simply blows his mind if anything's out of place in the apartment," Michelle says. "Everything has its place. If there's even a magazine lying around, it's enough to unnerve him a little."

Their apartment does reflect an orderliness but also a creative charm. Each room is done in a different period.

"When we feel early American we go into the den. If we feel Spanish, we go into the bedroom. All these pieces here we've selected to fit what we want. We don't like bright, gaudy colors. We like quiet shades of browns and greens and some golds."

Tom and Michelle can afford to live in a house if they want to. But right now, they would just as soon keep the six-room apartment in a fashionable affluent area of Maryland.

Something else they like to do is buy mementos from all the states they've been in. A beautiful Indian wall tapestry hangs in the living room. One summer they both decided to spend two weeks in the West living with an Indian friend who went to college with Tom. Before they left, the villagers showered them with handmade gifts. Tom says: "For Michelle and me this was one of the most marvelous, meaningful trips we have ever taken. And every summer, even if we have only four days, we'll fly out and be met by Pete and driven up to see his family and some beautiful people living on that reservation."

Tom and Michelle are very much travelers. Tom says, "We don't belong to the jet-set, because it's really meaningless, we just take off and go. Stop where we want to. We have swinging friends all over the country. The West, Midwest, East—and even in the deep South."

INTERVIEWER: *How did both of you develop an interest in swinging?*

TOM: I was first introduced to it by an airline hostess.

INT.: *Michelle, how did you get started?*

MICHELLE: I like to think I was swinging most of my life. It wasn't called that, and I didn't know what swinging was until after I became a swinger.

INT.: *You said most of your life?*

MICHELLE: I grew up very free in speaking and acting out my sexual fantasies. My family would tell me that certain things were wrong—masturbation, and just about anything that had to do with sex—but I didn't pay much attention to them. I went on and did whatever I felt I wanted to do and what I felt was right. I was an only child, but I had a lot of friends in school and we lived on ranches where there were other families, so I was around other children quite a bit . . . There were about eleven of us kids. We had chores to do like getting the cattle at night for milking. That was across the river, so we'd leave early, about four in the afternoon, and cross the river and play under the bridge. We'd change clothes—the boys would wear the girls' clothes and the girls would wear the boys' clothes. I believe I was seven years old. Some of the older kids, about twelve or thirteen years old, would be having intercourse; we did things like that together, in a group . . . We tried to make sure no grownups saw us because we felt we would really be in trouble if they did.

INT.: *So you consider that your first swinging encounter?*

MICHELLE: Yes, until my family moved to a Southern city when I was twelve-years-old. I didn't know what a big city was like, so the move was quite an adjustment. My parents were very conservative and never talked about sex. They never showed any affection toward one another. I didn't think any sign of affection would be appreciated, so for a matter of two or three years I wasn't involved in sex with other people. I just kept to myself as I was going to school and indulged in a considerable amount of masturbation . . .

INT.: *Tom, how did you and Michelle meet?*

TOM: At a swinging party . . . We had never met before but

during the course of the evening, we got to know each other rather well. About three days later I called Michelle for a date and wrangled an invitation to dinner at her place . . . Five months later we were married.

INT.: *Has swinging been good for your marriage?*

MICHELLE: It give us a head start, a better chance to make a go of it. You see, because we're swingers we don't hide our feelings from each other.

TOM: Look, we have problems. Some of them we iron out right away. Others, obviously, will take much more time. I think if a marriage is bad, swinging isn't going to help it. I know when we continued swinging as a married couple, we engaged in a lot of self-evaluation, and, at times, even extreme criticism . . . At first, we overdid the sexual freedom and honesty in terms of how we treated each other outside of swinging. Like anything else that's new, you tend to stretch it beyond its limits . . . There are still times when Michelle and I have pretty heated arguments.

MICHELLE: Except the best way for married couples to make up, I think, is in bed, and we swingers are pretty good at that.

INT.: *Tom, did being black create problems for you in the swinging world?*

TOM: Yes, in the beginning I did find some evidence of prejudice at certain parties. It seems that most white people are inculcated with the old wives' tale about a black person being superior and overpowering, sexually. Therefore, many white men believe that the black man is, in a sense, supersexed; they say, "Watch out for a black man when he gets near your wife or your girlfriend!" It's funny how difficult it is even for a fairly intelligent white man to shed this myth. Every man is basically the same sexually; the differences depend on what you put into sex and how another person responds to you, rather than to the color of your skin.

INT.: *We've been told that there are more black men than black women in the swinging scene.*

TOM: I'd agree with that. Many black women I know fear that swinging may hurt their dignity and encourage a general lowering of their moral standards. They also tend to feel that, even in swinging, the white man is really using them again in a sexual way.

INT.: *Do you ever feel used by white women?*

TOM: No. We have sex as equals.

INT.: *Why can't a black woman share this feeling?*

TOM: It's her past, mainly, the role that she assumed in her own family. Often the black woman is the main breadwinner because of the depressing restrictions that are put on the black man . . . I think a black woman feels it's safer to swing behind closed doors rather than to do it openly.

INT.: *Do you think swinging is helpful in breaking down racial barriers?*

TOM: I think so. Very much so.

MICHELLE: In my opinion, there aren't enough people who are able to accept the freedom they're allowed in swinging . . . We have many black friends who want to be swingers and attempt to join our parties but their upbringing causes them so much anxiety. They expect to be rejected constantly and don't seem to be able to get over this feeling very easily.

INT.: *I would think that this fear of rejection goes way beyond the color of your skin, that this would be one of the biggest fears for anyone who thinks about entering the swinging scene.*

TOM: A lot of people misinterpret what swinging is all about. They think that swingers are people who are always lying down and having intercourse, doing odd, erotic sex acts all the time. This is simply not the case. Swinging is a form of therapy. Most people who swing are very understanding, very open-minded in comparison with the general level of prejudice that you find in straight-world people.

INT.: *You never did go into those instances where you encountered prejudice in swinging.*

TOM: I've been swinging for seven years now, and I haven't encountered many such incidents . . . I used to travel a southern route a few years back when I first started working for my company, and I had two- and three-day lay-overs in——— (a Southern town) before I flew back East. When I had some free evenings I'd often go to local swinging parties.

INT.: *Were you the only black there?*

TOM: No, there were usually three or four other black men around.

INT.: *And how many whites?*

TOM: An average of ten to twelve couples, mostly husbands and wives, except for the politicians who attended. They'd bring dates along—airline hostesses or girls on their staffs who could be trusted not to say anything.

INT.: *How did you feel about that kind of gathering?*

TOM: I didn't have one general feeling that I wore to all these occasions . . .

INT.: *Can you be more specific?*

TOM: When I attended the first swinging party in————, I didn't know there would be any politicians around. I went to the party with a black girl. When we arrived I recognized one man who was in politics. I'd seen a picture of him in the newspaper. After a while I went up to him and we started talking. Then a white girl walked up to both of us and took my arm, leaving him standing there alone. We walked off to one of the bedrooms.

INT.: *How did he react to all of this?*

TOM: As I left, I remember seeing him smile and that was all until I finished having sex with the girl . . . We chatted in bed for a while. Then I headed for the kitchen and I saw him coming in. Again, he sort of smiled. I paused just for a second, wondering if he was going to tell the girl to bathe in Oxydol or something like that before they had intercourse, but he didn't say anything, so I walked out . . . A few hours later when the party had slowed down a little, I was at the buffet and he came up to me. I still felt he was forcing that smile, but he put his arm around my shoulder and started talking about how nice it was of him to let me have the girl first and that he couldn't be much of a racist if he allowed that and then went to bed with the same girl afterward . . . I think he was a real sonofabitch. But he put it all out in the open. He told me that, while he had to talk "white supremacy," he didn't really take it all that seriously . . . I told him that I figured as much, since his father and grand-father probably learned about sex from my black sisters who

86

taught their white masters all there was to know about screwing. He laughed at that. Out loud. And then I needled him some more about why he didn't bring his wife to the party. He didn't like that bit at all and after some vague, apologetic small talk, he disappeared in a hurry. I don't mean to single him out, or for that matter, imply that southern politicians are different than northern representatives. There's no great secrecy about the fact that sex crosses party lines and I'd presume that politicians, regardless of party affiliations or georgraphic locations, have hangups that are comparable to the rest of the electorate.

INT.: *Well, did you feel that your knowledge of the congressman's sexual activities gave you power over him?*

TOM: Oh, no . . . Who's going to print that kind of stuff? Everyone knows it's happening, and knows enough to ignore it— until someone gets caught and there's a public record of it. Then that poor fellow is made out to be the only one who's doing it.

INT.: *What about swinging outside the South? Is it different in the North?*

TOM: I don't know what you mean by "different." People are different, unique. So it's the people you're with, the level of intelligence they have, that would dictate the specific setting of a party, wherever it is. Because of my job, I've been afforded the opportunity to swing throughout the country. I've got swinging friends in every city I visit.

INT.: *Every city?*

TOM: (Nodding) There's not one city or town that I've been in where I haven't swung at least once . . . And what I'm saying is no great secret. Pick up any of the swinging publications with their list of clubs. They're everywhere.

INT.: *Do you use them as reference guides?*

TOM: No, I don't party that way. I go with people I know personally or people I've been referred to by friends.

INT.: *Is that because you're status-conscious?*

TOM: Could be.

INT.: *Do blacks make good swingers?*

TOM: Let's say we work hard at it.

INT.: *Then swinging gives you status.*

TOM: No, it's sex—doing it with people you like.

INT.: *Do you discriminate?*

TOM: I've learned not to, from experience.

INT.: *Have you had any "bad" trips as a swinger?*

TOM: If you mean have I met any bad swingers, the answer is "yes," and there have been bad scenes, too. But I've met far fewer creeps in swinging than I have in the straight world.

INT.: *Has your swinging changed the manner in which you relate to people in the straight world?*

TOM: And how! Right now, I'm teaching a class at my company, and I never would have been willing to undertake such a situation before. Now I'm able to transfer the freedom I've learned in swinging to other day-to-day relationships. I never would have been able to communicate as well as I do with the people I'm teaching without the background I've picked up from swinging . . . I can take on each individual in that classroom and psyche him out, recognize how we react to each other in a given situation. I know, for example, that a few of the men sitting in the back of the room are saying, "Prove it to me, black boy." Well, it doesn't phase me anymore. I've gained confidence. I can talk with the best of them, screw with the best of them, and nobody can hold me down or keep me from getting to the finish line—with them or ahead of them . . . Swinging is a great leveler, a great equalizer. Once you've taken off your clothes, well, there's not much status in a group of naked bodies, regardless of color. Basically, we've all got the same kind of equipment.

(NOTE: At this point, we took a break and went out for supper. Then Michelle stopped off at the neighborhood department store to pick up some items for a layette which she had ordered. Then we all settled down again in the comfort of their living room and started the second session of taping.)

INT.: *Do you have any feelings about preferring a boy or a girl for your first child?*

MICHELLE: No.

TOM: Yes, I'd prefer twins, actually—a boy and a girl.

MICHELLES Ha! He'd prefer the Dionne quintuplets, the more the merrier. Because he still doesn't accept the reality of what it is to have a child.

TOM: Aw, come on, now, I wanted to have this child as much as you did.

MICHELLE: I'm not denying that. I'm just saying that it's a little easier for you when and if things get rough, you've got a built-in occupational excuse.

TOM: Yeah, any time the going gets too rough, it's "Gee, darling, I'm sorry but I've got to take a plane to Kansas City."

MICHELLE: (Laughing) That's what I mean.

INT.: *How far along are you, Michelle?*

MICHELLE: Let's see, in two more days, it'll be the end of the seventh month.

INT.: *Has that affected your swinging?*

MICHELLE: It's been very restricted. My desires are different now. I have to consider my health as well as the baby's, so I don't take any chances . . . I'm not having intercourse at this point, but I can still go to parties with Tom and pleasure men orally by giving them head.

INT.: *How do you feel about your husband swinging while you're limiting your sexual activities?*

MICHELLE: I'm all for it. Even before I was pregnant, there were times when I didn't feel up to having sex because I had a hard day or I was sick or something. Why should my husband be forced to suffer along with me? We'll still go to parties together and I'm happy to see that he's having sex with someone because I care for him.

INT.: *Do either one of you have any feelings about how to handle your progeny's sex education?*

MICHELLE: (Shaking her head and laughing) He isn't even born yet.

TOM: But we certainly have talked about it. We want the atmosphere at home to be very open.

MICHELLE: Not at all like the background I had where my parents taught me so little and forced me to learn by myself. I'm not too proud of what happened back there. I'm lucky I ended up as well put-together as I am. What I'm saying is that I don't want to expose our children to those risks. I think it's

89

important for a child to learn about sex gradually as he's growing up and at his own pace.

INT.: *Please be a little more specific.*

MICHELLE: For instance, suppose he's four years old and asks what a word means or maybe he's seen animals mating or he wants to know how humans do it. He should be told right there and then. Maybe there's a proper way of telling him at his age level, but the main thing is not to give him the wrong idea, not to deny what exists or make excuses. It's best to be straightforward.

TOM: I'd go a step further. If I were in bed with Michelle and one of our children came into the bedroom, I wouldn't cover up, hide or act as if we were ashamed of what we were doing.

INT.: *Are you now talking about a situation where you and Michelle might be having intercourse?*

TOM: That's right. If that were to happen, and we've discussed this, neither one of us would object to any of our children witnessing the act.

MICHELLE: Definitely not. Because if he sees the parents whom he loves doing a loving thing, he's not going to misunderstand . . . I remember when I was a child my parents locked the bedroom door on me. I had a pretty good idea of what was going on, and when I heard my mother crying out, I thought my father was hurting her. I associated sex with pain, with a man doing something physical and bad to a woman. I don't want our children to grow up with those misconceptions.

TOM: When our children grow up and want to have sex on their own, we would hope that the atmosphere at home would encourage them to discuss these issues with us. Frankly, I'd prefer my children bringing their sexual partners into our home rather than resorting to a motel or places like that.

MICHELLE: I'd consider myself at fault if my daughter came back pregnant because she didn't know enough about protective devices or if she got involved with people in a promiscuous way and didn't know who the father was.

INT.: *Doesn't that sometimes happen in swinging?*

TOM: No, not that I know of. The women there are very careful about this situation. They know it's their responsibility, and they do a good job protecting themselves.

INT.: *Okay—suppose your kids are at the age of consent, how would you feel about their swinging?*

MICHELLE: Why should we object? It's good enough for us. We're doing something as a family without shame or guilt . . . We were at a swinging party not so long ago where a girl who was twenty brought along her mother and father. I'm not sure, but I think in this case her parents had never swung before. They were willing to experiment. After they saw the kinds of people that were there, they really loosened up and got into the swing of it. From what I hear, they still swing right along with their daughter.

INT.: *How do you feel about this, Tom?*

TOM: It was beautiful, just great, to see a mother, father and daughter able to communicate with each other on such a deep level . . . How many kids can go up to their parents and tell them they met this guy or this girl and had intercourse with them without the father or the mother tearing up the place?

INT.: *What about swinging parents who won't tell their children about swinging?*

MICHELLE: I'd rather not comment on that. It's a personal matter. But I'd hope they'd change their views.

TOM: We're lucky, I think, that we feel the way we do. We're looser about it than others.

MICHELLE: Swinging has changed our whole life in so many ways.

TOM: Before I was married to Michelle, I was making an average of $1,500 a month and I couldn't save a penny. Now that we're doing things together, we're able to set limits and save money.

INT.: *Do you credit swinging for this, or Michelle?*

MICHELLE: I'm the penny-pincher—give me the credit. And this brings up something important for me, personally. Before I started swinging and met Tom, I didn't have a very good image of myself. I was very dependent on other people in every aspect of my life. I'd laze around, watching television, vegetating. You can't get very far in swinging with that kind of attitude. You begin to see yourself much more realistically for the woman that you are. I don't think I could have handled a mixed marriage without the security that I got out of swinging. After I married Tom, I began to get a clear picture of the kind of life I wanted to lead. We have goals now, things we want to do, to achieve. I've enrolled in some classes at college in the night division and I'm doing some volunteer work at the university at a free clinic . . . I want to make something of myself, of our life together and our children. I look at them as a piece of ourselves that's put together in a new combination.

TOM: Amen . . .

INT.: *Can't you find this openness and frankness in the nonswinging environment?*

MICHELLE: I'd like to think I could, but I haven't.

TOM: And I don't know many people who have.

MICHELLE: People are much more uptight about our mixed marriage, for example, in the nonswinging world.

TOM: I have black friends that we don't feel comfortable with. I try to see people first as human beings, with their attributes and faults; the color of one's skin doesn't have much to do with the whole person, the good or the bad aspects of a particular soul.

MICHELLE: Frankly, I'm more comfortable around people who are prejudiced and don't mind saying it than I am with people who keep saying they're not and really are. That's what we mean about bringing things out into the open. I can understand it if someone says, "Look, this is the way I feel, it may not be right, but that's the way it is for me." I came from a background where most people were prejudiced and their attitude was—"We're right and everyone else is wrong."

TOM: I've learned that prejudice is hardly ever black or white. Especially in our affluent, over-indulgent society, it comes in all shapes and colors and in at least thirty-one flavors.

9

Some Observations About Swinging Couples

Sixty-four percent of the married couples we interviewed were in their thirties, twenty-eight percent were in their forties, and eight percent were fifty and over. Eighty-five percent of the married couples had children, of whom approximately fifty-five percent were in the prepuberty ages. Approximately twenty-seven percent of the couples had one child; approximately forty-nine percent two children, and twenty-four percent had three or more children.

Almost ninety percent of the married couples in our sampling preferred small, planned parties, averaging six to fifteen couples, as opposed to the so-called "orgies." Approximately the same percentage of the "marrieds" felt that groupsex parties replaced the nonswinging cocktail or weekend social party on their calendar. They insisted rather vehemently that sex for them never was a compulsive, obsessive affair.

These above statistics may belie the myth that suppressed sexual impulses encourage creative activities. Dr. William Masters and Mrs Virginia Johnson have debunked this myth and suggest that healthy release of sexual tensions may actually create a more freeing atmosphere for the exploration of other life realities. A majority of the married couples in our sampling appear to be coping rather well with other life priorities. They told us:

"I function better on my job now because I am less preoccupied with sexual thoughts . . ." ". . . The pressure on my husband and me to be at our best, sexually, whenever we go to bed has lessened considerably . . ." ". . . The openness and honesty I have found in swinging helps me relate better to non-swinging friends and business associates . . ." ". . . I'm not afraid any more . . ."

It also appears that almost all the married couples, like the singles, over-indulge in swinging in the beginning. With the marrieds, in most instances, the man appeared to be the initiator. However, once the woman overcame her initial timidity, she appeared to adjust much more easily to the groupsex experience. In fact, on the basis of our sampling at least, the woman tends to become the controlling factor in how the married couple continues their participation in the swinging scene.

Married couples tend to reach a point of satiation later than the singles. They start dropping out, on the average, after the first twelve to eighteen months. In contrast to the behavior of the singles, over eighty percent of the married couples we interviewed returned to the groupsex scene two or three months after they dropped out. They continued partying, preferring the structured system that the singles shunned. And though they continued to drop out occasionally for a variety of reasons beyond satiation—illnesses, or the desire to have another child and be sure of its paternity—swinging has become a rather permanent part of their lives.

Almost all the married couples in our sampling indicated that they had found friendships in swinging and that these relationships carried over into nonswinging activities, principally vacations, cultural or sports activities. It appears that these swingers feel more comfortable with swinging rather than "straight" friends.

However, in contrast to the prevailing attitude of the singles, the majority of married couples indicated that as their friendships with other swinging couples grew, their sex relationships with those particular people diminished. This new closeness apparently promotes an emotional commitment between the parties which, in turn, governs the decision about sexual encounters.

The married couples in our sampling, much more than the singles, felt a constant need for new partners. However, the couples indicated that if a particular sexual encounter with a new person was enjoyable, there were repeat performances.

The married couples were clearly much more concerned than the singles about how their new bed partners were selected. Surprisingly, they were less concerned about the partners' sex appeal than they were about possible exposure to venereal diseases and law enforcement authorities. Because of their status in the non-swinging community and their regard for their families, they tended to be much more secretive than the singles about their involvement in groupsex.

Thirty-three percent of the married couples in our sampling had been swinging for one to five years; sixty percent for five to twelve years; and seven percent for more than twelve years. The main reasons for their involvement in the groupsex phenomenon appared to be: (a) finding sexual variety with the consent of their own partners; (b) little likelihood of rejection; (c) experiencing extra-marital sex with little or no guilt (in fact, the group scene produces group approval and encouragement which tend to lessen jealously and competitiveness. Much more so than among singles, groupsex also encourages a kind of religious fervor in married couples, a desire to proselytize and bring new converts into the fold).

Approximately eighty-three percent of the married couples in our sampling felt that the expanded sexual knowledge they had gained from swinging enabled them to develop a better understanding of themselves as men and women. They felt that it took much of the anger and hostility out of the marriage bed and substituted a tolerance and freedom that enabled them to share deeper levels of communication and become their own best bed partners.

Almost seventy-five percent of the married couples and an equal percentage of the singles indicated that when they paired off in odd numbers (threesomes, fivesomes, etc.), both men and women preferred that the "extra" be another woman. The men indicated that they enjoyed having two women pleasure them, and, in turn, they were stimulated by the sight of a woman pleasuring another woman.

The greatest anxiety and difficulty relates to the children of married swingers. How should children be told about their parents' swinging? Should they be told at all? How much should they be told, and when? Few swinging parents are untroubled by these questions.

In sharp contrast to the singles, almost eighty percent of the married couples indicated that most of their "bad scenes" in groupsex tended to happen in small gatherings such as threesomes and fivesomes. The most trouble-prone pairing-off was the foursome consisting of two married couples. Problems developed when one partner didn't like the alternate "him" or "her." This situation seems to duplicate the same feelings of imprisonment, demand to perform, and lack of variety that their own marriage held for them.

PART III

The Singles

---

10 CATHY:

"For Me It's a Turn-On"

Cathy is twenty-four years old and single. She lives with two other girls, sharing an expensive Manhattan apartment, furnished in do-it-yourself, used, and midtown modern style. She has been swinging for two years and describes her family background as "New England rebellion."

Her father is a high school principal and her mother spends more time with Cathy's younger sister and brother than she does with other women friends: "She's like a pal as well as my mom—she's really great. My father's always trying to crack us up, and is always pulling some kind of stunt."

Cathy spent most of her childhood in the comfortable surroundings of a New England community. She had a choice of going to a girl's prep school for her secondary education or continuing in public school. She chose to stay with her friends.

Cathy valued those friendships. Weekends usually meant staying over at someone's house or having them over to her home; "We had slumber parties where we'd talk all the way into the night, and my mom and dad would finally have to tell us to get some sleep or it would be breakfast-on-Zombie-time in the morning."

She achieved all but a straight "A" average in high school, found time to be in the chorus, participated in school sports, and dated the "older guys from the Ivy League schools."

But once in college, she became tired of the dating routine, becoming a man's "possession" and being shown off as "please do not touch the merchandise."

One day she told the campus he-men to stay away, that she had more important things to do. Writing was one of them. "Nothing really that spectacular," she told us. "But I enjoyed it."

Following graduation from her eastern conservative college with a B.A. in English, she left for New York. For a while she felt that she would become part of the traffic, swallowed up before the light changed to green. But she has become used to a life crowded with things to see, things to do and places to go. Now the pace of life only makes Cathy shake her honey-blonde hair, cock her head to one side and wink and smile about what's next. Sometimes uncertainties that can't be winked or smiled away do surface, but Cathy has an answer: "I try not to think about the confusing things, so I keep myself busy all the time."

During the week keeping busy means working as an editorial assistant for a large New York publishing house. Busy at night means one evening a week at night school where she is accumulating credits toward a master's degree. That leaves little time for socializing until the weekends. Then she can let go and not feel guilty because she has accomplished as much as she can.

For Cathy, a bundle of energy wrapped in a five-foot-three-inch frame, one hundred seven pounds, everything comes in time if you don't wish for it to happen. Her prescription is simple: "Let it, that's all."

She has no plans for marriage; at least not yet. Cathy has time. And she still has a few things she wants to put together first.

Somewhere along the way she is also trying to understand why things are so different when she returns home these days. The man she had been dating before she left, the one she liked very much, hasn't changed. Cathy has. When she last saw him during one of her visits, she didn't want to do anything with him, not even pet.

Cathy often quotes the Thomas Wolfe title, "You Can't Go Home Again." She represents many single swingers: college graduates, professional young women, all of whom "can't go home again." Not to the way it was.

INTERVIEWER: *Cathy, how did you get into the swinging scene?*

CATHY: I was always the kind of girl who dated only one man at a time. Then, about a year ago, I was going with a fellow who had been swinging and liked it. At first, I felt that I couldn't do it . . . you know, having the kind of sex where I was sharing myself with more than one person. I still had that hangup. So he suggested that I go with him to a nudist camp. I didn't have to take my clothes off if I didn't want to, but at least I could see there how other people handled nudity.

INT.: *How did it work out?*

CATHY: It was a nice-looking place, set back in the hills. We went along a winding path, up toward a swimming pool . . . Most of the people were naked but some, like myself, still had clothes on. The women were wearing bikinis and the men bathing suits. Then, maybe, oh, about three hours later, after I had gotten used to seeing all these naked people, my friend asked me if I would mind taking my clothes off. By this time, since so many other people were nude, I felt I could try it out and see what would happen.

INT.: *Had you ever undressed in front of a lot of people before?*

CATHY: No. I did in my sorority, but then it was around girls and of course that's quite different from walking around nude where there are men. But, surprisingly enough, it didn't bother me too much. I think a lot had to do with the fact that I saw parents and their children undressed and enjoying the outdoors. Seeing these kids and their parents having such a good old normal time helped me relax and not be so conscious of the fact that I was naked . . . Some people were playing volleyball, others were pitching horseshoes. There

99

were children in the swimming pool. It was like going to a country club or being in a park. The only difference was that here the people had their clothes off. After a while, I got used to seeing penises wobbling when someone went up to knock the volleyball over the net, and breasts bouncing when women were running down the grass.

INT.: *Did you have sex with the fellow you were with?*

CATHY: Oh no, not at the nudist camp. The camp is quite strict about that. All he did was occasionally talk to me about swinging. There were a lot of questions I had about it.

INT.: *Like what?*

CATHY: Well, what the parties were like, what the people were like. He told me that it was really fun, that the people who came to swinging parties experienced being totally free and uninhibited and were quite open. The more he spoke about swinging, the more I became interested. So at the end of that day we agreed that he would take me to my first swinging party the following week. And for the first time in my life I really was looking forward to having a special kind of sexual experience, something unique. I wasn't sure what I would be like, exactly, but I had lots of wild fantasies.

INT.: *For instance?*

CATHY: Oh, having more than one man pleasure me sexually at the same time. I think every girl has these fantasies just as, I suppose, a man fantasizes over making it with more than one woman at the same time. Until recently it's been a man's world when it came to sex. I think people are beginning to realize that women also have these dreams, these fantasies, and once they shed those old anxieties that have been pounded into them about sex being dirty, they can also start enjoying sex.

INT.: *Did you have any fears about that first swinging party?*

CATHY: I think my anxieties were more anticipatory rather than being scared about what I would do or how I would react. I'm the kind of person who puts her mind to something, works it out in her head, and when the experience actually happens, I've at least gone through it in my thoughts. I feel that process helped me, especially at my first swinging party.

INT.: *Where was it held?*

100

CATHY: At the home of a friend, my date's friend. We went out to dinner first and arrived at the party about nine o'clock. There were people inside drinking a little bit, talking to each other. I didn't see anybody undressed, at least not in the beginning. I stayed with my date and we talked about my work and his day. Maybe an hour later another fellow walked up and introduced himself and joined us in more conversation . . . I guess it was a few minutes later that a girl walked over to where we were sitting. The man I was with, who had known her from other parties, started talking to her. Then he excused himself and left me with the other fellow whose name was Ralph.

INT.: *Did it bother you that your date left?*

CATHY: Not really; he had explained that this would probably happen. It was a way for new people to meet other new people and this was one of the aspects of swinging . . . Ralph seemed nice. After a while when I felt more relaxed, he asked me if I wanted to go into one of the bedrooms. I nodded "okay" and we walked into the nearest one. I saw two couples who were already in bed, and, quite frankly, it took me a while to get used to that situation.

INT.: *Do you remember how you felt?*

CATHY: It's difficult to select your specific feelings when you're seeing all this go on. I know I was embarrassed. I had never seen another couple having sex before and here there were two couples in the same bed and that boggled my mind a bit, I'll tell you. But the couples seemed to be having a good time, and I don't think they were aware of our being there . . . I stood near one of the corners of the room and took it all in. I watched the other couples and listened to them. There were noises: I mean, groaning and sighing, you know, sounds that we all make when we're having sex and enjoying it. I don't think any normal person with normal desires could have been turned off by all this. I didn't want to run out of the room or anything like that. It was really what I considered something beautiful to watch . . . Maybe about twenty minutes later, the guy I was with sort of looked at me and smiled. He didn't say, "C'mon, let's go to bed". He let me make that decision and I thought to myself, "Okay, why not? If I'm going to feel uneasy, I might as well find out now." I started getting undressed and found a bench to put my clothes on—fastidious me, everything was folded over neatly. I had to move somebody else's clothes out of the way to make room for mine.

INT.: *And the man you were with?*

CATHY: He was getting undressed, too, and after that he led me by the hand to the bed and we found some room on the side . . . At first, all I did was look out of the corner of my eye at the couples who were next to us. I never had seen the back of a man's testicles before . . . It was funny. The whole scene made me laugh and that turned Ralph on. He started caressing me and he knew what to do.

INT.: *Can you explain to a nonswinger what it's like to have sex with a group of people in the same bed?*

CATHY: It's a feeling that you don't have emotional ties with the guy you're with. You can just be with him and pleasure him and be pleasured by him, and then, if you want, move to somebody else in the same bed and have sex with him, too. I don't feel that I have to be in love with each guy I'm swinging with. That's the beauty of swinging . . . I'm having more dates and fewer problems with men than I've ever had before. With each guy, I really participate, give him the kind of sex he wants. And when we're finished, I'm exhausted, and, damn it, the fellow I'm with better leave exhausted, too. As I said before, I like to talk to a guy I'm with afterward, too, and I do get a little hurt if I see him leaving me and walking off with someone else.

INT.: *Is it a matter of pride or ego?*

CATHY: Something like that. I feel that perhaps I didn't satisfy him the way I should have or maybe we both were not in the right mood. The mind has a lot to do with swinging, too, you know. If I don't want to have sex during a particular evening or something happened earlier in the day that still seems to be bothering me, this can interfere with my swinging. It's like anything else in life. If I'm preoccupied, then it will interfere with whatever else I'm doing. But usually the feeling of being hurt or turned down doesn't last the whole

102

evening or ruin my evening. There are always other men to swing with.

INT.: *Do you try to get back to a fellow who leaves you too quickly?*

CATHY: (Shaking her head) Unless I really like him, no. I very seldom ball a man more than once in an evening.

INT.: *Isn't it inhibiting to have sex with so many other people in the room?*

CATHY: (Giggling) It depends on the party and the people. Swinging, when it's good, is sort of a group communication. If it's inhibiting, then it may be that the person can't feel relaxed with a large group of people, whether it's at a swinging party or a concert in Rockefeller Center. Groupsex for me and most of the people I know is a turn-on. But I'll grant you, it does take a certain kind of person, and, in varying degrees, some kind of conditioning, to be able to handle it. For instance, I won't deny the fact that there have been times when I didn't reach a climax.

INT.: *Do you know what caused that?*

CATHY: Sometimes I want to have sex so much that I anticipate it, go over it in my mind so many times, building up how great it's going to be. Then the first guy I get it on with at a party, well, it just doesn't work out for him or me. If he's not enjoying himself, I don't climax. At times, I think this happens when the party itself doesn't start off well and doesn't create its own "natural high."

INT.: *How do you get a good swinging party going?*

CATHY: It depends a lot on the host and hostess. Sometimes they'll try to separate married couples and have them mix with other people. The hostess keeps an eye on the food, if it's a dinner affair, or the snacks to make sure there's enough. If she sees that someone is uncomfortable, and this usually happens with new couples, she'll go over and try to put them at ease. The real trick is to get people to start pairing off. Sometimes we play games, touching games of the type used in sensitivity training. Or some of us take off our clothes so that the others pick up the vibrations. There are times when the host and hostess are naked before we come in. This,

103

usually, is stimulating. And sometimes it just happens—and you don't even know what causes it—a couple will start having sex in the middle of the room and the rest of us watch for a while. And I want to tell you, that gets things going fast.

INT.: *When a party is creating its own "natural high"—and you're part of it—do you feel impelled in this mood to swing with every man there?*

CATHY: No. Most of the girls I know who swing are just as selective as girls who don't swing . . . I like a man who's intelligent. I don't like a guy who goes to a swinging party just to get all the sex he wants, as if each girl is a conquest and nothing more. I remember going to one party where everyone had to pay ten dollars a couple for food and drinks and one guy made a *stupid* comment, something like, "Well, it's costing me ten bucks to get into this party and to make it worthwhile I'll have to make it with at least four chicks, at two-fifty a head." That type of person and that kind of attitude really upsets me because he's not there to experience what groupsex is all about. We're sharing ourselves with other people, nor for a price or for conquest, but just to enjoy sex together in a group. I don't go to bed with lots of men at a party just because there are available males there . . . I sort of look around the room and watch the guys and see how they act and, after a while, I know who I'd like to go to bed with. Sometimes I know a man wants to swing with me, but for some reason I don't go for him, so I'll very graciously say no.

INT.: *How do you say that without putting the man down?*

CATHY: You, can excuse yourself by saying, "I'm a little tired now," or "Maybe later in the evening," or "I was thinking about having a drink now," or "I have to go to the bathroom." There are swingers whom I love dearly but there's nothing physical between us—they know it, I know it—and we're still good friends.

INT.: *Are you saying that there are men who turn you off permanently?*

CATHY: There have been times when I'm at a party and I see someone whom I've said no to before, maybe on two or three occasions. But this night, something happens between us—I can't explain it—and I want to go to bed with him.

INT.: *How do you communicate that to the man?*

CATHY: (Giggling) That's not very difficult. I just let him know I want him. It's a look or the way I touch his hand, rub his shoulder—he gets the message.

INT.: *What happens if a fellow says no to you?*

CATHY: I try to say to myself that I've made the wrong choice. My pride is hurt; sometimes there's a certain amount of ego involved, but it's still much more honest than what happens at a straight party.

INT.: *What do you mean?*

CATHY: At a nonswinging party, people usually get drunk. They're dancing, trying to play around and sneak in a few moments of necking with someone else's wife or girlfriend before they leave. I hate that. In swinging, sex is no issue, and this is very important. It's there for those who want it, and without having to grab or hassle for it on the side . . . When someone doesn't want it, they can talk . . . Seriously, we do a lot of talking. There's an openness that I've hardly ever found at a straight party. Swingers are very frank with their opinions; whether it's an argument or discussion on politics or religion or whatever . . . I went to a conservative little college in the East, and when I dated a guy for any length of time, I was supposed to do what he wanted me to do, say what he wanted me to say, as if I was his possession. That was a very restricted feeling. I really didn't feel like a person. In swinging, people are interested in knowing you, how you feel about certain things . . . This kind of communication makes you feel like a freer person. I'm convinced that I'll marry a swinger because a man who swings is a very giving person, and I'm a giving person, and that's what I'm looking for in a mate.

INT.: *What kind of man did you want to marry before you started swinging?*

CATHY: I don't exactly know. I don't think I'd ever figured it out, but I'm sure he would have been rather straight-laced . . . Before I started swinging I didn't want the man I married to know any more about sex than I did. Wow, would that have been dull! Until I was twenty-one I wouldn't even let a guy get inside me. I didn't even like the idea of touching his penis and I wouldn't have known what to do with it. Now I'm learning all about the sexual things that a man enjoys, and I also find that I'm having multiple orgasms. I can reach a climax and, maybe five minutes later I can reach another one. There's no telling how many climaxes I'll have in one evening. Before I was swinging, if I felt that I wanted to go to bed with a guy I was dating, I was lucky if I had even one orgasm. In a swinging situation, there's much more equality between the sexes. I admit that the guys and the girls are performing to a degree. But as equals. Swinging women are beautiful women, sensuous women. And we can experience one orgasm after another because we are not inhibited or hungup or afraid to learn ways to achieve these sensations.

INT.: *How do you account for your ability to achieve multiple orgasms?*

CATHY: I know how to relax. I also know how to tighten my muscles. I've been told that when a girl has multiple orgasms it makes a man feel he is sexually attractive. Most fellows like that feeling and compliment me on my sexual abilities, which makes me feel very good. Really, how many straight men take time to tell their wives how good they were after they had intercourse? I'll bet that not too many do that . . . Well, swinging women receive the kind of attention every woman needs if she is to be a good lover . . . Of course, swinging men *do* know more and are willing to take the time to pleasure a woman instead of expecting everything to be done to them. Especially when it comes to control, a male swinger knows how to keep from coming too soon, and that gives the woman more time to enjoy being satisfied.

INT.: *How do you personally achieve satisfaction?*

CATHY: I find that I like a man to give me head to begin with. A man who can do this well makes me feel as if there's a vibrator down there. This helps me to become loose and to think of ways to pleasure him. Every man is different, but after you've been swinging for a certain period of time, you start knowing these needs almost intuitively. I can just sense what a man likes, what will turn him on the most. Sometimes, I'll gently start running my fingers down him, starting below his navel and continuing down until I reach his testicles. I scratch them underneath, around, on top, not in a rough way but as gently and softly as I can. Then I'll start stroking his penis all the way down to the bottom, just slightly, barely touching the skin. Sometimes I play with his pubic hairs, curling them with my fingers or my nails. Other times I'll start by circling my fingers around his stomach. Even though what I do with one guy may be different from another, I've found most men like sixty-nine.

INT.: *How do you feel about that?*

CATHY: Sometimes it's difficult to know at what moment I should enjoy the sensation of being stimulated by his tongue and mouth, and at what moment I should give him the same pleasure. I don't want to feel selfish. When I kiss and stimulate a penis, I like to put my whole self into it.

INT.: *Do swingers go in for a lot of oral sex?*

CATHY: To start things off, yes . . . But most of the time it ends up with the man coming inside the woman.

INT.: *Are you saying that swingers prefer the traditional one-to-one, man/woman relationship?*

CATHY: I guess so, most of them do. But there's also variety. When you get wound up in a group situation, things sort of happen . . . I remember one time when I was in bed with three men. One of them was on top of me, his penis inside my mouth, and I was turning my tongue on it in different ways. At the same time, the other two men were caressing me, squeezing, hugging, kissing, and I heard their sighs and groans. That really gets to me, those sounds, because they tell me I'm really pleasuring my partners. It was great, a truly fantastic experience . . . And that's what sex is and should be when it's uninhibited. It's experimenting, trying different techniques, positions . . . Sex is something to learn, just like talking and walking and skipping and hopping and jumping. You learn by doing.

INT.: *How long have you been swinging, Cathy?*

CATHY: Over two years now.

INT.: *Have you learned all there is to know about sex?*

CATHY: Oh heavens, no. Do you ever stop learning about anything? Only recently I learned how a fellow can hit my clitoris even when he's on top. I'm constantly learning. There's so little communication between the sexes, especially about sex . . . I gather that most women, when they're finished with sex, are very loose, their vaginal muscles are too relaxed. Now I've taught myself to tighten up a lot and how to use my vaginal and pelvic muscles. I was told that there are certain muscles inside the woman, in the abdomen and the lower thigh area, that can contract to give more pleasure to the male . . . At first I started contracting my muscles *after* a man and I had reached our climaxes. Now I'm able to contract and expand my muscles while a man is moving in and out of me. From what my partners tell me, this provides an especially exciting sensation.

INT.: *Do you think a lot of this sex talk—I mean, the detailing of it and the emphasis on performing—is exhibitionistic?*

CATHY: If the nonswingers could just accept the fact that sex is a natural thing, then there wouldn't be such an emphasis on it. It's no more exhibitionistic than talking about a gourmet dinner for four hours or buying new clothes or anything else that pleases you. For me, it's really part of being a woman, a complete woman. That's the best way I can describe it. Maybe it's also part of Women's Lib in a very direct way. In swinging I can, if I want, display as much of my sexuality as I have ever wanted to do. I don't feel restricted. I don't think I could ever go back to that middle-class morality that followed me around before, although I'm not going to march around City Hall or down Fifth Avenue with a placard pleading the cause of swinging; I don't think that's necessary.

INT.: *Let's get back to your feeling of being a complete woman. Are you saying that swinging and sex for you also embrace a concept of feeling—love, perhaps?*

CATHY: No. I think you're missing the point. I don't have to love a man to have sex with him. I don't have to feel tied down to a man, indebted to him, possessed by him, just because I've gone to bed with him. But I do have feelings for the men I have sex with.

INT.: *There still seems to be an overemphasis on the sexual act at these parties.*

CATHY: I've attended many groupsex parties where the emphasis was on sensory perception, doing silly, crazy things that hardly ever ended up in sexual intercourse. One of the best times I ever had was at a birthday party for a swinging friend. For dessert—I'm not putting you on—a lot of us girls took a bath in chocolate syrup. Then we went into another room where the hostess started spraying whipped cream all over us, and whoever wanted—men, women, it didn't matter— started to lick it off.

INT.: *And I always thought sex was nonfattening.*

CATHY: (Giggling) I know you don't believe me, but it really did happen. Then we formed an aisle by lining up on two sides and, one at a time, each person was lifted up at the beginning of the line and passed through the center. As you were carried from one person to another, people began touching and massaging parts of your body. It was a feeling of floating off the ground while you were being fondled by hands, fingers, lips and tongues, completely trusting those who were carrying you. It was as if your whole body was expanding, becoming part of the whole room, the whole atmosphere.

INT.: *In your experimenting, did you observe women pleasuring women?*

CATHY: Yes, a lot of that goes on in the swinging scene.

INT.: *How do you feel about that?*

CATHY: When I started I couldn't see myself doing it. At first, I thought that if I ever got involved with a woman, I wouldn't be able to pleasure her back . . . But as time went on and I saw how enjoyable it was for some other women, my initial feelings began to change. I think this usually happens when a woman's sexual desires are not completely met by the men at a swinging party. Most of the time this happens because the men are tired out, they've had it, but some of the women are just starting to have orgasms and are in need of more satisfaction.

INT.: *Have you ever participated in this form of sex?*

CATHY: Yes . . . The first time I ever became involved with another girl it was someone I had known for quite a while. We had developed a rapport with each other. We were at a small party and we got on the subject of teaching—she was a teacher—and we continued to talk about one thing or another. It just developed, just happened that we started kidding around. She did things like hug and kiss me on the face and then massage my back and my legs. Then she touched my vaginal area, and it developed into a very sensual thing. We ended up giving each other head and it really was a very pleasing experience.

INT.: *How do the men of some of these women feel about this?*

CATHY: I recall one discussion with a husband. I think he put it something like this: "A woman understands another woman's feelings at times even better than a man can." Then I asked him, and I remember now I was kind of embarrassed myself, about how he felt when he saw me pleasuring his wife. He said it didn't bother him. He didn't have any qualms about what she did to me or what I did to her, because she still gave him good sex and he loved her very much. He wasn't afraid that she was going to run off with another woman.

INT.: *Do you think that some people would consider this an act of lesbianism?*

CATHY: I'm sure some people would. It isn't, as far as I'm concerned. I still prefer having sex with men. I think I always will. I'm not saying that some of these women aren't bisexual. I suppose some are. But most of the women I know who occasionally give head to another woman appear to be very normal. Many of them are married and have children.

INT.: *I gather that most swingers don't tell their children anything about swinging?*

CATHY: I think it's a personal matter, an individual decision . . . I have wonderful, marvelous parents, but I think if I ever told them about my swinging, they'd be concerned, even though they're aware that I have a lot more sexual freedom than they ever had when they were my age.

INT.: *What do you think would bother your parents most about your swinging?*

CATHY: I think they'd prefer me to find a lasting relationship, even though they realize I don't want to get married for at least two or three more years . . . I just want to find *me* first.

INT.: *Are you finding yourself in swinging?*

CATHY: Most of the time. The openness, the freedom of being yourself, with no vulgarity in sex, all this is important to me. The fact that there is no sneaking around, trying to get it on with a guy or a girl behind someone else's back as if sex is ugly, dirty, something evil, all this makes sex for me now very liberating in a deep sense. It's much more than just a physical thing and that's what I think it can be for most women.

INT.: *What would you say to women who may want to swing but are too inhibited to take the first big step?*

CATHY: That's difficult to answer because each person is so different when it comes to individual hangups. Perhaps one of the easiest ways is to attend a few swinging parties just as an observer.

INT.: *You mean like a voyeur?*

CATHY: Maybe in the beginning they could just go even if they don't get undressed, see what the swinging scene is like and get rid of some of those fantasies that most nonswingers have about what goes on . . . If you're up on grass or alcohol, sometimes that can help to relax you a bit.

INT.: *Do you feel it also helps you enjoy sex more?*

CATHY: No. For others it may, but not for me. I feel it depends on an individual's body chemistry, just as with liquor. Some people can drink and still function and be aware of things around them; other people who drink can't.

INT.: *What about drugs like hallucinagenics?*

CATHY: I've never used speed or acid, and very few of the people I swing with do. When you get into heavy stuff, you *do* become separated from reality.

INT.: *Is swinging a reality to you?*

CATHY: Yes . . . Getting rid of my sexual frustrations frees me so that I can handle the other parts of my day better—my work, interacting with people. I've gained some insights into myself from all this. Now I'm ready to say much more of the time: "Hey! You out there! This is me and damn it, if you don't like me for what I am, too bad!" Sure, sometimes I talk too loudly and sometimes I giggle too much, and there are still times when I'm walking sideways . . . But more of the pieces fit now. I know where my head's at most of the time.

11

GENE:

He Never Stops

Gene is thirty-eight years old. He was divorced after sixteen years of marriage. His three children live with his wife, who left the Southeastern city where he lives shortly after they split up. He has been swinging for eight years.

"I'm making it now—don't laugh, I'm not kidding—in business as well as in bed," he says.

Gene wasn't kidding. He still lives in the city. His life hasn't changed much in thirty-eight years. Still the same hustler and wheeler dealer, the same "Old Gene," always on the make. With money and with women. His mother always made a point of teasing him about his successes, but when he made his first million she agreed with all his family and friends that Gene was the best. He was the brightest of her sons. And when he began losing money, he was the black sheep again.

His oldest brother is an accountant. The younger one is an account executive for an advertising agency. The other boys are college graduates, Gene is not.

From the time he was a kid, Gene was always looking for

an angle for making a fast buck. His first big break came when he learned of an inexpensive way to produce a costly essential component for a certain machine. He was able to corner the market, but the next time he tried the scheme, it backfired and he suffered disastrous losses.

Then he ran into a group of real estate men and learned how they operated. "I discovered I could do the same thing, without any cash of my own, by simply putting people together. One guy needed one thing. Another guy needed something else. So I put the two together, got my finder's fee and off I went again."

All five-feet-eight inches of him are active: always a little bulky but not paunchy. He's constantly exercising and keeping in shape. He has to, because Gene is the kind who decides on Tuesday to take up tennis. On Wednesday he buys a racquet and some balls. Thursday he signs up for lessons, and the next two weeks it's a crash program. The third week he is on the phone calling the best tennis players he knows to spend afternoons with him, helping improve his game. A week later, he's playing for small money, and winning.

This is his way in anything he tries, including sex. Driving, total devotion, and then packing it all up and going on to something else. It's also this way with scuba diving, golf: he always gets the best expert to teach him how to do it, and then tries to beat him at his own game.

Gene wanted to learn how to ride a horse, so he bought one. Gene wanted to learn how to play music, so he bought a guitar. He bought his kids guitars and everyone played. Now he's on a sports-car kick.

He reads, but often doesn't care about the last hundred pages or the ending. He can recite, line by line, passages from the classics with the dramatic intensity of a Burton or a Gielgud. In the next breath he can tell you who is doing what to whom in the National Football League. He loves modern music, but only listens until the sounds become meaningless, at least to him.

Gene's life is always spinning around him. He operates best that way—winning and losing.

Gene likes to drop names and important people know they need him. He doesn't have to remind them. He never would.

He's a spray of energy, missing, scoring: "The best way to

hit the top is to know what it's like sliding on your bottom on the bottom."

He goes to swinging parties, but he doesn't need to swing. He's not necessarily interested in new friendships. His interest is finding new sex partners. Swinging happens to be an easy way of doing just that.

The girls he dates know him only as much as Gene wants them to know him and they accept Gene for what he is. What he won't do is intentionally hurt someone. He's too busy to hurt. And he has been hurt himself, although Gene will not dwell on it. But it seems that's why Gene runs fast until he's exhausted, sleeps soundly until he thinks it's time to run again.

And his sex? He claims that he is always satisfied. Others doubt it: "Some swingers think I'm a male nymphomaniac . . . a satyr. I think they're nuts."

Regardless of who thinks what—or how right or wrong they are about Gene—he does represent a small category of swingers: the man who is out to get as much as he can without denying it.

GENE: . . . That should hold the phone calls for a while, I hope. I think I was born with an extension cord as my umbilical.

INTERVIEWER: *Is the phone always this busy?*

GENE: Seven days a week when I'm home . . .

INT.: *You were talking about how your attitudes about swinging have changed in the last two years.*

GENE: Yeah, in the beginning about eight years ago, swinging was kind of a kick for me. It was different then, the people were different; they didn't have to find all sorts of psychological reasons to justify their swinging. They just fucked and didn't have to talk about it afterward. Now I can't even take my prick out without having to analyze why I'm doing it. Most of the people I know who swing today seem to be practicing psyching each other out in bed more than they screw . . . at least in my personal experience.

INT.: *Is this true at every swinging party you attend?*

GENE: I wouldn't say it's true of every party I go to, but nearly all of them. Swingers are just too goddamn cultish now, too fanatic about their conditions, rules and regulations. At some parties it has to be fifty percent men and fifty percent women, and if I happen to walk in with a bachelor friend of mine, the whole place gets jumpy. They say, "We told you not to bring anybody else," that kind of crap. A week later, another party wants more women there than men because the women outlast the men. To me, it's a lot of childish bullshit. And then there's a thing about smoking pot. I know several swinging groups who say, "No pot, no dope of any kind." Others say, "Yeah, grass is okay but not heavy stuff." Even the ones who smoke grass at these parties tell me that it isn't necessary to have pot in order to be sexually stimulated. And yet they get stoned all the time on the stuff. You try and figure it out! I think swingers are getting to be as conformist as the straight people they knock.

INT.: *How do swingers feel about you?*

GENE: I haven't made it a point to walk up and ask each one, "Do you like me? You don't? How come?" that kind of nonsense. But sometimes that's just about how they act to each other, with all that "Who do you like best?" crap. I've been with them where they've talked for hours about who was the best in bed and she has a mole or she has too much hair, or his prick is so small someone reported it missing in action. They tear other swingers down and have petty jealousies like fishwives.

INT.: *But married couples say that swinging reduces or eliminates petty jealousies and competition.*

GENE: Like hell it does. Take ten couples, put them in the same room and watch the wives fuck other husbands and the other way around, and watch the look on the women's faces when they catch their husbands squirming and groaning and eating these chicks out like they've never done with their wives. They're about ready to cut their husbands' balls off. And the same holds true for the husbands. They see their wives getting it on with other men for maybe three hours and they're ready to call their attorneys for a quick divorce. Again I'm speaking from personal experience.

INT.: *They say it's fun and swinging leads to an open kind of communication.*

GENE: Porpoises have an open kind of communication, and they're

115

supposed to have a high order of intelligence. Do you see them swinging? You know, man is the only animal who has to go out of his way to invent new kinds of sexuality.

INT.: *Why do you think that's true?*

GENE: Because he's lazy, he's bored and because he's afraid to say, "I fuck because I want to fuck and for no other reason but that one."

INT.: *And you're different?*

GENE: I don't make excuses about my need to have sex and I don't need strength in numbers to find the excuse to go out and screw. I don't need a group of people around me who are having sex to make sex more comfortable for me. I screw because I want to screw, because I have a need to screw and because I don't ask myself why I have this need. I do, I have, and I'll always have it until the day I'm laid—to rest.

INT.: *Even with your attitude, are you still invited to swinging parties?*

GENE: I ball a chick and I make it a conquest and then I move on to ball another chick. I'm there to have sex—not to talk about the stock market or the PTA.

(The phone rings. He answers it and talks for a few minutes.)

INT.: *Did your wife swing?*

GENE: Hell, no. I was married at nineteen. She was scared about sex from that day on until we got divorced three years ago.

INT.: *How long were you married?*

GENE: Too long; sixteen years.

INT.: *And you have children?*

GENE: Three—a daughter in high school, a son in junior high, and the little one's in grammar school. But that boy—watch him, he's gonna out-hustle his father.

INT.: *You must have had sex with your wife to conceive.*

GENE: That's all she thought it was for.

INT.: *Do you think that came from religious conditioning?*

GENE: Not in her case. Her family wasn't particularly religious. She just didn't like having sex.

INT.: *Generally, or with you specifically?*

GENE: Go ask her. As far as I'm concerned, there was always an excuse. My favorite one was, "You look tired and you *do* have that big meeting tomorrow." (He shakes his head.) I

116

always liked that one because she knew I'm the kind of person who feels wide awake after I screw. Everyone else I talk to tells me that after having sex for, say two or three hours, they get tired and a little lazy. With me it's different. If I have a big meeting or I've got to tie a deal together, I'm in the sack with a chick the night before and the next morning I can negotiate like a hawk . . . Anyway, back to my ex: I started cheating on her and I was scared—because of the kids, not because of her. But I didn't want her to cheat.

INT.: *Were you afraid she would offer you competition?*

GENE: Not that way at all. She couldn't handle sex, so I was afraid she'd do something emotional, something out of spite for me, and it would wind up hurting her even more than my cheating on her, which was bad enough.

INT.: *Did you ever feel she knew you were cheating on her?*

GENE: I'm convinced she didn't know until the very end. But that wasn't the only reason for the divorce. I made a lot of money—my first million when I was under thirty—and I did it all on my own. I lost it all on my own, too. Maybe I was *too* good at making money. I lost my money about the same time I lost my marriage. Maybe my wife would rather have had a rich man fucking around on the side than a poor man—I don't know. We got the divorce and whatever I had left, she got, too. That was three years ago. It's a great game, counting the friends you have left after you've lost a lot of money and a marriage. I played that game a lot—alone.

INT.: *How did you make the adjustment?*

GENE: In retrospect, I don't think that it was really a question of adjustment. I'm sure I did then. It was hard, and it was lonely and frightening at times. I was thirty-five then and had already lost one future. I did something about three months after my divorce, on impulse or whatever you want to call it. I hitched cross-country to Los Angeles and then back again. I was used to traveling first class in jets or flying my own plane and now I was bumming it on the highway with a beard, jeans, the whole bit. When I stopped in New Mexico a couple of hippie kids picked me up and I lived at their commune for a while. I fucked their chicks, ate their food—our food, because I tilled the land with them—raised crops, even helped deliver a baby. I got my manliness back again. These young chicks really dug me. They had the same attitude, the same kind of appetite for sex. We screwed a lot, in the morning, in the afternoon, at night, anytime we wanted to. But we also worked together and we respected each other. Everything was up front.

INT.: *How long were you there?*

GENE: Oh, it was about four months before I took off.

INT.: *Why did you leave?*

GENE: The work was too hard. Even to get all that fucking free, I didn't want to work that hard. So I just hit the road, came down to Los Angeles. I thought L.A. was hyper-dull—nothing but a lot of big talk from empty heads. Then I thumbed my way back East again, stayed in Denver for a while. I used to like to ski, but not once did I go up to Aspen. I just didn't feel like it.

INT.: *Maybe because you might see some old friends?*

GENE: Possibly . . . I just didn't go there . . . left Denver, stayed up in the northern peninsula of Michigan for a while and fished and then came back home. I still had some connections. I'd get deals together, take my five percent and split. Then I started going out. I think it was the first time out with a woman that we got invited to a swinging party. I hadn't been to one in years and I got embarrassed balling her in the bedroom because people were walking in and out. I lost a hard-on and realized this was really a dumb way of getting it. I don't need an audience. But I started back swinging to find new girls. Then I'd convince them to forget the swinging parties and make it with me—in private.

INT.: *I have the feeling you're not the sharing type.*

GENE: All I'm saying is that if I see a groovy chick, I've got enough to keep her occupied all night. Why should I share her?

INT.: *Suppose she wants to share herself? After all, you're talking about girls you pick up in the swinging scene.*

GENE: That's up to her. I'm not trying to run her life. If she wants to go back to swinging after she's swung a little with me—fine.

(The phone rang again. This time it was a woman's voice, and Gene made an involved series of arrangements for her to come to visit him from another city. When he hung up, he was all smiles and boastful again.)

My system's working so great now, who's got time for swinging?

INT.: *What's your system?*

GENE: Take that chick who just called . . . I've got a week's vacation for her all planned. Not with me, just for herself. I bought her the plane reservation and paid for a week in the Bahamas. She digs it; she gives me good sex, she's entitled to a week off. I'm a bachelor and I plan my week around sex and maybe a business deal if I see a good one coming. I start the week by calling girls and making dates through Wednesday. If I think I can get a better girl for one of those days, I make two dates and cancel the other one out. I may even tell a girl that I have another date and will make it for some other time. I don't lie, and the chicks like it that way. Or I'll say, "I have a business appointment and maybe after that something will happen and I don't want to hang you up, so let's do it another night." Some of the girls I screw have jobs that take them in and out of town and others are from out of town. I may get a call from one girl who's a buyer in New York. She comes into town every other week during the season and stays at my place overnight on Wednesdays. So every other Wednesday I keep free, but I have a stand-by date if she doesn't come in. As I said, it's all up front, no bullshit, and the chicks I date are the same way. They're playing the same kind of a game.

INT.: *You do admit that you're playing a game?*

GENE: Hell, yes, but no one lies in this game and no one cheats. I haven't made it with another married woman and I won't. I don't like dating divorcees with children, either. I've got three kids of my own. My time is for them, and not anyone else's.

INT.: *Do you prefer certain types of women over others?*

GENE: I like 'em young, and I don't want 'em to have sexual hang-ups or as few as possible. As it turns out, I've found more swinging women who have hangups that nonswinging women.

INT.: *What's the difference?*

GENE: Swinging women are exhibitionists. I want to fuck in bed —not in a circus. Chicks who want to know "Why?" and have

119

to ask a lot of other questions and analyze my prick, they shouldn't screw, at least not with me. And the girls that I ball have got to have been balled by other men before me. I'm no Albert Schweitzer with any sense of missionary zeal when it comes to sex. In fact, what I like to do after I make it with a girl a couple of times is to introduce her to some of my friends. This way, I can split with her without any bad feelings. I tell her I talked to the other guy and he's really gone for her. My friend is getting jealous and I think it's best to cut things off between her and me. The girls dig this and as long as they groove with the other guy, what's the difference? A couple of girls I've laid off on some of my friends have actually gotten married. One has a baby now and I was best man at the wedding.

INT.: *Don't you ever tire of so much sex?*

GENE: Why should I? It's a great body-builder: good for the stomach, leg and back muscles, besides the muscles that I lift a number of times a day. The girls I screw are in good shape, too. They have to be able to keep up with me.

INT.: *How many times in one day can you have intercourse?*

GENE: I've fucked ten times in an afternoon and evening. It depends where I am and who I'm screwing. I remember once there were four of us on a twenty-five-foot cabin cruiser and the water got very choppy. You can get squalls off the coast and sometimes you're lucky to come out alive. We hit some bad weather about four miles offshore. One guy got sick and heaved; his girlfriend tried to help him and she fell overboard. It was fierce trying to pick her out of the drink because of the goddamn waves that were so high. After it was all over we steered toward the beach, I dropped anchor in a pretty calm area and we all relaxed for a while. My friend was still down in the galley, out of it. We were in pretty shallow water, so I took the girl I was with, the one who didn't fall overboard, into the water. I don't know how I did it but I managed to get a hard-on, even though the water was chest-high. We had two Mae West life jackets on, but we kept slipping away from each other. I lost my hard-on because the damn seaweed kept tripping us up. Finally she got a rise out of me again, but this time some idiot came screaming by with his speedboat and the girl couldn't hold onto me, even with the life jacket on. Eventually we held onto each other and couldn't stop from laughing, like two sick porpoises. I think it was the laughing more than anything else that made us come together.

INT.: *In water?*

GENE: Oh, yes, and it can be done in the air, too. I think the wildest time was in my plane. We must have been five thousand feet up. This chick started undressing as we were taking off, so she was all set when I leveled off. She wanted it . . . now! I put the plane on automatic pilot and she just about tore me out of my chair. I started reaching for the controls and she pulled me away again. I mean, she was really out to rape me. She had me pinned to the floor. I don't know how she managed to do it, but she straddled me sideways and began pumping up and down, knocking the wind out of me. Then we hit turbulence, and I must have gone all the way up to the roof of her mouth, but she was digging every minute of this except when the plane started shaking wildly. I came in her like a gusher because I'd kept holding back so long. She was screaming. I was hollering for her to get off me so we could land, but she was so into it, I don't think she knew what was happening to the plane. I never came with so much force and excitement in my life. I think it was probably the sense of danger that did it.

INT.: *Do you ever wonder why you like sex so much?*

GENE: No, why should I? I said earlier I have a strong need to screw, so I feed that need when I can, as much as I can. But I wouldn't recommend my life-style to someone else.

INT.: *Why not?*

GENE: Because mine's a need. I know it is. I need a lot of sex. For others, I think all this sex would be the most impotency-inducing experience anyone could ever have. Just thinking about how much I get a week would turn some men soft, and make 'em stay that way. I know my own kids couldn't handle all this sex. I don't think any young person can. It's too much.

INT.: *Good for you and not good for them?*

GENE: Not that so much. A boy and a girl should postpone going to bed until they both know there's a deep, meaningful feeling between them. That's the time for romance. When they're young, they should get it out of their systems. When you reach maturity, you're wise enough to know how to separate sex from love or any strong emotion.

INT.: *Are you recommending, then, a kind of nonswinging sexuality for the younger generation?*

GENE: Yes, except for those young, under-age girls that I screw . . . I don't go out looking for them, don't get me wrong. But at some of the orgies I meet a girl who looks under age and says she is, and there's a special thrill doing it under those circumstances. I remember one girl—I think she took me on as a challenge—who nearly out-screwed me every time, just to prove she could handle my kind of sex.

INT.: *Where is all this leading to?*

GENE: I don't think it's leading me anywhere, it's all part of my life-style.

INT.: *But you sound like a one-man sex machine, purely mechanical . . .*

GENE: I'm not, though. I don't need a rationale for doing it.

INT.: *How did you arrive at that feeling? It must have taken thought.*

GENE: It did. When I lost my marriage and lost my money, I had nothing: no one, nothing—except my kids, and it was hard for a while to see them. I've been told that everyone has suicidal tendencies at one point or another, and I used to joke about that when things were good. Then, when everything got bad, I did think about suicide and it wasn't a joke. Sometimes I spent hours thinking about the best way to end everything. I imagined how many cars would be at my funeral and who would cry and who wouldn't.

INT.: *Did you try taking your life?*

GENE: Nearly. Once I hadn't seen anyone in weeks. A girl I knew called and we got together one night. The fact that she wanted to go to bed with me, despite the way I looked and the way I must have acted, meant something to me. Here I was at the bottom and she didn't care who I was or what happened— only that she wanted to please me and maybe that I could get out of my pit long enough to please her. I was so low and here was someone accepting me and not asking questions or trying to figure me out. I didn't think I was a man or capable of manly things, but she did. All she wanted was me. I hadn't had that kind of request in a long time, so it took the act of sex to bring me out—so what! That's better than spending thousands on analysis or existing on tranquilizers. I don't know, maybe you can't understand it, but there's no other way I can put it: sex to me is life—that's the way I am.

12

GIL:

A "Head-Jockey"

Gil is twenty-seven years old, single, and has been swinging for the past three years. He was graduated from a well-known university in Massachusetts with a degree in applied mathematics, continued on a fellowship and received his master's degree two years later. He lived in a university town and led what he called a quiet life, dating every now and then, but spending most of his time studying and working on research projects.

After receiving his post-graduate degree, he was interviewed by a number of leading marketing and research firms and chose one with offices in the East.

Gil comes from a large family; two older brothers and an older sister. He is the only one still unmarried.

In his early childhood and later in his teens Gil thought he was somewhat removed from his family. His father and mother both worked. His older brothers and sister seemingly received more attention. Whatever, the reasons, Gil was always the last to be listened to and the last to be cared for.

He found himself slowly withdrawing from family involvement and from outside relationships as well. It seemed more comfortable that way.

Mathematics appealed to him because it was nonpersonal, devoid of emotion, and he did exceptionally well in it.

Throughout college he was basically a loner, relegating his sexual life to fantasy, to excessive reading of sexual literature, including the works of Ellis and Freud, and to masturbating.

As he reflects back on his college days, Gil admits that he was not much of a ladies' man. He was never a good dancer and no better as a lover. Failures bred other failures, and they deepened his doubts about his own masculinity.

Though he is of average height, five-feet-eight, he is not unattractive. His face is strong, square jawed, and he wears glasses. Although he is not muscular, he appears to be in fine physical shape.

Gil heard about swinging through a college buddy. He was quite curious about it, but it took him a while to get his friend to take him along to a party. He really went as a voyeur. And that's all he was at the first few parties until he became more comfortable and found his own way of pleasuring women. He insists that it not only satisfies them, but also is rewarding to him.

INTERVIEWER: *What kind of a swinger would you call yourself?*
GIL: I don't like to categorize people, whether they swing or not, but if you want a description, I prefer giving oral sex to women rather than having straight intercourse.
INT.: *Have you had straight intercourse at a swinging party?*
GIL: Occasionally, yes, but not very often.
INT.: *I've heard other swingers talk about head-jockeys.*
GIL: I'm familiar with the term . . . If it means anything, then that's what I am.
INT.: *Is there a reason?*
GIL: You sound like a psychiatrist friend of mine . . . I have a problem of impotency . . . I don't know if you've ever heard about it, but some men who are impotent find it difficult to keep from coming. This has happened to me quite often.
INT.: *Did you ever seek psychiatric help?*
GIL: Yes, but what do they really know? The psychiatrist I went

to was more interested in hearing me talk about swinging than he was about my own problem of impotency . . . He *did* say that if I could find sexual satisfaction in swinging, then I probably was doing the right thing anyway.

INT.: *Do you feel set apart from the rest of the men who swing?*

GIL: Not so much. I mean, sometimes there will be men who joke about what I do. Sometimes I take it seriously and I suppose some of the ribbing is intentional.

INT.: *Are swingers more willing to accept your problem than non-swingers?*

GIL: First I have to challenge the way you said, "accept your problem." I know what you're thinking: the first step in solving any difficulty is admitting that the difficulty exists, that's true; but I'm not so sure my problem is an obstacle when it comes to my own sexuality.

INT.: *Do you feel your form of sex is limiting?*

GIL: No, not really. There's an awful lot of oral sex at swinging parties. So, what's so limiting about giving head or receiving it? . . . Some men have a difficult time in coming more than once in an evening, although others can reach several orgasms. The point is that swinging can be a strain and, especially with new swingers, it often is. It's not easy to perform in front of a group of people for the first time. A lot of truth comes out in groupsex. Everyone can see just how good a lover you really are. For some men, this is embarrassing, especially if they boast about how great they are in bed and then everyone else sees the lie.

INT.: *Did something like that happen to you?*

GIL: I didn't let it—I knew I couldn't control myself that much, and that was one of the reasons I decided to swing. At any rate, with me, the concern about sustaining an erection and keeping from coming isn't there any more. Many women at swinging parties are not fulfilled, at least not always, because it's their sexual nature to reach more orgasms than a man during a given evening. I give them head. I probably have more sex with women who swing than most swinging men do.

INT.: *Have you ever felt sexually inadequate at a swinging party?*

GIL: I get the feeling that you're having more of a problem coping with my kind of sexuality than I have. I don't think there

126

is any man, whether he screws standing on his head or lying on top of a woman, who doesn't find himself inadequate at one time or another.

INT.: *Some swingers have told me they always feel satisfied at a swinging party.*

GIL: There are fools who swing, too, you know. Look at it this way: wouldn't sex turn out to be a total bore if everything was always perfect?

INT.: *Do you ever tire of your kind of sexuality?*

GIL: No, that's one of the advantages. I can pleasure an unending amount of women at a given party, and let me tell you something else about this kind of sex: if you have an open mind about it, it's really a much more unselfish form, and I've learned a lot about women. It's great to turn them on in this way—to see, to hear and to feel them enjoying multiple orgasms . . . There is really much more that a man can do to pleasure a woman by giving head.

INT.: *I don't quite follow you.*

GIL: You use much more of your own body—your mouth, your whole face, your hands, the way your position them on the woman's body, caressing her buttocks or massaging her breasts. It's much more intimate way of meeting a woman's sexuality. I can pleasure her so much longer this way, with much more intimacy. I can't describe it adequately, but there is something very moving about being able to see a woman come, feeling the contractions of her muscles, sensing her whole bodily warmth becoming a part of you.

INT.: *What about the old adage, "if you've seen one . . ."*

GIL: ". . . you've seen them all"? Well, not exactly. Some women have fairly big openings, others are tight. I know a number of swinging women who keep their pubic hair short-cropped and sometimes that can be rough on a face. Each woman has her own . . . I guess you could call it, their own vaginal identity . . . personality . . . sweet, soft, sometimes a little bitter to the taste. It all depends on the kinds of soaps they wash with. Lately many of the women have been using feminine sprays that pose a little problem for me. I have allergies, and perfumes can cause my nose to burn. It's difficult to give head when you're sneezing and sniffling. So I have

127

to be careful. Fortunately, there are some nonallergenic sprays.

INT.: *Do you feel you can get all the variety you want out of sex by giving head?*

GIL: Not at all parties or with every woman I give head to, but sometimes when the mood is right you'd be surprised at the things I do. Take, for example, whipped cream desserts. A couple of times when I've gotten a girl really going, she's poured beer over herself and it's something else to have head with a head on it . . . I'm not trying to be funny; this is the kind of stuff that goes on. I can think of a lot of ways I've given head which have been appetizing and created my own kind of sexuality. There's always something new and different that I'm up to my head in.

INT.: *You honestly feel that you're not missing straight intercourse?*

GIL: There are times when I am. I have straight intercourse every now and then, but I'm more comfortable with what I do, so I stick to my specialty.

INT.: *Do you find you're giving more head than you're receiving?*

GIL: I don't keep a percentage card in my pocket, but I'd say I like to give as much as I can before I receive it.

INT.: *Do you think your sexual preferences will change?*

GIL: Is that a kind way of asking whether I will ever learn not to come so fast?

INT.: *Not that so much . . .*

GIL: I'm sure one day I will . . . In the meantime I'm having a good time. And if you're talking about marriage, one of these days I'll settle down and raise a family and be a good husband and father. Right now, I've found a way to fit into a group of people and be liked for my mind and for what I can contribute, so I'm in no rush to change the scene.

13

JENNY:

On a Total Reality Trip

Jenny is twenty-six years old, single, and has been swinging for five years. She is not a big girl; five-foot-five, thin, brunette hair cropped close to the front and turning up in curls around the sides of her face and the back of her neck. She said: "It's my ape look, somebody told me. I cut my hair myself. I don't like long hair especially. It gets in the way of things." Her greenish eyes flare when she recalls good times. She has many of them.

Jenny was rather reluctant to talk about Jenny in the beginning of the interview. She was careful to channel the flow of her dialogue, waiting at times, almost impatiently, for us to respond. If we didn't, she'd pull back and turn listener. Jenny is an excellent listener, and as the interview progressed we began to realize why.

She was born and raised in the deep South. All through her early childhood, into her teens and when she reached the age of "being legal," she questioned nearly everything that tradition dictated in her community. But she did her questioning in her thoughts instead of embarking on a campaign to challenge her elders.

There would be a time, she thought, when all the built-in

emotions and ambiguities would explode, but in a soft, genteel, Southern way.

Jenny did explode out of her shell and it happened in a series of revelations rather than one big pop. With each successive stage a girl-child grew into a girl-woman.

Jenny is not particularly attractive. She said, "I wasn't one of those Southern belles who kept having a coming-out party once in the fall and then again in the summer."

Therefore, Jenny, early in life, embraced the solitude and privacy of the outdoors. She loved taking long walks by herself in the summer, smelling the fragrance that Williams and Faulkner wrote about: "It was all there and it was all mine, to touch, to taste."

Jenny now works at a West Coast television station where she is a writer and assistant producer. She left her hometown a year ago. Life to Jenny is the best of past, present, and future.

She is a mover and every bit an original person. She loves to paint and sculpt. When she has the time she visits the nearby art museum and the local galleries. However, she's not one to memorize artist's names, nor is she able to recall any style or period.

Jenny has a natural eye for texture and feeling. She has shown some of her work in the small galleries along the "let it happen" streets where the young people who walk them are art forms themselves. This is Jenny's world. The small leathercraft stores, the restaurants with funny-looking doors and half-hidden windows. And the ocean. The ocean where she spends as many weekend hours as possible crewing aboard a friend's boat.

On Saturdays and Sundays, short trips lead them to a point enough miles out to enjoy relationships with the others aboard. Some are actor friends whose movies gross millions: "But when we're sailing nobody really cares who's made it and who hasn't, because we're out to be with each other, not with what we all represent."

When Jenny talks about her newly found life-style, her face responds with enthusiasm, a lovely smile that slowly opens, blossoming. Free, relaxed. That's how Jenny wants to be thought of. Because she is that way.

For Jenny time is an ally rather than an adversary. The week ahead is always a challenge instead of a struggle. It lets her function on her own terms, at her own speed.

She puts in her eight to ten hours a day on her job. She knows that when supper is over, there is a clay mold on her worktable to be formed or a painting waiting to continue its creative unfolding—if not that night, then the next. But call her an organized person? Forget it. Instead of worrying about how to organize or what to organize, she just does it. Little pressure. Much more enjoyment.

Maybe that's why she is out of organized swinging and into another cycle of life. Jenny may well be a new breed of swinger. She typifies young, single people who feel that the idea of organizing swinging parties just for the sake of sex is self-defeating. If it happens, fine. If it doesn't now, it will later.

In our research, we were surprised to discover that in the South, even in the deep South where tradition is thought to be unyielding, swinging is just as popular as in the North, East, and West. The feeling of commitment to the moment, however long or short that moment is, and not in a careless way, dominates the thinking of many single young people who swing in the South as well as anywhere in the country.

If there is one phrase that best characterizes Jenny, she is, as she says, "on a total reality trip."

INTERVIEWER: *Jenny, how old are you?*

JENNY: Twenty-six.

INT.: *Where were you born?*

JENNY: In New York. I was a war baby, the middle child in a family of six. My parents were originally from the South, and just after I was born they moved back to ———— (a Southern town).

INT.: *What kind of area was it?*

JENNY: Like any other thriving city in the South. There was a lot of emphasis on material things, competition for material things . . . Everybody knew everybody else. And everybody was striving for the same thing, for the same country club to belong to . . . It all seemed to be a part of the game.

INT.: *What do you mean by game?*

JENNY: Because it was all so artificial.

INT.: *Was your family a part of it, too?*

JENNY: In a way, yes. My father still has a very good food business. So the value of the dollar and its importance in the community was always talked about. And when it wasn't talked about it was quite evident.

INT.: *Weren't you benefiting by your family's success?*

JENNY: Well, I had a nice roof over my head, good food and the use of a car, if I wanted it. But I was never much on buying clothes when I was younger. I'd just as soon stay in my jeans as anything else.

INT.: *How did your parents feel about your attitude?*

JENNY: They managed . . . I wasn't the town rebel by any means. I was always home for supper on time. I went to church. I studied hard in school. Believe me, I was quite the normal one.

INT.: *Was your household religious?*

JENNY: My parents were very religious, but they never pushed their beliefs on me or any of my brothers and sisters. I wasn't forced to say prayers at night. When I did, I did because I wanted to. I went to church every Sunday until I was twelve, although there were some things that turned my head around about organized religion. When you go to church and you see all the political deals and big business deals that are made on the front sidewalk of the church . . . between Sunday school and church, and all the ladies look like a herd of peacocks, it becomes fairly obvious why they attend church. I think more politicians in my town were elected on a Sunday than any other day in the year.

INT.: *Perhaps I shouldn't say here that politics make strange bedfellows.*

JENNY: (smiling) It's a matter of appearances mostly, and that was important in my town, too. There was a lot of gossip going around, hush-hush things, little tidbits that everybody managed to know about everyone else. I think when a man went to bed with his wife at night the whole town shared in the excitement—or lack of it.

INT.: *What were the sexual attitudes of the town?*

JENNY: When I was growing up I was oblivious to that because I was a tomboy, and the male friends I had were not gentlemen callers, as such, but rather buddies. If they ever scored with me it was usually rounding third base on the way to homeplate. I was one of the "guys" for a long time. They

132

would come to me and cry on my shoulders about their relationships with their girlfriends . . . Mostly they had the same problem about sex that I had: not being able to talk to my parents.

INT.: *Your parents taught you very little?*

JENNY: Yes, considering what kids know about sex today there was very little discussion about it . . . I remember when I started my menstrual period I received a little pamphlet that told me about birds and bees and little else . . . It was indicated to me that sex was a forbidden and dirty thing that was not to be discussed. The easiest thing for my parents and my friends' parents to do, I suppose, was to hand out the pamphlets. In effect, our parents were saying, "Don't talk to me. Check page 15 instead." As I was growing up some of my friends would make references about sex, and I reacted like a dummy because I didn't know what they were talking about. It wasn't in any of my pamphlets. They all had a good laugh and I had to find things out mostly by myself. I managed to do it by the time I graduated from high school.

INT.: *Did you go to college?*

JENNY: I was accepted at the University, but I turned it down and turned down my father's offer for a job working for him. Instead, I went to one of the large Southern cities for a year where somehow I was lucky enough to get a job as a production assistant at one of the television stations. It meant nothing more than tagging after my boss and making sure he didn't make any mistakes big enough to get him fired. I learned his job so well that I suppose I posed a threat to him, so I was let go. Then I returned home. I found a job working for one of the local radio stations as a secretary, and I went back to living at home . . . The job was fascinating and later on I was writing news stories and doing some on-location reporting of my own.

INT.: *It sounds as if you were enjoying life.*

JENNY: Wrong. I was beginning to learn about life, but not able to do much about it. I still had the problem of dating guys more on a buddy-buddy basis than anything else.

INT.: *Were you afraid of sex?*

JENNY: Yes, damnit, I was. I had a notion about romance and

being swept off my feet by some virile-looking male who also had compassion for people. I found it safer with my thoughts. Thoughts don't demand a quick smile or an interested look. And there's something about the privacy of the mind that I can feel comfortable with. It's something you don't have to share . . . I guess that was one of my problems. A fear of sharing. Even that word: "share!" Five meaningless letters until you put them together. Well, I wanted to share myself with someone and I was also afraid to . . . I went on in that fashion until I met Dan. He was a free-lance photographer working out of ———, the capital of a Southern state. I met him when I was working for the television station, and I met him again one night in my town when one of the politicos in the state held a party for media people. Dan was working on a story about integration. For the next few months he was in and out of town and we became good friends.

INT.: *What kind of a man was he?*

JENNY: Intense, with a delightful wit, and much older than I was.

INT.: *Did he have a family?*

JENNY: No, divorced. And he didn't talk much about his ex-wife. I gathered they weren't ever able to have children . . . As time went on he and I became very close. He was the first man that I ever went to bed with, but it was flat. Losing my virginity wasn't at all a mind-blowing affair.

INT.: *Was it your fear of sharing again?*

JENNY: It was more a lack of knowing what to do . . . Dan knew what he was doing, and I simply didn't. I was a plumber when it came to sex . . . Dan was good for me though, and patient. But no matter how much I learned I was still having sex only with him . . . I could hardly walk down the street looking for an available bachelor in town and say, "Pardon me, but guess what I've been learning the last few months! Would you mind terribly if I could show you, say tonight at your place after dinner?" Most of the men in town who weren't married were the same ones I played baseball with when I was a kid. I was good at that sport, and that reputation followed me around more than the boys did . . . One night when I was with Dan I really opened up and cried like a baby. When it was all over he said he would introduce me to some people in town who were a lot of fun. "Jenny," he said, "You're about ready to meet some swingers." I had heard about swinging. There were supposed to be big groups in certain cities. But not in my town.

INT.: *You didn't believe him?*

JENNY: Not about the swingers . . . I felt I knew all the people who lived there. So in the next days every time I saw someone I knew, Dan had me wondering: does she or doesn't she, or does he or doesn't he? . . . In two weeks, sure enough, Dan came back and picked me up one night and we drove to a section of town that I knew. But I didn't know the couple who met us at the door. In fact, the surprising thing was that I didn't know anybody there . . .

INT.: *Were you apprehensive?*

JENNY: Startled, really, but I still thought this was going to turn out to be some kind of joke on me. It wasn't.

INT.: *How may people were there?*

JENNY: I think around ten couples. Most of the people were in their late thirties, married couples. That didn't bother me because I like being around older people . . . They were all middle-class and respectable, and I didn't associate well-placed people with swinging.

INT.: *Were any young people there besides you?*

JENNY: No. There was an elaborate food setting, and a lot of camaraderie. It all made me feel very much at ease.

INT.: *How did the party start?*

JENNY: It just did. I think it was the host and hostess who got things started. They undressed and helped a few others undress in a playful way, and before I knew it two couples were going at it next to the fireplace. I didn't have time to sort things out. One minute I saw the action next to the fireplace, and the next minute it was happening on the couch where I was sitting, and the next minute somebody had me by the hand and I was led to the den. He took me in, helped me undress and all I can say is he did everything to make me feel like a woman. He helped me loosen up. He stayed with me until I reached a climax, and then he stayed with me some more because I felt a kind of surge, and I climaxed again. I opened my eyes, I think once, to see a number of people standing in the room watching me.

INT.: *Did that bother you?*

135

JENNY: Listen, nothing can bother you when you're reaching that kind of sexual satisfaction. It was one sensation after another. I was shocked when Dan told me later that in four hours I had no less than six men, one after another. I never had been so fucked out in my whole life. It was incredible. I was never so exhausted, yet never so lifted in spirit.

INT.: *How long did this euphoria last?*

JENNY: From about seven-thirty in the evening until two in the morning.

INT.: *Were you in bed all the time?*

JENNY: Oh, no. I'd get up in the middle of things and leave. I'd say I had to make a "pit stop" and quit for a while, have a sandwich, talk to some people, and then find my way back into that room again.

INT.: *Did you feel you had to say "yes" to all the men there?*

JENNY: Almost, yes. Actually, I had that feeling about a lot of the parties I attended. I think it was possibly because at almost every party I attended I picked up a sense of competitiveness —the men mostly did that, and some of the women did, too— about getting around to everybody.

INT.: *That sounds rather compulsive.*

JENNY: Well, swingers have such an enthusiasm about everyone having sex. They tend to feel badly if someone comes to their party and doesn't have a good time and receive enough attention. In a way it *is* a compulsion.

INT.: *Is that what led you to have intercourse with so many men at your first party?*

JENNY: No. It was something that happened: you're in the middle of it and you're not aware of the momentum, so to speak. Every man that I balled that night knocked himself out to make me have an orgasm, and everyone did beautifully. Consequently, it was almost a pyramid effect, as far as my orgasms were concerned, because every time I reached a climax it was at a different level. It's a whole thing about women. A woman's sexuality is different. A lot of women can experience this change radically; they can be brought up without ever having an orgasm, and then they get into swinging and discover they can have orgasms on orgasms, and each one mounts onto a more beautiful plane . . . I'd had orgasms before, but I hardly ever felt good about being a woman, and that was the level

136

of feeling those men brought me to. It was such a rare experience for me—this sudden sureness about my womanly powers—that I wanted to keep the experience going. So I don't think that handling so many men that first time was a compulsion for me. I can assure anyone and everyone that what I went through that night was not a gang-bang or anything like that.

INT.: *Did you feel emotionally involved or was it just sex without love?*

JENNY: I felt emotion with some of the men and a lot of it with Dan. With others it was more of a very satisfying feeling for me to observe that they were having such a good time and that I was principally responsible for this. You have to consider that most of the people there were married. For those men it was just good sex. I would even say that a lot of marriages are held together by swinging.

INT.: *Doesn't that indicate a weakness in such a marriage?*

JENNY: (shrugging) I suppose there are as many reasons for getting into swinging and hanging in there as there are stars in the sky. Swinging goes against the grain of what our society decrees to be right when it comes to sex. And everyone who swings can't help but think about that either: sex is supposedly for making babies, and God help us because that's the way it's been taught. Think about all those people who've been raised in this kind of atmosphere and then take all their clothes off and throw them in a room with a bunch of people and say, "Okay, get in a big pile and do it." A lot of them are bound to think, even if they don't say it, that this is Sodom and Gomorrah.

INT.: *What makes them hang in then?*

JENNY: Married couples whom I've talked to at any great length usually have had the experience of being attracted to some person outside of their marriage. They've wanted to get it on with this person and couldn't because they were married. That can really fuck a person up. Ultimately, if that person can't live without getting it on with this other person it becomes a sneaky affair. If they get caught, it creates a big hassle. There's no big hassle about sex in swinging, and that's what the magnet is for married couples.

INT.: *What does it do for a single girl like yourself?*

137

JENNY: After a while I found that organized groupsex didn't do too much for me. During the first months I kept feeling that I was the young cupcake, as it were. I was younger than most of the other women, I enjoyed sex, and I liked the feeling of discovering my womanly powers. And because of the relative smallness of the city I was becoming alarmingly popular among the swingers. The invitations came, and I found it difficult to say no. After the newness wore off and it got beyond exchanging certain amenities, I didn't have much in common with most of the swingers who were married. For instance, I didn't have children to talk about. What really broke it up for me was that I was constantly being referred to other men who came into town, friends of the local swingers. Sometimes I even got calls from a married man saying his wife was sick or having her period. His wife called to assure me that she didn't want her husband to miss out on a party, and would I mind going along as his date . . . All in all, I began to feel hassled into going places and having sex as if I was some sort of sexual target. Another thing happened: doing it weekend after weekend, I was constantly in a state of satisfaction. I can't possibly enjoy sex in a state of satisfaction. Then it becomes very passé for me. I'd lost a lot of my inhibitions, swinging had loosened me up as to my womanliness, and now it was undermining me. As I began to reason it out I saw that I could have more fun as an uninhibited single girl in the straight world, and I could be much more selective about my men. And now I was very reassured about my capacity to attract them.

INT.: *So swinging was rather rewarding for you?*

JENNY: For a period of time, yes . . . But I have another observation: I found that groupsex for married swingers was a way of achieving group approval, permission to have sex outside of marriage. It was just that group approval that turned me off. I don't want to plan, to count the days before a party. And then again it was the town itself. There was some anxiety about my parents and other members of my family finding out. Sooner or later it would have to happen. One of them would be on the phone outraged and uptight . . .

INT.: *So you quit?*

JENNY: And moved to the West Coast where I rented an apartment close to the ocean. Sink or swim, whatever, I was on
my own. And my interests broadened. I learned to sail,
started to paint, which came to me naturally. And when Dan
was away on a story I dated fellows who loved the outdoors.

INT.: *What about you and Dan at this point?*

JENNY: We were friends and still are, and I hope always will be.
Whenever he is in town he is free to stay at my place. But
there are no limits on what either of us does beyond that.
That's the way sex has been since I came to the Coast:
unplanned.

INT.: *What do you mean?*

JENNY: For example, in the summer months I've been crewing a
lot aboard a friend's sailboat. At times other people join us
for a sail. Sometimes couples are matched off, but usually it's
an uneven pairing, a couple of extra guys or girls. We can
be out for miles taking in the sheer joy of the day and the
ocean and if some of us want to get it on we do. Maybe it's
two guys and me or two other girls with me and one guy.

INT.: *In a group way?*

JENNY: Yes, but casually: some of us may do it, others are just
sacked out. Nobody cares. If it happens, fine. For me, sex has
found its place. It's much more natural now. In that sense it's
a radical change from what I, as a single girl, went through
in the organized group scene. I don't have to worry about
maybe spending too much time with a particular guy; or tell
myself that I don't want to hurt so-and-so's feelings, so maybe
I'd better ball him, too, tonight.

INT.: *Do you think that this is where group sex is heading—toward
the casual sexual happening that you've been talking about?*

JENNY: No. Swinging for marrieds does require considerable
planning and organization. They need a more complicated
structure because of their family obligations. There's a big
difference between the single personality and the characteristics of the swinging married couple.

INT.: (smiling) *What happens if sometime in the future you are
swept off your feet by that "virile-looking male with compassion?"*

JENNY: It could happen, I suppose.

INT.: *Then would your sexually-liberated self envision getting married?*

JENNY: Yes, damnit. And I know what you're leading up to. I have not purged myself totally of the red, white and blue aspects of romance and love—and I am using love the way I think you are laying it on me. But I never could go back just to getting it on with one guy. I suppose that if I got married, I'd go back to organized group sex.

INT.: *I've been meaning to ask: was there a problem about swinging with black people in the South?*

JENNY: (after a pause) I'd rather not get into that rift with you.

INT.: *Why not?*

JENNY: You'd start asking me whether I ever went to bed with a black stud, and was he better than a white dude, and how would I feel if this black stud balled my sister and said she was better than me in bed, and still didn't marry her.

INT.: *I won't get into that if you don't want to.*

JENNY: I don't because there is no end to it. I grew up with "black" people. They were an integral part of my life. I have deep and stony feelings about them.

INT.: *Do you care to share those feelings with me?*

JENNY: We're back to the word "share." No. I don't trust you enough. This whole black issue has been rapped over so much that I don't think I have any new insights to express on the subject, and I don't want to be misquoted and misunderstood. I admit to an initial prejudice about how far black people should rise in our Southern society, what they could and couldn't do. But I've changed my views radically. I have a deep sympathy for their condition and their need to improve their life and the urgency of this happening. I like black people very much. They have great soul, great give . . .

INT.: *Thank you, Jenny, for deciding not to talk about it.*

14

Some Observations About Single Swingers

Seventy-two percent of the single men and women we interviewed were under thirty. The remaining twenty-eight percent consisted of separated or divorced people in their thirties; of these, twenty-five percent had one or more children.

Approximately seventy-five percent of the single men and women preferred smaller groupsex gatherings; i.e., parties with anywhere from two to fifteen couples and/or singles. These singles disliked, with varying degrees of intensity, the larger parties, which were commonly referred to as "orgies." The general feeling was that these affairs were too impersonal, dehumanizing. ("After a while, you don't know who is doing what to whom, and why.") There was general agreement among the singles (and marrieds as well) that the orgy is the riskiest and least controllable aspect of groupsex because of its attendant dangers: venereal disease, underage participants (almost always young girls), freaks, voyeurs, hard drugs, and bestiality.

Nevertheless, approximately twenty-five percent of the single men and women attended orgies on an average of once a month because they offered the widest possible choice of new bedmates with little or no emotional involvement. Most of the time, people never even knew each other's names. Yet when a sex-mate was particularly satisfying, the relationship could be continued outside the groupsex scene.

For the women the most frequently mentioned value was the opportunity for experimentation with many positions, techniques and couplings with several men and/or women. Almost all the single women who preferred orgies thought of themselves as extremely "good" and "responsive" in bed, and they seemed to enjoy the opportunity to exhibit those characteristics in a crowded environment.

For the men the most frequently cited benefit of orgies was "the marketplace atmosphere," "instant new blood," with sex available at a fast and furious rate. We had the feeling, though, that the most appealing (though unstated) advantage seen by most men was the atmosphere of anonymity, much like the feeling of being lost in a crowd. This seemed to allay many of the men's anxieties about achieving and maintaining erections or ejaculating too quickly. So much happens in an overcrowded bedroom that little attention was paid to anything in particular; therefore, there was less chance for disapproval of a man's performance. Also, orgy sex satisfied the man's need to "do it" rather than "feel it."

It appears from our sampling that male and female singles went through similar phases with regard to the ebb and flow of swinging activities. At first, they all tended to overdo it: two to five parties in a weekend—Friday and Saturday night, Sunday brunches, etc. For the singles this phase usually lasted from six months to a year. By then approximately sixty-five percent dropped out of organized groupsex encounters.

The main reason for dropping out was a general resistance to planned sexual activities; and singles clearly were more flexible than married couples in their ability to move out and explore casual sexual encounters.

Approximately seventy-five percent of the female singles permanently dropped out of organized groupsex parties; approximately sixty percent of the single men did likewise. But almost ninety-eight percent of the single men and women continued their swinging sexual activities informally and in smaller groups, often after a social get-together, perhaps an athletic event or a culturral evening.

Unorganized groupsex appears to be sharply on the increase among singles because it offers the widest freedom in time, place, and choice of bed partners. Also, the selection process is less haphazard and therefore poses minimum risks of disease and exposure. The singles, as a group, seemed far less concerned with the dangers of public exposure than the married couples.

Participation in swinging did not last as long for singles as for the married couples in our survey. Almost seventy-two percent of the males had been swinging for one to five years; twenty-three percent from five to twelve years; and only five percent longer than that. Sixty-nine percent of the females had been swinging for one to five years; twenty-nine percent from five to twelve years, and two percent longer than that.

Almost eighteen percent of the single swingers under thirty were still attending college on a full or part-time basis. These singles often carry a full load of undergraduate or postgraduate courses and are much more involved with non-swinging people than the married couples in our sampling. For example, many singles live in apartment buildings catering solely to singles. Many of them do not call themselves swingers, yet they share in the new trends of sexual freedom, including groupsex.

Over sixty-five percent of the singles insisted that their plural sex activities created deep and abiding friendships with many different sexual partners, lasting, in some instances, several years.

When we questioned them about the separation of love from sex, about eighty-five percent of the single men and women felt that they were capable of having sex without love, but not without feeling. They insisted that their relationships were always selective. We heard words like "empathy" and "vibes." They felt "so close" to this person or that person. They could be "open" and "honest" with many of their sexual mates. Though they consistently shunned the use of the word "love," their activities seemed to encompass something more than impersonal, no-names-please sex. One of the words most often voiced by them to cover the love gap was "caring."

PART IV
Fathers, Mothers, and Their Children

---

15 SCOTT:

"A More Open Atmosphere At Home"

At forty-two, Scott is a successful surgeon in the Midwest. He heads his own practice and has other doctors working under him.

Talking to Scott, you can see why. Almost as quickly as we began our questioning, Scott analyzed what we were asking, making a mental outline and preparing himself for his dynamic, thrustful answers. Like a surgeon working with a scalpel, he would get to the core of the matter with a semantic discipline that is well learned but not rigid, unlike people who stick to one track and seldom, if ever, vary.

When his wife died, his life changed considerably. He was faced with the task of bringing up two girls—Lynn who was then nine, and Beth who was sixteen. His responsibilities were dual: to maintain the figure of masculine authority and, at the same time, taking on those qualities of understanding and caring that usually belong to the mother.

Scott dates. Mostly younger women. Which means he must stay young himself and stay in shape. When he can, he jogs early in the morning, tries to spend evenings exercising and, at least three times a week and every Sunday afternoon, he goes bicycle riding with his daughters. He says:

"I don't consider myself handsome in the sense that some women are going to drop everything and come running. But I feel confident and comfortable enough to hold my own."

Scott is trying to find a life-style of his own. "A middle ground," as he says.

His home shows that. Open, modern in many ways. It's a fairly new nine-room split-level on an acre of land with some of the idealistic quality of a Walden. Most of what he has was built or designed by himself. He takes great care and pride in his home. And it shows:

"A man's home should also be his retreat. I'm trying to make ours that way, the best I can."

INTERVIEWER: *Would you give me some brief biographical background about yourself?*

SCOTT: My childhood was quite conventional. One older sister. No broken home. Not many trials or tribulations. Generally, a rather happy home. I was raised as a Roman Catholic. The religious persuasion was pushed harder by my mother than my father. After graduation from high school I entered the University as a pre-med student and then went on to medical school in the Midwest, where I trained in surgery.

INT.: *How do you feel about nudity generally?*

SCOTT: I certainly liked the idea of having a natural attitude in the family—parents and their children being nude in front of each other. This met with varying acceptance and rejection from my wife when she was alive . . . And my kids had their own psychology of life. Girls have a strong desire to dress up, and their sense of modesty comes out of that.

INT.: *Are you suggesting that nudity at home became a controversial issue?*

SCOTT: Not really. If we stepped out of a shower, for example, it wasn't necessary to put on a robe before leaving the bathroom. No one was running out the front door and down the street without any clothes. But the kids knew that if they wanted to they were perfectly free to walk around the house unclothed. That was their decision.

INT.: *Did you find this kind of behavior compatible with your religious upbringing?*

SCOTT: As this was happening at home I began to uproot myself from that background except for the preservation of the basic values of life, a continuity of ethics that I continue to live by.

INT.: *Did you consider nudity a form of sex education at home?*

SCOTT: You could call it that . . . Our Judeo-Christian background probably led us to experience many of the same things . . . We all went through the period of masturbation; and we were all told that if we did this we were going to go blind or insane or some other terrible disaster would strike us. Then, approaching teen-age, we began petting in the back seat of cars, or wherever else we could . . . That too was bad because at that time it involved the possibility of pregnancy. The pill has helped reduce that risk, but kids still pet. Well, I feel that children should be told about sex and where babies come from. I know from my own experience that a child himself will dictate the process by asking questions when he feels the need to do so. At that point I think the parent should answer unabashedly, because if you are too embarrassed to talk about sex to your kids then you shouldn't be participating in it yourself.

INT.: *Do you feel some people might say, since your views run counter to the mainstream, that you are forcing them on your children?*

SCOTT: You'll have to ask my children. I think they should have their privacy, but they should also have their sex questions answered. If they ask, how can I be forcing answers? I would rather have them be sexually informed than be on drugs and ruin their minds *and* bodies . . .

INT.: *Do you feel this open sex attitude in the home is therapeutic?*

SCOTT: Wait a minute! Don't confuse shamelessness about the human body with a sex act . . . There is probably more promiscuity going on on a public beach than there is in our home. Every day, with my kids, is a brand new experience.

146

Whether you agree with my feelings or not, every parent who raises children knows that every day is fraught with new and unpredictable encounters . . . I know with my oldest daughter Beth, she started dating a guy and liked him. When they became emotionally involved with each other I decided that she should go on birth-control pills. I didn't tell her this is what she had to do . . . I called up our family doctor and gave him my approval to prescribe the type of pills he felt was best for her *if* she ever called him with that kind of request . . . Therefore, in the end it would be her decision, and I thought I had given her a more comfortable way to make it. Personally, I didn't know if she was old enough to get married, and I didn't want her to get pregnant prematurely, but I didn't want to deprive her of having sex if she wanted it. My youngest daughter Lynn started masturbating a while ago, and I encouraged it. I think it is a good thing. I remember feeling good when I used to do it. So why deprive her of this feeling? This also leads to a more open atmosphere in our home. I'll have several friends over for a small supper party and my children know they're free to join in if they want to, sit and talk, or listen, get involved in conversation with any of my friends. I think, for example, my twelve-year-old daughter Lynn can talk more freely about sex than some of the adult straight friends I know. She can handle it perfectly well.

INT.: *Does your swinging create problems with your straight friends?*

SCOTT: A lot of different people make up our society. I feel that I can adhere not only to my own beliefs, but I also have a responsibility to respect other views as well. I have to be one thing at work in my office and another kind of person at home with straight friends. And there is still another side of me to explore when I am in my group environment. I'm resolving these differences slowly. I'm finding a middle ground . . . You see, for myself and for some of my friends sex is a by-product of swinging. Some of us go to parties to meet new people, to make new friendships, to see or be a part of this feeling toward sex as much or as little as we want.

INT.: *Could you explore these deeper aspects of swinging further?*

SCOTT: It's a search for the real values. What is life all about? For some time after my wife passed away I had no experience with swinging. Then I met a friend who told me about a lodge up north, where professionals like myself gather, especially on weekends, to relax, to do what they want. Some were swingers, others were not. I went up there with girlfriends on different occasions and enjoyed the atmosphere and the stimulating alternatives. After my first six months of swinging I reached a point where I just didn't think it was worth the effort to go to a swinging party just to take a girl to bed. When I go to a swinging party now there are times when I am inactive sexually. If I do find someone I like and we establish a rapport then we will see if we can enjoy each other. But for some swingers I know, there is the feeling of wanting to be possessed by someone rather than wanting to possess someone. Wanting to give, I think, can be a good thing. So for some, experiences in a group scene can be rewarding. For others, the consequences can be unsatisfactory.

INT.: *What are you personally seeking from these groupsex experiences?*

SCOTT: I feel that in certain swinging groups you can reach an intense closeness with people; not always sexually and not always sensually, but a strong bond between people can be created. I've been surprised to find a lot of people who want this kind of closeness, a tribal feeling of concern for one another in sort of an extended family as opposed to one-to-one, individual selfishness . . . This becomes an emotional investment in someone outside of yourself. I honestly feel that this group involvement, from what I have seen, is a possible answer for the man in the city after a day's confrontation with the remoteness of the technological world. It's a way to maintain his sanity through a rejuvenation of feeling.

INT.: *Others say that this emphasis on sexual freedom in the group scene can become dehumanizing.*

SCOTT: Seeing other people copulate in front of me used to be a turn-on. I don't think it is anymore. It's become commonplace. But I think feminine nudity is a beautiful thing . . . Women in that condition are never dull for me as long as copulating does not become mandatory.

148

INT.: *Do you sense pressure to participate at a swinging party?*

SCOTT: At some gatherings people seem to insist that everyone swing. If you walk in with a girl she may be obliged to swing with someone she may not care for. In other words, she is your donation for the evening to permit you to come in, look around and see what else you want yourself. To me that is far more regimented than the so-called normal society. The reason I go to my friend's lodge is to become unregimented.

INT.: *Is there a contradiction then—does the theory of freedom in swinging become regimented in practice?*

SCOTT: If there is a mutual decision on the part of the partici-pants (husband and wife or other consenting couples), then I think swinging is a good thing for them to do . . . However, some aspects of it can be dangerous if there is a dominant member who imposes his or her swinging on the other partner and the other mate goes along as the only means of keeping the marriage together. Then swinging can be destructive. I have seen this happen. The poor wife is petrified by all that's going on, and sits in a corner with the look of panic instead of love in her eyes . . . I have also seen it work the other way. A husband brings his wife as his entrance fee to find another sexual partner, and before the evening is over his wife is having a ball and he is not making it very well in the swinging scene . . . It's an individual experience and the judg-ment is deeply personal.

INT.: *Will you continue swinging?*

SCOTT: I'm in a little different position than the married couples who go to parties because I bring girlfriends, which is not exactly the same as "trading" with a wife . . . I do intend to get married again, and the woman I marry doesn't have to be a swinger. I can't really say in advance if I would bring my wife to a swinging party. I'm not sure . . . I am sure of this, however: any man-woman relationship should come from the mind first. When two people can enjoy the process of living together, completely apart from sex, then in that mean-ingful relationship, sex will find its own level.

BETH:

"The Children of Swingers Are Very Free with Their Feelings"

Beth, Scott's older daughter, is fairly tall, five-feet-six, has long brown hair that ignores style and dark brown eyes. She is a freshman in college.

Beth is a sum of things that go into making a lovely eighteen-year-old girl. She is not really beautiful. Her attractiveness comes from a balance of separate features that fit together well.

She is unconcerned with artificial things and very concerned about artificial people. Life to her has too much depth, too much that is undiscovered, to allow for shallow people. She is extremely perceptive, listens carefully to a question, thinks her answers through, and then is as precise as possible in a quiet, yet intense, manner. She organizes her feelings so that when she finishes answering a difficult question, you feel she is giving you a complete thought, not fragments.

Beth has her own unique identity without trying to manufacture it as she goes along. At times fragile, at times taking the lead, one characteristic never competes with others.

She is dating one man. He has his own place and when they

feel like it they live together: sometimes for a week, sometimes as long as a month. But they're not living together because so many people of their age are doing so. They form their own unit when they feel it's right. Nothing is pushed or forced; no one has to be convinced into doing anything.

Beth dresses to fit the mood: sometimes in "freaky" clothes, sometimes in simple, traditional styles. Her boyfriend does the same.

One thing she doesn't want—or even experiments with—is drugs. That's not her scene. If she can't feel the vitality of life on her own, there's something awfully wrong. She doesn't want to burn her brain out and become a "senile twenty-year-old" in the next two years.

INTERVIEWER: *How old are you?*
BETH: Eighteen.
INT.: *Where you were born?*
BETH: On the West Coast. I lived there for five years and then moved here. We've been living here ever since I entered the university.
INT.: *What about your family?*
BETH: My mother died three years ago and it's had an effect on us, especially my younger sister who is twelve now. But things are working out and we're managing to stay together as a family.
INT.: *Was there a religious atmosphere in your home?*
BETH: My parents were Catholic, and my grandfather had finished his instruction to become a priest. Shortly before being ordained, he decided against it.
INT.: *Do you know why?*
BETH: It must have been a long struggle that finally surfaced. When he talked about it, he said something to the effect that he couldn't serve in the ministry because he had serious questions about celibacy.
INT.: *Did this have any impact on your home life?*
BETH: I wouldn't really know. But little by little, my father, I think, more so than my mother, was going away from the Church, not necessarily alienating himself from Catholicism,

151

but trying to adopt his religion to a more contemporary way of life. My mother, on the other hand, continued the concept that people keep their ideas and their thoughts to themselves. I think what she meant mainly referred to negative thoughts and feelings.

INT.: *Such as?*

BETH: Well, if we didn't feel that someone was right or if we got mad at somebody, we had to keep it to ourselves.

INT.: *That's what you were told to do?*

BETH: Mostly it was what we were told to do.

INT.: *Did this lead you to become rebellious?*

BETH: No. At that time we felt our parents were right in their thinking and so we never really made an issue of it.

INT.: *Did this religious tone at home affect the sexual education you received?*

BETH: No. In that area, things were fairly open, particularly when it came to nudity. My father felt it was all right for us to walk around the house semi-undressed or without any clothes on. I was eight when my father started telling me the facts of life, and I didn't feel he was embarrassed about it. He encouraged me to ask a lot of questions which was not too easy for me to do, especially in this area, and he was quite patient with me.

INT.: *What about your mother?*

BETH: She let my father do most of the explaining. My Mom was more inhibited when it came to the discussion of sex or things related to that.

INT.: *How did she feel about household nudity?*

BETH: Mostly she went along with it, but I do know later on she had misgivings.

INT.: *Did she say what they were?*

BETH: I think her personal involvement with nudity bothered her more than the idea that the rest of the family was doing it.

INT.: *How did you and your sister feel about this exposure of the body?*

BETH: I didn't mind at all. I felt it was being pushed on me a little bit, but I didn't mind seeing the human body. My father explained it rather well, I think, back in the beginning. He said that God created us and it was a wondrous creation, something that we should be proud of, not ashamed of.

152

INT.: *Then you did experience a rather liberal sex education at home.*

BETH: I'd have known very little if I'd had to rely on what they taught me in school. The grammar school classroom instruction was quite rigid and "square." As I recall, the teachers were making the whole subject look bad. It was almost as if they themselves were extensions of parents who didn't want to discuss these things with their children at home and were doing it reluctantly at school to strangers because they were being paid to do so.

INT.: *What's the answer, then?*

BETH: That's so personal. I know I learned quite a bit at home and it was very helpful to me. If I'd had very "straight" parents, I don't know where I'd be now.

INT.: *It's startling to hear this from you, Beth, growing up in a Catholic household.*

BETH: You're bringing some of your prejudices into it, aren't you?

INT.: *I'm thinking not only of what I presume goes on in most Catholic homes but in Jewish or Protestant homes as well.*

BETH: I understand it better now.

INT.: *How did your friends and neighbors feel about nudity in your home?*

BETH: In the beginning they didn't know about it. (She smiles) That did create some embarrassment. When friends came to the door I had to keep them waiting outside until I made sure that whoever was inside put on some clothes.

INT.: *Did you discuss family nudity with your friends?*

BETH: No, I didn't think they'd understand. I didn't feel embarrassed or frightened about sex or nudity. Thanks to my upbringing, I never have. But I do feel uptight around people who might not like this free behavior.

INT.: *Why did you have this feeling if it's been helpful for you?*

BETH: Because I'm not a proselytizer by nature. I wouldn't know what to say to them. I feel very guarded and I have to be very careful about what I say around straight people. I feel there's a wall between us, that we can't communicate very well, that they're trying to hide something and I am, too.

INT.: *Is that the way you still feel?*

BETH: About proselytizing, yes. But now I've got lots of friends who are very loose about nudity and share my feelings about the openness of sex. Many of them have swinging parents—some of them don't, but we've all got a good thing going between us. I mean, we communicate and we don't really care to argue with uptight people because we're happy with what we're doing by ourselves.

INT.: *I still don't get a clear picture of how your family reconciled an uninhibited home life with regard to nudity and the constrictions that your religion would impose on that.*

BETH: It was a gradual process. Religion was always there. We went to church. We were tight unto ourselves and didn't talk to others about the things we did at home. Then, after my father started swinging, the Catholic Church went into the background, and now we have our own ideas about religion. We think of God in a completely different way.

INT.: *Would you care to explain it?*

BETH: I don't believe God had in mind for us to have one set plan: "No, don't do this" or "Yes, that's all right." Different kinds of people develop different life-styles. Some of each is good and some is bad, according to individual judgments. But I don't think you can put down permanently in advance, for all time, what is good and right for everyone.

INT.: *What do you feel is the Catholic Church's attitude toward what you're doing?*

BETH: They probably feel we're all damned.

INT.: *Do you feel damned?*

BETH: No. I feel a lot more honest the way I am than I would if I were trying to follow the precepts of the Catholic Church and not believing in it. I also feel honest toward myself and toward other people. I can relate to people a lot easier and say what I feel a lot easier. And I do attribute this to my parents, especially my father's attitudes toward sexuality.

INT.: *When did you find out that your father was swinging?*

BETH: For about a year after my mother died, my father stayed home quite a bit. He had friends, couples who encouraged him to go out with them. But too often their conversations came back to what they were doing together as couples. And this was hard for my father to listen to. Then, maybe nine months after my mother was gone, some of the same people tried to sort of match up my father with people they knew, either a widow, a divorcee, or someone who'd never married. My dad wasn't ready for all this . . . A few months after the end of that first year he started meeting some new people, people that I'd never been introduced to before . . . They all seemed nice and quite interested in my sister and me. And, not long after that, my dad started going out . . . Sometimes when he came home and I was still up, we talked. He didn't say that he was swinging, but the way he talked, the way he said he was having a lot of fun and doing things he'd never done before, made me get the feeling that there *was* something different going on in his life. Then one day he told me . . . that he was swinging.

INT.: *How did you feel when he told you?*

BETH: First, I thought that he might lose himself, that he might not be able to find someone else to attach himself to, that swinging was a way where he just couldn't find someone whom he'd consider marrying. He'd get too turned-on about swinging and be lonely half the time and satisfied sexually half the time. But now I feel that he is searching around, looking for that one person, and swinging is how he is going about it.

INT.: *Do you really think he wants to settle down again?*

BETH: He does want to. He just hasn't found the right person.

INT.: *Was the concept of your father swinging in any way upsetting to you?*

BETH: Not really, except for those reasons I already mentioned. I wasn't shocked, if that's what your're getting at.

INT.: *How did you feel about your father's swinging friends?*

BETH: Well, I hope that they're being honest about swinging. I hope they're swinging because they feel it's right and not because they want to follow the crowd.

INT.: *Do you think sex should be an important part of most people's lives?*

BETH: It's there . . . I mean, it's something that shouldn't be ignored. But I don't think sex should be overstressed either. To me, it's not as important as love, but it has a lot to do with love.

INT.: *Swingers say that you can have sex without love. How does that concept strike you?*

155

BETH: It depends totally on the individual. I'm living with Roger. He's my boyfriend, and we have sex together. We also eat together, ride bicycles together, go on nature hunts, sometimes argue. We even cry together, and I like him very much.

INT.: *Does he share your views about sex and nudity?*

BETH: I wouldn't be living with him if he didn't.

INT.: *Do you feel sexual freedom leads to other kinds of open-mindedness when it comes to social and political issues?*

BETH: Hmm, I never thought about it that way before. Possibly. I guess it would come down to knowing enough about a swinger's prejudices before he started swinging and then to see if his views have changed.

INT.: *Do you feel that swinging over-emphasizes sex to the point where it becomes compulsive?*

BETH: Not really. My father, for example, has less preoccupation about sex now than before he started swinging . . . If you say "No!" to sex over and over again, it's quite obvious that a person will desire it even more. I think once you've broken the barrier of "getting sex" then people are freer, more able to search each others minds . . . It's part of a relationship, and unless you have other things going for you, then sex alone simply will not sustain a bond between two people or more than two people.

INT.: *You think groupsex has a future or is it just a passing phenomenon?*

BETH: I can't really predict anything. I'd like to think that swinging will become more accepted and generally a natural thing to do.

INT.: *Do you feel that swingers consider themselves a persecuted minority?*

BETH: Probably so. I think they feel they have to keep to themselves quite a bit because other people feel threatened by them and because it's a new thing, a new idea, and most people don't know what it's about.

INT.: *How does this affect your relationships with square friends?*

BETH: I'm usually very quiet and stay in the background. My views on almost everything are different from most of my "square" friends. When I'm with these people, we don't have things to talk about.

156

INT.: *Why do you think you're so far apart?*

BETH: Well, if you say sex is important, then I feel that you must also say that love is important. So, if you're very free with sex, you're going to be equally free with your feelings. But an uptight person withdraws into an almost frightened, catatonic state if you as much as go up to him and hug him, especially if you do it without a little warning.

INT.: *Why, then, do you go on seeing these straight friends?*

BETH: There are so many parts to everyone's life. I've started painting, and I do quite a bit of it now. I'm also majoring in political science, so I have to go to class with lots of straight students. There are a lot of things I have to do with regard to my interests that bring me in contact with straight people.

INT.: *You're the child of a swinging parent. Do you know others?*

BETH: (smiling) What's that terrible phrase—"Some of my best friends are . . ."

INT.: *How has this kind of life-style affected them?*

BETH: The children of swingers that I know are very free with their feelings—that's the biggest thing. Extremely honest.

INT.: *But some swingers don't tell their children.*

BETH: That's not true. They're not honest swingers then.

INT.: *Do you feel a swinging parent should tell his or her children?*

BETH: Definitely.

INT.: *Is there a limit in terms of age?*

BETH: No . . . I mean, it's just when it's made out to be bad that it might hurt to tell a child the fact that his parents are swingers. If you start out by telling a child that sex isn't bad and that his parents feel it's right to have a very honest, open feeling toward sex, then why hide it from a child? There's nothing bad about it.

INT.: *But in our culture, will children be threatened by this kind of revelation?*

BETH: I don't think so. The parents would have to be very honest with them and explain to the children as much as possible why they swing, what's behind it all. If a child knows that his father or mother is going out and having all sorts of relationships with other people because the parent really loves or likes these people, he's not going to be worried about it,

157

I don't think. It's only if parents hide something from a child, if their reasons for swinging are dishonest and ambiguous, then there would be something wrong in terms of the children.

INT.: *Are there any things that kids shouldn't see in the swinging environment?*

BETH: It would depend a lot on their upbringing and their parents. If, say, the sexual act had been hidden from them and made to seem like, "You should never see anything like that," then I don't think they should until their parents maybe slowly change their own thinking toward it. But if you've been brought up, you know, to where you can accept anything like that, any sort of natural human act, then I don't think there should be any limits.

INT.: *Would it bother you to observe a sexual act?*

BETH: Umm . . . I think I'd feel embarrassed if I walked in on my father. But it wouldn't have any big, horrible affect on me. I personally feel that it's something private and *I* wouldn't like anybody walking in on *me*. That's probably why I'd feel embarrassed if I walked in on my father.

INT.: *Beth, you've lived in the middle of the swinging and nonswinging worlds; have you decided how you personally feel about swinging?*

BETH: Do you mean, will I swing, have I swung? (she smiles) No, I haven't. I don't feel that swinging is for me.

INT.: *Why not?*

BETH: I have all the sex I want with Roger. I want to marry him after I finish college. I want to travel and develop an awareness of myself, an awareness of life, and I want to be able to function within that system. I feel I can.

INT.: *And Roger?*

BETH: He shares these views . . . But our exposure to swinging will have a definite effect on our marriage . . . Our observations of the openness and the honesty that it offers to so many people have brought us closer to our feelings. I think Roger and I can make a go of our marriage. Now may I ask *you* one question? Don't you ever get tired of asking all these questions on sex, sex, sex?

INT.: *Sometimes . . .*

17

LYNN:

A Twelve-Year-Old Is Told About Her Father's Swinging

Lynn, Scott's younger daughter, is Beth six years younger—winsome in a delicate, almost elflike way, reminding one at times of a Keane painting. Huge, saucer eyes that sparkle and settle, looking almost infinitely forward, quiet shades of darkness beneath. Soft, almost translucent skin.

With a mixture of innocence and coyness she is much like most twelve-year-old girls. She asks for the right to wander a little, and change thoughts when she finds a better way of saying something.

The first thing that she did when she raced through the doorway after a day of school was to give us a quick nod and smile, then off she went to the kitchen for a glass of milk and cookies, which she then as quickly carried into the den, asking Beth "What did you do with the album that was sitting here this morning? You know the one, *that* one."

The record album was uncovered beneath a pile of others to which she had been listening the night before.

It was too bad our tape recorder could not pick up the

shrugs, the frowns, the inquisitiveness, the broad smile that we saw often during the interview.

She spoke with surprising ease, and no question we asked seemed too difficult to understand or answer.

INTERVIEWER: *Lynn, you know that we've talked about this with your father and received his permission to interview you?*

LYNN: Yes, he told me.

INT.: *How old were you, Lynn, when your father first told you about his swinging?*

LYNN: It was last year. I'd just turned eleven.

INT.: *How did you feel about it?*

LYNN: I felt better when he told me . . . I was kind of surprised though, a teensy little bit.

INT.: *Was it a long talk?*

LYNN: Yes. It was about his reasons. He came into my room one night before I went to bed. I knew he'd been taking out a few women, and I knew he liked them because he'd bring them home for dinner, but I knew he had things on his mind.

INT.: *Was it the way he acted?*

LYNN: Things like that. He felt like he always had to explain why he was going out after my mom passed away . . . He'd ask me if it was okay, you know; if I didn't want him seeing another woman right away he wouldn't. He'd wait. So I knew things like that were troubling him.

INT.: *Did you understand what he told you about swinging? What it was all about?*

LYNN: Well, kind of. The general idea. And Beth told me the rest.

INT.: *You asked?*

LYNN: (She nods and smiles softly) Uh, huh. I was curious about the people doing it. Did they have children, too . . . Were their parents telling them about swinging like my dad did? Well, I thought about these things for a while and then, finally, asked my father.

INT.: *Were you embarrassed about asking?*

LYNN: Maybe a little . . . He said some of the parents told their kids and others didn't . . . And if I wanted I could even

160

meet the other kids and the moms and dads, too, at a friend of my father's. This man has a real neat lodge up in the hills, about a two-hour ride from here. It's real great, you know. During the winter there is skiing, and in the summertime there are lots of trails and things to do on a weekend.

INT.: *Had your father been up there alone before?*

LYNN: Not alone exactly. He said he took some of his women friends there. But once a month there's a "family day" and my dad said he would like to take Beth and me up there at that time, if we wanted to go.

INT.: *Did it work out?*

LYNN: Yes. And the people up there were very nice. They do anything they feel like doing. You don't have to wear clothes if you don't want to.

INT.: *Did anything you saw up there bother you?*

LYNN: People walking around naked and stuff . . . ? Well, it's there. I kind of liked it. I don't care.

INT.: *Beth said that there was a lot of nudity in the family while you were growing up.*

LYNN: Well, when my mother was still living my dad didn't much mind if all of us walked around the house naked. Before I was nine I was too bashful . . . And at my dad's friend's place many people go around that way, so after a while you don't really notice it . . . And we all had a good time.

INT.: *What did you do there?*

LYNN: I liked swimming in the pool. Roaming around. Taking walks. I like the people up there and things to do.

INT.: *What about your other friends who don't go in for this sort of thing?*

LYNN: Well, my friends whose parents swing we all pretty much think alike. We feel free to say what's on our minds to each other. And we can talk to our parents about things that I don't think my straight friends can . . . I have two girlfriends who live close to us. One girl is pretty free and we can talk about things, but the other girl, sometimes I'll say something and she'll give me a bad look.

INT.: *Does that separate you from your straight friends?*

LYNN: What do you mean by that word?

INT.: *Well, like you aren't comfortable or at ease with them.*

161

LYNN: That's true . . . When I'm around kids who are not like myself I try not to say anything. Maybe I'm missing out on some fun that the other kids have, but I feel freer to say things on my mind . . . It doesn't bother me to talk about sex to my sister or my dad, or to listen to some of my father's friends talking about it . . . I like my father's friends.

INT.: *Do you spend a lot of time with them?*

LYNN: (nodding) We're a very close family since my mother . . . You know. We go out lots of places and do lots of things as a family with some of my father's friends. Like to the lake. Up into the hills. And we talk a lot, too, about almost anything, I mean. There is a lot of talking and laughing.

INT.: *Have you any other feelings you would like to express on the subject of swinging?*

LYNN: No, not really. I don't think swinging should be done in front of anybody who doesn't like it. It should be done if the people who want to swing really want to. I don't think that people who like to swing should force it too hard on the people who don't like to.

INT.: *Do you think some people who swing do try to force it on others?*

LYNN: Well, they don't try too hard, but they may try in words. I think people who want to swing should have a free choice, not feel that because everyone else is swinging they have to do it also.

INT.: *In your home you've had the opportunity, Lynn, to enjoy a much more open sex education than most children your age.*

LYNN: Yes, I know that. We sort of all share things—like problems in school, even.

INT.: *Do you like school?*

LYNN: It depends on my grades. They're pretty good now. And we talk about religion, a lot about that.

INT.: *How do you feel about religion?*

LYNN: I'm not the kind of person who says prayers when I go to bed at night. I feel that God is not as straight as people say he is. He's had a couple of good times, too.

18

TAMMY:

An Underage Runaway Who Swings

Thousands of young people run away every year, drop out of family and school to see what life is all about. Tammy is one of them. At fifteen she ran away from an Eastern family which, as she puts it, "had all the material stuff, but couldn't put things together." She had been enrolled in a prep school, had made the honor roll, and was in her sophomore year when she left an environment that some would consider offered an abundance of security.

Maybe that was one of the reasons she left. The realities of anxieties and uncertainties are not always obvious in a two-story colonial home held together by all the trimmings of luxury. Tammy felt something was missing, and, at seventeen, she still feels the same.

Tammy doesn't care about style. She puts on the first thing that fits her mood for that day—any day. She's constantly at her hair, pulling the long brown strands away from her eyes. She looks as if molded by the wind, but never settled, always searching.

Tammy has been swinging for one year. Since she is under

age, she runs a special risk, but she says she can handle herself with no one's help.

She lives "somewhere" in the Los Angeles area.

Unlike the children of swinging parents we interviewed, Tammy plays a role in the groupsex scene that a majority of swinging parents would never want for their children. But, no matter how strict the rules are in swinging, the Tammys, although small in number, have a way of turning up when you least expect them.

The temptation is to dismiss Tammy as a juvenile delinquent; except the more you "read" her, the more you feel yourself touched by her story.

Tammy has an answer for everything. The world's bad, so she knows a way to change it. Give her a brick to throw in a window, and she'll tell you what you can do with it. She can't be passed off as a militant because she really isn't. She can't be called a street freak, because she's not any more. She can't be called sloppy and careless, because she takes good care of herself. She's not an easy mark for anyone, because she has learned the hard way what it's like to stay on top of things.

Tammy eludes an easy excuse to place her in the category of a social misfit so you can rid yourself of justifications for being angry with her. After a while, you become less angry and more intrigued about what makes Tammy run. Until you realize that maybe it's you who are doing the running, not Tammy.

It was difficult for us to like her. But she is real. And that made it hard for us to forget her.

INTERVIEWER: *How long have you been around Los Angeles?*

TAMMY: Almost two years . . . I left home and bummed around the country for a while and then, I dunno, I guess I was lucky, and I hitched in from wherever it was that I was last in.

INT.: *Your parents . . .*

TAMMY: Worried, I suppose . . . Hey, I did call them once when I was in Missouri. They said the same old crap, you know, like, "Come on home, we're sorry, things will be different," that kind of bullshit.

INT.: *And you didn't buy any of that?*

164

TAMMY: Maybe for a few moments I did, you know, but then I know them.

INT.: *What are they like?*

TAMMY: Rich, running around the world all the time, the whole bit—big house, big cars, big friends, no class.

INT.: *Do you think they love you?*

TAMMY: If you mean that one night my father stuck it in my mother and nine months later I popped out, then, yeah, they love me.

INT.: *Isn't that being rather hard on them?*

TAMMY: They were too busy, you know, too busy to have children. They had three anyway. I have a younger brother and an older sister. But still, I really think they're happily married in their own way.

INT.: *Do you love them?*

TAMMY: Probably somewhere inside me I have a little feeling for them.

INT.: *Why did you leave home?*

TAMMY: Why did I leave? Um, to seek fame and fortune . . . You don't buy that, do you?

INT.: *No.*

TAMMY: Okay, let's see. I left because everything around me was screwed up, including me, I suppose. Maybe I was even more messed up than anybody else.

INT.: *What about now?*

TAMMY: Things are more together. My head's more here than there, but in the beginning when I sort of dropped into Los Angeles, it wasn't.

INT.: *Why?*

TAMMY: Okay, you're in a city alone, right? And you don't know anybody, so you bum and that's what I did for a while—I bummed. Like sometimes I'd hitch into the San Fernando Valley and stay outside of one of the supermarkets in a rich neighborhood and just stand around and rap with the guys who'd wheel out the groceries, and we'd have a deal going. They'd wink whenever they were taking out a big order for a man and wife. I'd come up to the man and look real sad and lonely, and I'd usually come up with a couple of quarters and sometimes more—like this one guy who wanted to take me up to his home, it was up high in the hills. I told him I'd yell rape right out in the parking lot and, man, did he empty out his wallet! I mean, I didn't come out and ask him for money, but he gave anyway.

INT.: *Is that how you made all your money, hustling off the street?*

TAMMY: I don't like the word hustling . . . it sounds cheap. More like making my expenses every day until I could find something.

INT.: *Did you?*

TAMMY: Uh huh. I got into making clothes. I'd sell them to the head shops or the boutiques around town. I still do that and I'm pretty good at it.

INT.: *What's it like, living on the streets?*

TAMMY: It's a world no different, really, than the world where The Man controls things.

INT.: *What do you mean "The Man?"*

TAMMY: The Corporation. It's a funny thing, but the street freaks who think they've dropped out really haven't, except the Hill People and even they have to make enough to exist . . . I mean, you see a bunch of us walking together at night like in packs, but we're really scraping for ourselves: barter and exchange—the whole bit; it's the same on the streets as in the straight world.

INT.: *How long were you living that way?*

TAMMY: A couple of months, but I could do without it, really. Then one of the girls I was bumming with got a bundle from a relative of hers who died, so she rented this old, run-down home and two of us moved in with her.

INT.: *You and who else?*

TAMMY: This other girl we'd both met on the street.

INT.: *How old were these two other girls?*

TAMMY: One had dropped out of college, I think she was maybe twenty-two, and Cindy was nineteen.

INT.: *Is that when you stopped hitting the street?*

TAMMY: (nodding) Like, we thought we could hold out for quite a while if we watched how we spent the money . . . then some of the guys the other girls knew at college started dropping over, little by little, and my two roommates would sort of encourage me to go to bed with them. I mean, *they* were doing it, so why not me?

INT.: *Did you?*

TAMMY: Yes . . . I really didn't enjoy it with these big-shot college guys who thought they knew everything. I had to be on grass when I went to bed with them, and after a while even that didn't help except maybe when I really got stoned.

INT.: *Did you stop doing it after a while?*

TAMMY: Yes . . . One night this cat who was in bed with me got stoned and started laughing and telling me about all the money I was making for him. He thought I knew that my two room-mates had gotten him to pimp for me and that the money I was giving them was going to him . . . It really blew my mind, I mean I'd become a sixteen-year-old prostitute! I really didn't have to find sex that way.

INT.: *You said you didn't like doing it with these guys, and yet you continued doing it for quite a while.*

TAMMY: I don't know . . . They got me grass, that's one reason. And it wasn't more than two or three times a day on an average.

INT.: *Don't you think that's a high "average" for someone your age?*

TAMMY: Yeah, I guess so . . . but there were dry spells. I mean, a couple of days a week nothing like that happened . . . Of course, after I found out how they were using me, those cunty roommates, I split.

INT.: *What happened then?*

TAMMY: The street again for a couple of days. Also, libraries. I read a lot and I went to those free concerts at college and listened to the music. I met a guy at one of those concerts and we hit it off real well.

INT.: *What was he like?*

TAMMY: He was different than the other guys I knew.

INT.: *In what way?*

TAMMY: He cared about me, and he didn't have to have sex with me all the time to show that he cared . . . We saw a lot of each other, and I moved into his pad . . .

INT.: *What did he do for a living?*

TAMMY: He was a musician . . . He was about twenty-nine. I think he was twenty-nine, but he looked younger. He played with a pretty popular group. I met a lot of his friends and found out he knew them through swinging.

167

INT.: *How did you feel about that?*

TAMMY: I wanted to go to one of his swinging parties and see what it was like.

INT.: *How did your boyfriend react to this?*

TAMMY: Big deal . . . I wanted to go, so he said okay, and I'm glad I did, especially that first night. I was a bit of a sensation, and I was also a little upsetting to some of the people there, especially the women. I was the age of their daughters, and here I was swinging with their husbands.

INT.: *Maybe you were looking for a father figure?*

TAMMY: Get off it . . . I don't dig that psychological introspective crap. These older men dug me because I was young and good-looking. And I dug them because they knew what they were doing. I still dig older guys who swing. They're gentle; they don't just stick it in and groan. They know how to ride a woman, they know how to excite a woman. One older guy I swing with grabs my rear and squeezes it so that it's nearly touching his penis. It doesn't hurt and it really turns me on.

INT.: *What kind of swinging parties do you like?*

TAMMY: All kinds. I like orgies once in a while; I mean, there it's easier . . . I hardly know who I'm screwing with. Somebody can have his finger up me while I'm eating some other guy out, I mean really going at it. It's fun and not personal. And I like to experiment a lot. Sometimes I give head to three guys at one time. I go from one guy's penis to another like three straws lined up one after the other, and I have a contest to see if I can have them all reach their climax at the same time.

INT.: *Do you try to reach your climax with them?*

TAMMY: Oh, no. I sit back and watch them squirt all over the place. That's the way it is when I swing. I have fun, play games, that's the way I want to swing. When I'm with my boyfriend, it's another thing . . . we're emotional . . . We can have sex in bed for hours at a time—it's different.

INT.: *Do you think that swinging for you is really some kind of rebellion?*

TAMMY: From what? My parents? I'm living just like my parents now: rich people, big cars, big homes, except that I've got my head, I'm on top of it. They're not and never will be . . . Like the orgies I go to. I've had sex with some important people,

168

politicians, doctors, people that my parents would consider a must at every party they throw—except they don't swing.

INT.: *Hasn't the fact that you're underage ever caused any trouble?*

TAMMY: Are you a cop or something? I kinda dig it, making it with these older guys, going up to Vegas or the Salton Sea or to Big Sur, and they make me feel like everyone else . . . One time we crossed the California border, going into —————— (a Southwestern state) and the border cops checked to see if we're taking in or bringing out any fruit or vegetables that might bring in bugs or something. I had this urge to yell back at the cops as we were leaving the checkpoint, "Hey, you dumbheads, you forgot to check me! I'm the ripest thing in this car, and I'm all ready to be eaten."

INT.: *I can't buy that you haven't had any trouble with the law.*

TAMMY: Don't be so picky . . . There were times, sure . . . There's this guy I know—he's a big name. Well, he digs chicks who are underage and he called me once from New York. He told be that a friend of his was shooting a movie on location in ——————. He wanted me to meet him there. He'd make arrangements for my plane ticket and he'd have someone at the airport drive me out to where they were filming. So I told him I didn't know, just to hear him get a little anxious over the phone. That was funny: here's this famous celebrity and I was making him stutter . . . Finally I said yes. Well, the first day up there I really dug it. I'd never seen a flick being shot before, and I just kept walking around and taking everything in.

INT.: *What about your friend?*

TAMMY: I kept ignoring him during the day, and some of the other men were bugging me about getting it on with them that night after the day's shooting, and I told them to cool it. I mean, there were other girls up there my age and they were available, except I think I was the cutest . . . Well, that evening my friend had to kind of remind me why I was invited up there and what I was supposed to be with him for. So I told him, you know, yawning in his face, "I have an early call, dahling," and he'd just have to wait another day, which blew his mind. The next day it was really hot. They broke in the afternoon, and all of us headed for one of the air-conditioned trailers, and we all started to get it on. This one actor, who was the star of the film, looked like he really was a great lover, so I decided to start off with him and we went into his private trailer and some other cat came in to give him a massage. Then some chick walked in and she was going to give me a massage and she did until she stuck her hand around my crotch and started playing around . . . I told him to get his hired hands out of the trailer if he wanted to have me. He was a great big disappointment. I mean, all he wanted me to do was lie on my back. He didn't want me sitting on top of him because he had strained his stomach muscles riding a horse in a scene earlier in the day, and like it must have taken him five minutes before he could finally come. He screwed like he acted—five takes before he could wrap anything up.

INT.: *How long were you there?*

TAMMY: Two days, over the weekend. Then I flew back to L.A.

INT.: *Didn't you say you almost got into trouble?*

TAMMY: Oh, yeah, I forgot . . . One of the ranchers who owned some property, he and his wife came onto the set and I guess she heard about what was going to happen that night, you know, the swinging. The cops came and somebody told them the lady was making everything up, that what she heard was a rehearsal of a scene. I think the head cop got a few bucks and an autograph and everything blew over, but it was close for a while.

INT.: *Aren't some of the older men afraid to go to bed with you, knowing that you're underage?*

TAMMY: A few. That's their hangup, because I know they'd probably like to make it with their teen-age daughters and would if they could.

INT.: *And the legal age bit doesn't bother you?*

TAMMY: Why, does it bother you? I see nothing wrong with what I'm doing. I'm a woman, I do woman things now. I love as a woman, I think as a woman, I'm expected to act like an adult and I do.

INT.: *What about marriage?*

TAMMY: You mean the guy I'm living with?

INT.: *Yes.*

TAMMY: Not now. Maybe someday. I do know this: I want to have his child and live together until the baby is maybe seven or eight years old. Then if he and I still want to get married, if we still dig each other, then maybe . . . If not, then I have my child and can go anywhere I please.

INT.: *Anywhere?*

TAMMY: Until I find another place . . . Um, I had a couple of friends who lived in Israel for a while on a kibbutz. They told me about how everyone lived together and worked together, but still were separate. I mean, they were individuals, too, but working and sharing for all the common, natural needs and desires. I think maybe this is the kind of life I'd like to give by child. I'm not Jewish, but this kind of communal living is close to what I think would be a productive environment to raise a child in, and for that matter, productive for adults, too.

INT.: *Do you think everybody of your generation should lead the kind of life you lead?*

TAMMY: I'm not an activist. I'm not trying to set trends or tell anyone else what to do. It's better if we're doing our own thing our own way. If someone else's bag is burning down a building or a bank, I'm not gonna go along with them and carry the matches. But I'm also not gonna burn them down for burning down the bank. I think a lot of this activity is just another way of avoiding the issue.

INT.: *What is the issue?*

TAMMY: The issue is the problem which affects everyone, not just the conservative or the liberal. I mean, the issue that threatens every one of us. I don't know what it is, but I know it exists. As far as those young people today, most of them are going to demonstrate until they start paying taxes and putting their kids through school, and then they'll just back off, play middle-class suburbia with each other and forget how they looked tossing the brick into the science building window when they were still in college.

INT.: *But you'll still be tossing the brick, so-to-speak, even when you're older?*

TAMMY: I didn't say that. I'm not desperate. I don't have to search to find, because I've found.

INT.: *It seems to me you're basing all your attitudes on the fact that you swing and what you're saying is that for you, sex is the answer.*

171

TAMMY: I'm not saying that. I'm saying that I've found a balance in sex at the age of seventeen where a lot of women at the age of thirty-seven still haven't found it. But I don't go into chills and convulsions when I'm not having sex with someone. I may swing for three nights in a row and then not have sex for another seven weeks.

INT.: *Have you thought about when you'll stop swinging?*

TAMMY: I haven't given it much thought, and I don't think I will. It's there when I want it and that's how I've always wanted to have sex, not as an obsession, but something that's there when it's needed . . . And when it comes to swinging, I still like to make it with the older men, the married guys. How do you like that?

INT.: *Obviously you like it. How do you feel about seeing a married man outside the swinging scene?*

TAMMY: It depends on the guy.

INT.: *Does it matter if his wife knows about it?*

TAMMY: Not to me. It just matters how the guy can handle us and how he can also handle them.

INT.: *It sounds to me like you're choosing up sides again: "us" and "them."*

TAMMY: Am I? I don't think so. If I felt that a man was hurting his family, hurting his wife and kids, I'd tell him so and end it right there!

INT.: *How can you be so sure?*

TAMMY: From experience, that's how. I've dated a few married men whose wives didn't know about it. One fellow in particular tells me that since he's been seeing me, he feels more relaxed at home. So if you want to say anything about me, then say I'm saving a marriage and not that I'm breaking it up. That's what you're thinking, isn't it?

INT.: *Yes, I guess I was.*

TAMMY: You have a right, but you're wrong. I make judgments and then I live with them and forget about the anxieties of second-guessing. I know a lot of people who breathe and eat and screw, but who really are dead inside. I live.

INT.: *It doesn't sound like you're all that sure of yourself.*

TAMMY: Who is?

INT.: *But I'd think that anyone like yourself who had a problem*

172

with home life and family would want to make sure that it wouldn't happen again.

TAMMY: Are you saying that swinging is bad for me?

INT.: *I don't know. I'm suggesting . . .*

TAMMY: You know, I think you're uptight about just about everything I've been doing.

INT.: *Maybe.*

TAMMY: All I'm saying is that marriage is a bummer from what I've seen about the people who are into that thing. I'm being more honest with my guy the way I am now than if I were married to him.

INT.: *Do you really enjoy the swinging scene?*

TAMMY: Not all of it. Like grass: I used to dig the stuff, but not any more. When a guy's really stoned on grass at a swinging party and he wants to make it with me, I tell him to shove off. You know, if he can't turn on with me, then forget it. And I don't like the creeps and the bores, the guys that are sloppy and have to manhandle me and lay their paws all over me and don't care about who I am, only that I'm another hole to be filled.

INT.: *Aren't you contradicting yourself? Earlier you said you liked orgies because you didn't know whom you were going to bed with.*

TAMMY: Picky again! I was telling you my feelings at a different time. I'm into different things now, so I feel differently about swinging. I don't need to swing all that often, like every week or once a month, unless I really feel like it.

INT.: *What kind of life-style is that?*

TAMMY: The kind of life that I feel anybody who makes an effort at finding it wants: a balance. I don't mean an evenness, but a blend of things, like a painting where the colors and the textures each have a life of their own, but they mix, they move without any interruption. That's what I mean.

INT.: *What do you want to do with yourself?*

TAMMY: There you go again, trying to pin me down. I don't have any fantastic loyalty to any one way, to any special life-style. I'm into painting, I'm into writing, I'm gonna keep on testing until one day I find something and say, "Yeah, that's it" and groove with it.

173

INT.: *What about the world, the "straight world"—how are you relating to that?*

TAMMY: That's changing all the time, too, and I'm for change. I guess I'll work for it more actively, but only when everyone gets their heads together, finally, all at once. Black, brown, yellow, red, green, magenta, everybody at the same time, not one group getting what they want one year, and the next group the following year.

INT.: *That's how you feel?*

TAMMY: Right. That's how I feel, that's what I see, and that's what I want. At seventeen, I have a right to, don't I?

19

JIM AND DONNA:

"There Were Two Couples Using Teddy's Bedroom"

Jim and Donna live in a fashionable two-story home in one the oldest West Coast communities, set back from a small, almost private street, shaded by tall maples on each side. At night the scene looks like a Christmas picture postcard—graceful, stable, warm.

Jim, a pharmacist, was in the garage working on his car when we drove up. He said, "Thought maybe you'd have a pretty hard time finding the place; that's why I gave you those long instructions."

"No problems at all," we told him.

Jim welcomed us into his home, excused himself for a minute to wash his hands and told us that Donna was still upstairs getting dressed. The news was on in the den, so we watched the color television and looked around.

Nothing was out of place or left to be cleaned up later. A lot of antiques, Early American furniture. Everything showed pride of accomplishment and good taste.

A few minutes later, Jim and Donna walked into the den.

Jim was dressed in a crew-knit sweater-shirt and slacks; his wife in a simple skirt and blouse. Donna is by no means a beautiful woman. Light brown hair, pulled back in a ponytail. Soft blue eyes. A pleasant smile, and proud of the fact that, as a woman of forty, she could still hold her own with girls ten years younger. She has the kind of face that grows old imperceptibly, even after the age of thirty-five: creamy, with traces of redness when she got excited and wanted to make a point in the conversation.

Donna gives the impression of being taller than she is, which, as she said, is "close to five-feet-four-inches." Slim, a well-trimmed figure, with a cheerleader's wholesomeness.

Their fifteen-year-old son, Teddy, wasn't home during the interview. He was playing football somewhere, said Jim, who is his stepfather. This is a second marriage for Donna and Jim's first. They have been swinging together ever since they were married ten years ago.

Jim is forty-five: black hair, receding a bit and with traces of thinning on top. His face has the kind of beard that requires at least two shaves a day—dark and heavy under the nose and chin. He is a well-groomed man, however, and works out with Teddy, using the barbells at least three times a week. The results showed mostly in his arms. Somehow one always pictures a pharmacist wearing a freshly pressed cotton uniform with short sleeves, his arms wiry with dark hairs, and that the way Jim's are.

"On Monday nights we always watch a television show about doctors at a medical center," Jim remarked. "One of these days they're going to give equal time to the pharmacists of the country, and there'll be an hour-long dramatic show about people like me. Maybe they'll call it 'The Young Pill-Pushers' or something like that."

It was a Monday night, and so we all watched the doctor's cure the patients at the medical center and afterward began our taped interview.

INTERVIEWER: *Which one of you got into the swinging scene first?*
DONNA: I did.
INT.: *How did it come about?*
DONNA: Through marriage. That doesn't sound right, but that's

really the way it happened. My late husband, Pete, said what I'm sure a lot of husbands feel: that he couldn't see spending the rest of his life going to bed with the same woman. He was honest about it and I loved him dearly for it, but when he first told me, I was a little upset. My feminine pride, you know what I mean. But the more I thought about it, the more he made sense. Because the same thing holds true for the woman. Part of having a good sex life is variety and having patience . . .

JIM: And having plenty of people.

DONNA: He's right.

JIM: I really feel that Donna probably reacted the same way I did when I first got into swinging.

DONNA: That's the truth. When I married, I was twenty-three. Before I met my first husband, I hadn't had much sex, but Pete helped me learn. He helped me enjoy sex, and he introduced me to a lot of beautiful people who felt the same way.

INT.: *What about you, Jim?*

JIM: If anyone had told me before I met Donna that I was going to turn out to be a swinger, I would have told them they had rocks in their heads . . . Well, a year or so after Donna's first husband died, we met. She had come into the drugstore a couple of times and we got talking. Finally I asked her out. One thing led to another and I proposed about seven months later.

DONNA: Would you believe that not once, not one single time while we were going together, did he ask or even hint at going to bed with me? A little hug, a "Thank you, I had a good time this evening" kiss, and then he left. If we hadn't held hands occasionally, I'd have thought I was dating the Invisible Man.

JIM: I wasn't that bad! I just didn't want Donna to get a wrong impression about me . . . You see, I didn't know she was a swinger.

DONNA: And I was afraid to tell him because he seemed so impossibly "square."

INT.: *Why did you go out with him then?*

DONNA: Because no matter what, he was a lot of fun to be with.

INT.: *And you survived all this dating without swinging?*

DONNA: (Smiling) Not exactly. I was also seeing another man who was a swinger . . . But I liked Jim better even though it *was* frustrating.

JIM: For me, also. I proposed no less than seven times.

DONNA: And I said no at least seven times on each occasion. I finally broke down and told him why.

JIM: She wouldn't marry me unless I agreed to swing. Would you believe that? That's the way I found out about her dark, deceiving past.

INT.: *Well, all marriages aren't made in heaven.*

JIM: This one almost wasn't made at all. At first I was real shook up. I thought swinging was wrong. I thought it would bust up a marriage . . . all those things. Then again, I saw how Donna was a wonderful mother to her boy. She was also active in the PTA, and, above all, worked as an administrative assistant to the president of a large corporation. Then I met some of Donna's swinging friends. I couldn't believe that those kind of people—they were really nice—were swingers. I remember saying to her, "These people? That couple—the one whose husband is a dentist? You've got to be kidding." She wasn't. So I could hardly say to her, "Look, they aren't normal, they're just hiding their horns in public."

DONNA: Jim finally said yes, he would swing, and I said, "Then you and I have a date to get married."

JIM: And we've all lived happily ever after—all 750 people we've been in bed with.

DONNA: Honey, we've been to bed with more than 750 people since we got married. We probably know more than 750 people right now, and most of them swing.

INT.: *How did you adjust to this kind of life style?*

JIM: It wasn't a matter of adjusting, exactly. It became a whole integrated thing.

INT.: *I'm not sure I understand. Don't your straight world activities ever interfere with your swinging life?*

DONNA: They don't have to. Look at it this way: Work, we put it up there; we're grateful to all those nice people in those giant companies that my husband and I toil for in the weekday heat and the cold for our daily bread. That is separate and apart from the rest of our life, which is almost totally dedicated to swinging.

JIM: I think you're confusing him again, dear. We're not talking now about "swinging" sex. We're talking about our doctor, say, who is a swinger. Also our dentist. Donna's gynecologist is a swinger. I buy my cars from a swinger who has his own automobile agency. Gee, the drapes, the rugs, the roofing we bought from a contractor who also swings. Let's see . . . (he looks around the living room), there's hardly anything that we've bought in the last year or so or any services that we've gotten from anybody who hasn't been a swinger. Even our lawyer and the accountant we switched our business to are swingers.

INT.: *You're talking about a local subculture that envelops your life.*

DONNA: It's the other way around. It's our choice, and it doesn't stop here in this city. We have swinging friends all over the country.

INT.: *Pen pals?*

DONNA: No, I'm talking about friends we see and spend time with. Married couples mainly.

JIM: When we take a vacation, we plan a swinging schedule. And sometimes when we're in another city, people there tell us, "If you're going to take such and such highway back, why don't you stop off in that city and call up so-and-so. I'm sure they'd like to meet you and have a get-together."

INT.: *A swinging get-together?*

JIM: (Laughing) Not necessarily. There have been times when we get together with swinging friends and, say, go down to San Diego for a long weekend and take in the bullfights. Or we'll drive to Las Vegas to see some shows and gamble a little. We're just socializing. Sometimes there's no sex at all. But almost all of our friends, the ones we spend our time with and have fun with on these recreational outings are swingers . . . And it's a great way to travel. More often than not, we're invited to stay with one of the couples and when they're in town here, we reciprocate. All of us save a lot of money that way and meet new and interesting people at the same time.

DONNA: We've been taking off a month each year making these trips. A few years ago we went to Honolulu, visited with some

179

friends we'd met here locally and had a ball. The same thing happened the year we went to the Caribbean.

INT.: *Now you're getting into the international swinging scene.*

DONNA: (Laughing) Hawaii is part of the United States. I'll go along with you on the Bahamas, though.

JIM: You see, we can afford all this. We're able to do so many things that way which we couldn't do as nonswingers. Donna and I are both doing well financially. The drugstore, knock on wood, is holding its own, and Donna takes home a very respectable salary.

DONNA: We don't like to be thought of as extravagant spenders. We're careful about saving money. Teddy, our son, will pretty soon be ready for college and right now we have enough money to pay for his education. Once he's through college, if he doesn't want to work for his father, we've saved up a little extra for him if he wants to go into a business of his own.

INT.: *Does Teddy know that you're swingers?*

DONNA: He does now. He didn't for a long time. Some swingers tell their children; others don't. We waited until we felt sure he was mature enough to understand.

INT.: *How did you manage things with your son before you told him?*

DONNA: It was not great problem when we went off to someone else's house for a party or on a weekend trip. It was a matter of arranging for a baby-sitter or having one of Jim's relatives —a few of whom live in the city—come and stay with Teddy. Whenever we had a party at our place, we just arranged for him to spend the weekend somewhere else.

INT.: *Do you think he knew what was going on?*

DONNA: No, I don't think he was too interested in sex. But even if he did he never told us, and I don't think it would have bothered him too much. You see, as he was growing up, Jim and I often took him to nudist camps. Not that we're active nudists ourselves, but we thought the whole experience, the opportunity for him to see the human body, see how natural it is, would be good for him.

INT.: *And Teddy grew up without facing problems due to your swinging?*

JIM: I think he's better off for it. He knows now how his parents

180

feel, what they do, and it's quite clear to us that he respects our opinions on that matter. And we've never been pushy, nor do we intend to, with regard to what he does when he grows up.

(During Jim's comment, Donna started laughing. At this point, he looked at her puzzled . . .)

DONNA: I'm sorry I'm laughing, Jim, but I was remembering that night Teddy came home early. It was a Sunday and he already knew we were swinging. We had thrown a party for about twenty couples at our place. It was supposed to be just a day-time affair but the party started late because the ball game on television was delayed due to rain. Anyway, by the time Teddy came home, some of our friends were still here.

JIM: (starting to laugh) Yeah, I remember that . . . Teddy seemed a little puzzled because he'd kept up his end of the bargain, coming home when he was supposed to. Well, Donna and I just told him to go to his room. He wasn't being punished or anything like that, but we thought it would be better if we handled things in that manner. Well, Donna and I sort of walked Teddy to his bedroom, opened the door, and we found quite a surprise inside . . .

DONNA: Several of them, actually. There were two couples using Teddy's bedroom.

JIM: His bed, to be exact.

INT.: *How did your son feel about that?*

JIM: I don't think you could say he was overjoyed and it caused some embarrassment. We don't like to march in on people like that, especially when we're hosts. But then our son was entitled to the privacy of his room.

INT.: *Even if it disturbed the privacy of others?*

DONNA: Well, it was just one of those things. Something had to give. I think our friends were more embarrassed than Teddy. Of course they got up as gracefully and quickly as they could and moved off to another bedroom.

INT.: *I see you have lots of bedrooms in this house. Was this built before or after you entered the swinging scene.*

JIM: (Laughing) Coincidentally with the start of those activities. You're forgetting that I couldn't marry Donna until I agreed to become a swinger. We did add a couple of bedrooms to the house later on. That whole back wing, in fact, and there's also a den.

INT.: *For swinging?*

DONNA: No, it's more of a workshop. Jim's a great tinkerer and Teddy often works with him fixing things out there.

INT.: *If you wouldn't mind, we would appreciate the opportunity of interviewing Teddy. We've interviewed several children of swingers.*

DONNA: I don't know . . . Teddy's a fairly shy boy. I don't think I'd want that. Jim?

JIM: Well, I don't care. I'm sure he has some of his own opinions. If it's all right with you, Donna, I suggest we let him decide.

DONNA: I think it's a good idea talking to children. I just don't want to single out our son as the only child. He's already an only child . . .

(Shortly afterward we received Jim and Donna's approval to interview Teddy.)

20

TEDDY:

"My Parents Are Honest With Me"

A week after we interviewed Donna and Jim, we drove up to their house again to meet their fifteen-year-old son, Teddy. It was early on a Monday evening and, to our surprise, Donna and Jim had delayed supper and welcomed us to join them.

We began talking to Teddy intermittently throughout the meal and started to get acquainted.

Teddy, as all fifteen-year-olds, has specialized interests—mostly football and girls—but, as Teddy's father put it, "One of these days, he's either going to have to hang up his cleats or buy a pair for his girlfriend."

Teddy looks as if he has the making of a running back. He has a tall, well-built frame, a milky complexion, freckles, and a sandy mop of hair that never manages to stay in place for more than two minutes.

There is much shyness in Teddy. He is an outdoor type. He feels more comfortable moving around, using his hands, and throughout our interview we noticed a restlessness. He could never sit still in one place very long.

One other point. Teddy requested, rather tentatively, that we tape the interview with him in privacy. His parents seemed to understand. As if it had been thought of before dinner, if not said, Jim took Donna bowling as soon as the kitchen was cleaned up.

INTERVIEWER: *Teddy, how old are you?*

TEDDY: Fifteen.

INT.: *Where were you born?*

TEDDY: Ohio.

INT.: *What's your grade level in high school?*

TEDDY: I'm a junior—second semester junior.

INT.: *You say that as if you want to be a senior in a hurry.*

TEDDY: I wouldn't mind it if I didn't lose that extra season of football.

INT.: *I gather you're pretty good at that.*

TEDDY: I guess so.

INT.: *Are you thinking of making a career out of it?*

TEDDY: No, I'm not *that* good . . . Medicine interests me more. I wouldn't mind becoming some kind of doctor.

INT.: *Teddy, you know, of course, we're taking this interview with the approval and consent of your parents.* (Teddy nods) *Did they discuss this with you?*

TEDDY: That's right, and I kind of liked the idea.

INT.: *Good. Now: your mother said she had brought you up with a nudist background.*

TEDDY: Yeah.

INT.: *Could you go into that?*

TEDDY: It started when I was around two . . . I used to go to these camps now and then until I was eleven.

INT.: *How did you feel about it?*

TEDDY: Good, I guess . . . I mean, I don't remember feeling bad.

INT.: *Your parents told me that they were swinging for quite a while before you were aware of it.*

TEDDY: Yeah, I guess so.

INT.: *How did they handle it when they had parties here?*

TEDDY: Well, they just said there was gonna be a grown-up party and I'd be bored anyway, so would I mind sleeping over at a friend's house? Things like that.

INT.: *Did you have any idea of the type of parties they were?*

184

TEDDY: No, not really.

INT.: *When your parents told you, how did you feel about it?*

TEDDY: I don't think I was permanently shocked or that it had any great effect on me. My parents wanted to make sure I was mature enough to handle it . . . It was their business, really.

INT.: *How did they happen to tell you?*

TEDDY: (shrugging) One night my mom and dad were sitting in the den and Mom began talking to me. She just told me, you know. She said something about because I was old enough to know now . . . I don't think I had any initial thoughts about it after my mom told me. Until I was alone in my room. And then the first thought about it was "Why?" I still don't know why my parents swing, really. I guess the people my parents swing with are all friends. It's all open.

INT.: *After you knew, did things change about your staying or leaving when there was a party?*

TEDDY: No. Only now I knew the reason I wasn't staying around: the adults felt funny about my being there, that was it.

INT.: *Did that bother you?*

TEDDY: I guess so, sometimes . . . My mom said that the people who are real close friends, it doesn't matter to them. But people my parents didn't know and who may be coming over for the first time, they were the ones who were uptight about it, I guess.

INT.: *Have things changed in the last couple of years?*

TEDDY: Yeah, I've gotten to know more of the people, the ones who come over a lot. I say "Hi" to them and talk to them for a while when I come home and they're still there.

INT.: *Have there been any problems when you come home early and a party is still going on?*

TEDDY: No, not really.

(He starts to laugh)

INT.: *Are you remembering something funny?*

(Teddy laughs some more)

TEDDY: I'd rather not go into that . . .

INT.: *Okay . . . do your friends know that your parents are swingers?*

TEDDY: (Firmly) I wouldn't tell them. I won't at all, that's that.

INT.: *Why?*

TEDDY: (Shrugging) Probably because I'm embarrassed about it.

185

Not embarrassed personally, but I feel uncomfortable explaining what swinging is all about to some of my friends.

INT.: *And the neighbors?*

TEDDY: One or two of the neighbors know something.

INT.: *Your father mentioned one party when one of your neighbors tried to climb a fence.*

TEDDY: Yeah, you want me to go into it? . . . I wasn't there, but my dad told me what happened . . . This guy next door—he's a real funny guy anyway—had a friend come over and the two of them climbed the fence. They ended up hiding under our car with binoculars, looking, and all they could see, my dad told me, were bare feet.

INT.: *Then someone noticed them?*

TEDDY: Yeah, and they ran off.

INT.: *Did he decide to fix the fence?*

TEDDY: Yeah, and I helped him. We built it up three or four more feet.

INT.: *Did that stop them from prying?*

TEDDY: I don't know; maybe they still do. It's really silly, isn't it? I mean, the human body—big deal!

INT.: *It's a big deal to lots of children and I guess even adults who weren't exposed to the kind of upbringing you've had.* (Teddy laughs) *Did I say something funny?*

TEDDY: (Nodding) . . . *Exposed.* I don't know what all the fuss is about. Even when I'm home studying while a party's going on, I try to keep to myself. I don't care.

INT.: *When won't you care enough to be able to tell your non-swinging friends about what your parents are doing?*

TEDDY: When I get older. Or maybe not until swinging is more out in the open. Until then, if I tell a friend of mine who happens to be religious and his parents are religious, they'd probably look at me and go into shock.

INT.: *I guess some of them would. Do you think knowing about the swinging scene in your home has brought you closer to your parents?*

TEDDY: (Paces, pauses, turns around . . .) It's still the same way. My mom and I were always close. I could say things, almost whatever I wanted, to my dad . . . (He crosses over to me.) Knowing that my folks are swinging, this is a Big Truth. Probably the most important thing they ever revealed to me.

186

I think that means there's nothing they'd ever keep from me. It's a trust in me. They ran a great risk telling me. They didn't know how I'd react . . . I could've blabbed it around and someone could've blabbed it to someone else, and it could've gotten back to people who work with my mom or dad.

INT.: *Did your parents ask you to keep things quiet?*

TEDDY: (Shaking his head) No, nothing like that. They left it up to me. They showed me they had all this trust in me . . . I feel I'm lucky to have parents like that.

INT.: *Suppose they hadn't told you and you had found out on your own?*

TEDDY: (He paces restlessly for a moment before answering . . .) Then I guess I'd have thought my parents were doing something behind my back, that they were ashamed of it and maybe it was wrong . . . But now I know how they feel. They believe in what they're doing and, as I said, it's their business, really. (Teddy stops pacing, drops down onto the sofa, musses his hair so that we can hardly see his eyes.) . . . Yeah, there are changes, I guess. I trust them more now and, like, I can even say what I feel about something that bugs me. It's easier.

INT.: *What bugs you?*

TEDDY: (He's back up and pacing) Well, when I come home sometimes and the party's a little late breaking up and I have school work to get done by Monday morning, I don't like to walk into my room and find "company," you know what I mean.

INT.: (Smiling) *Your parents did tell me something about that.*

TEDDY: This kind of thing doesn't happen often, but we've had our disagreements over it. I think I'm completely right. I think swinging is fine when it doesn't interfere with someone else . . . That's the only thing that really bugs me. I don't want to worry about using my own room when I have to.

INT.: *Have you worked this out with your parents?*

TEDDY: Well, yeah, they understand how I feel now much more than before and, like I said, it doesn't happen often.

INT.: *Do you know any other children with swinging parents?*

TEDDY: No. I don't want to, really. I've got my own friends.

INT.: *What do you mostly do with them?*

TEDDY: Well, like football and going hunting sometimes and going partying . . . (he laughs)

INT.: *What do you mean by that?*

187

TEDDY: I was trying to make a joke, like when I go out with a girl.

INT.: *Have your feelings about the boy/girl relationship changed?*

TEDDY: You mean, because my parents are swingers?

INT.: *Yes.*

TEDDY: No, but I think I'm more at ease with girls. And before I knew about my parents swinging, I liked to go steady. I did with one girl for quite a while. Now I want to hang loose, sort of.

INT.: *What about the old double standard?*

TEDDY: What's that?

INT.: *Men used to feel it was all right for them to go to bed with a girl, but that the girl they married had to be a virgin.*

TEDDY: (Grinning) You're kidding!

INT.: *That's the way it used to be when I was growing up about a thousand years ago.*

(Teddy is laughing and on the prowl again)

TEDDY: When you put it like that, I don't know what came first—the grown-ups swinging or the kids doing it.

INT.: *You think maybe the fact that the kids broke sexual taboos could have influenced their folks?*

TEDDY: (Shaking his head) I don't know. Honestly, I couldn't say. What came first—the chicken or the egg? Does it matter? What's happening is good, better, for both sexes. You have to grow with the times. You can't stay back in the Middle Ages where people couldn't have sex before they were married.

INT.: *You think swinging is changing all that?*

TEDDY: I think it's happening even without it. You know, most people aren't swingers, but I think in time swinging will be just a natural thing.

INT.: *What do you mean by "natural"?*

TEDDY: (still pacing) . . . like taking a walk. I mean, no one would say anything about it at all.

INT.: *Or bother to look over fences or hide under cars.*

TEDDY: That's it.

21

MELISSA:

"My Mom and I Have Had Some Funny Experiences Swinging Together"

Melissa lives with her parents in a comfortable home high on a hill in California. It seemed much higher because we had to walk up all those steps to get there. It is two-story, brick-frame place, more New England than California in flavor.

"Hi, I'm Melissa. You must be Herb and Paul. Come in. The place's a mess. Would you like anything to drink? Don't mind my dog, he looks big but he doesn't bite . . . Why don't you go into the living room and I'll bring out something for you."

We walked behind the dog who made sure we knew where to sit and where he was supposed to sit. We caught a glimpse of Melissa smiling at us in the not-too-distant kitchen: "Orange juice or apple juice is all we have—take your pick."

Melissa is twenty-one years old. When she talks she shakes her long, black hair away from her eyes and softly struggles with the remaining strands which never quite get back into place.

Her eyes are direct, never wandering around the room when she is talking.

She wears little makeup, probably none at all, because everything about her is natural, including a tan from a stretch of summery weather in San Francisco. Her clothes are simple but not sloppy: a freshly cleaned pair of jeans that flare at the bottom; a bright red blouse with long sleeves, open at the neck; and tennis shoes, a little spoiled but still part of her own style.

She isn't tall, probably around five-three, and although she told us that she has to watch her weight, it's difficult to tell why. She has a pixyish look when she anticipates something that is going to be said or reflects on how she is going to answer a question. First, her olive eyes dance, then she breaks into a warm smile or a contagious laugh or a little girl's innocent giggle.

An early shyness about our taping quickly left Melissa as the interview progressed.

INTERVIEWER: *Melissa, how old are you?*

MELISSA: I was twenty-one a few months ago . . .

INT.: *Where were you born?*

MELISSA: In the Midwest. I stayed there until I was through grammar school, so I must have been, let's see, twelve years old when my family left for California.

INT.: *How many were in your family?*

MELISSA: Then it was my dad, mom and my older brother, who's now a lawyer.

INT.: *Did you want to leave the Midwest?*

MELISSA: Well, things weren't going to well for us there. My first father's company okay'ed a transfer to one of their California offices. So we picked up our things, bundled into our Volkswagen, which only had about an inch of space left for our cocker spaniel, and off we went.

INT.: *You said your "first father?"*

MELISSA: Uh huh, because two years after we started living in California my parents separated and finally got a divorce.

INT.: *How were things in your family before the divorce?*

MELISSA: Our household wasn't happy. It was very difficult for everyone. Anytime we wanted to go anywhere, for a ride or out to a movie or maybe to get away for a weekend, there was always a fight before we left . . . There was even yelling at breakfast over pancakes before we left for church. I don't mean to say it was always my father's fault—except that it probably really was, as I look back . . . My mom worked hard. She even went back to college when we got there, got her bachelor's degree in English and enough credits to teach so that the financial burden wouldn't be so great on my dad. I think he resented her doing that.

INT.: *Were you a religious family?*

MELISSA: We were active in church, mainly because of my mother. I remember after my confirmation the pastor said to all of us, "Now, you're going to be good Christians, and you're not going to do anything bad." When he said that I felt that I wasn't free. And at that time I had to be. My life was very experimental. I had a lot of questions. As a matter of fact, at age thirteen I still wasn't too sure what the process was that made a woman pregnant.

INT.: *Did you try to talk to your parents about these things?*

MELISSA: It was awkard with my mother because she didn't know very much, and I didn't get along too well with my father . . . I have to be honest with you; I have a tendency not to like him, mainly because of his attitude toward sex. His feelings haven't changed to this day. Sex was and still is to him something to get from anyone, anywhere, anytime without respect for their feelings, and that I don't like.

INT.: *Wasn't there an opportunity for you to learn about sex in school?*

MELISSA: At that time teaching sex was still very controversial. My teacher wouldn't even mention about the man's penis being introduced into the woman's vagina. And here I was a budding kid starting to notice things about myself: like pubic hair and a secretion coming from inside me. I wanted to know what this was all about . . . I remember that some of my girlfriends and I would get together and talk and wonder if there wasn't something wrong with us . . . Then when I used to go to bed at night there wasn't anyone to talk to about these things. I mean, even if my brother had been at home—he was away at law school—I wouldn't have dared ask him about sex things. So I took to just studying my body, examining it in front of the bathroom mirror, and then I got to touching it. During one of those times I discovered my clitoris. I felt something. I didn't know what it was at first. I pushed it around this way and that way, and if I pushed too hard it would make me jump so I kept pushing it hard and let myself jump. I noticed how my body reacted to that movement. It was like getting hit with a doctor's hammer when he checks your reflexes. This was all part of my experimenting. It was really a super-good feeling . . . finding out so many things about myself, about growing into a woman.

INT.: *Were you worried about any of the changes that were happening to you?*

MELISSA: On and off I guess. I was anxious because of not knowing it all. Like, I could just dream about being with someone and that was the extent of my sexuality. One time my mother had taken be to a movie, and there was a guy sitting next to me. He was really good-looking and quite a bit older than I was. Probably in college. He was strong-looking, more an adult in my eyes. I could smell his cologne, I don't know what it was . . . I never could get his fragrance out of my mind after that. I could smell it at night for a long time. And then I listened to songs on the radio and I'd dream that those songs were about me.

INT.: *Were these romantic feelings about sex?*

MELISSA: Ohhh . . . I was the biggest romantic in the whole world, I thought. I was too much. I did a damn good job with my fantasies, too, my dreams. Books got me into these feelings, too . . . I remember I was a sophomore in high school at the time. I had just finished reading *The Ninth Wave* by Eugene Burdick, and I never forgot the philosophy in that book.

INT.: *What was it?*

MELISSA: Just being mobile. I related that to me, just having mobility about myself, in my social life, in my personal life, at school . . . and the way the character Mike Freesmith used people to get what he wanted—it was so fantastic. The machinery and his thinking . . . Anyway, I'm a very impressionable person, extremely gullible, okay? Now I met a guy in high school who fit the description of Mike Freesmith: very intelligent and he had a way with people. He was a junior,

192

so he must have been sixteen-years-old, I guess. Sherman was his name. We talked to each other. I mean like a couple of words in the corridor between classes. A "hi" and nothing much more when he's in a line ahead of me in the cafeteria. Suddenly, that day, he is actually turning around and talking to me and I am answering back, and you won't believe what he said, "Do you believe in premarital" how does the phrase go, "premarital intercourse?" Big words. First of all I had to think about the word "pre" because it was in front of "marital" and "intercourse" was vaguely familiar. Every time I heard a new word I'd run up to the school library on my free period and head for the Webster Dictionary sitting open-face on its stand . . . So I said to him, "Can I answer you later on that? I'm not quite sure." Anyway, he said he would meet me out in front of the auditorium after seventh period. Well, I got there a few minutes late. I looked at him and said, "Well, what are you talking about, c'mon, really!" So he said, "Sex." He said he wanted to talk to me about sex. He said "talk." So we took a walk to a nearby park and we talked. About the woman and the man and exactly, explicitly what happens. He made it all sound very interesting. After about two hours of talking he said, "I would like to screw you" or maybe, "I would like to have intercourse with you"—yes, he used the word "intercourse" and not "screw." At the time the only word I could think of was "WOW, now what!" Then he said, "We've been talking about this and we haven't even kissed each other yet." So I kissed him. It was just a quick kiss. And then he said, "I'm not going to ask you now to do this—I'll give you a week. You're coming to the game Friday night? The football game?" I said yes. "I'll meet you at so-and-so and such a place and you tell me then if you want to have intercourse with me." Okay, so I had a week to think about it. (laughing) And this was really one of the biggest weeks in my life because I was debating—should I or shouldn't I? It was not a Clairol solution.

INT.: *It must have been quite a week.*

MELISSA: The worst part was that he had given me too much time to think. Like, the game finally came that Friday night —our school won, by the way—and afterward as I was walking to meet him I still hadn't decided until I just said it. But as I look back on it now I think all along I was going to say no, and that's what I told him.

INT.: *How did he react?*

MELISSA: He understood just fine, he said. We could go on being good friends, that was all. Any questions I ever had about sex I could ask him without being embarrassed . . . Well, we got to know each other that year, going out on dates. At first nothing happened, but somehow I knew what was coming, and I wanted it to happen because by now it was kind of romantic between us. And he had been so patient . . . One night he asked if I would go to an apartment that one of his friends, another senior, had. Would I like to go there and have dinner—just the two of us. Okay? I knew it was coming and I was ready. Really over-ripe by now. But I still wasn't sure, in my sixteen-year-old-mind, how it would work out. Well, it was a super-great evening. We listened to some soft music on the stereo, we talked, we even took a shower together. One thing led to another, and then we were in bed laughing hysterically because he was too big to get inside me. I've heard since then that it's physiologically impossible for a penis to be too big for any vagina. I don't know, but the way it turned out was good because it left everything romantic. We petted a lot, and I tried to satisfy him. Nothing oral —just with my hands. I thought if I did more to him that would mean he would do less to me. Super logic! He even got me home on time, so Mom wasn't angry.

INT.: *What about your dad?*

MELISSA: My parents were divorced by then. Anyway, I had some bursting-at-the-seams dreams that night. And I think it was the next weekend after a movie, in Sherman's car, that it happened! I thought that either his penis got smaller or my vagina grew. But that night the parts fit together, and very nicely, too. And I just started having sex, even with other guys, after I would date them and get to like them. I was, in a sense, experimenting with guys more than with sex. I wouldn't, for instance, have oral sex with a guy. At the time I said, "Are you crazy? You pee out of that thing, why should I put my mouth on it?" That's how I felt initially . . .

194

Another thing was that never once did I experience an orgasm
. . . Most of the guys were still in high school, a few were in
college, so what did they really know about sex? Even when
I was a freshman in college I wasn't getting any great satisfaction . . . That all changed when I met Chris, who was
and still is a graduate student in English.

INT.: *What was he like?*

MELISSA: Mature, for one thing. He cared. He took his time with
me . . . I think that was the big difference. I was, in a sense,
a slow learner, certainly about sex. I never felt it was sinful
or that I should be punished for doing it before marriage,
but Chris made me understand there was so much more to
sex than just doing it. We saw a lot of each other during my
first semester in college. He was at my mother's wedding when
she married my stepfather, Dave. My mother thought the
world of Chris, and still does. Of all the guys I have dated,
Chris is the first who made that kind of impression on her
. . . So the four of us did a lot of things together, going
to movies, eating out, and things were also different with my
mother: having a man around the house again who really
liker her and me, too. There was a lot more laughter instead
of the yelling and the loneliness there used to be . . . A few
weeks before Thanksgiving, my mother and I planned a
special dinner for Chris and my stepfather, and afterwards
we all sat on the rug near the fireplace and roasted marsh-
mallows as we talked. I don't know how we got on the subject of love and sex. All of us got there about the same time.
Chris was the one who was saying funny, startling things that
he had never told me in private before—like a woman should
have as much choice in expressing her sexuality as a man
does. And then he mentioned swinging for the first time . . .

INT.: *How did your parents react?*

MELISSA: That was the most surprising part. My mom didn't say
anything. Not one word, just listened. But my stepfather
opened up and said he had heard about swinging. He felt
that if a couple had thought seriously enough about it and
wanted to try it—why not? I was all flushed and bothered
listening to this. Here's my stepfather, whom I really like,
taking the "young rebel" position, and I'm beginning to feel

like 199-years-old and out of touch with the times . . . Chris sensed this, I guess, because he made an early evening of it, and when I came back from saying goodnight to him my parents had already gone upstairs . . . But I couldn't possibly sleep with all those things swirling through my mind . . . About a half-hour later, like out of nowhere, my mother came back downstairs. She was wearing a bunny-type pajama outfit that Dave had bought for their honeymoon, and said she wanted to talk . . . We settled down by the fire. I poked around and got it going again . . . She didn't want to talk about Chris and me, just about herself, about her life with my natural father; how frustrating and full of aggravation it had become when he started cheating on her, and after the divorce how very lonely she was until she met Dave.

INT.: *Had your mother ever opened up like this before?*

MELISSA: No, never. That's the point. Sometimes you can live with a person all your life and never really know how they're put together or how they become unglued unless that person ignores every ego-centered bone and nerve and risks the consequences of a terrible exposure.

INT.: *How did you feel when your mother began to do that?*

MELISSA: Like she was, well trusting me . . . I mean, to have your mother, whom you always look up to, talk that way. It's like she was bringing me deep, deep into her world . . . You see, she had been so wary of men that when she met Dave and started to have meaningful sex again with a man—I felt funny hearing about this from her lips, but good also—she was kind of worried. I think she said "terrified"—that was her word—that she was going to lose him. And what she was saying about Dave was, in so many ways how I felt about Chris. I mean, we were younger and not even talking about marriage yet, but I did love him, and I was afraid that it wasn't going to last . . . Well, when my mom heard that she hugged me, and tried to reassure me . . . She didn't want me going through what she had faced in her first marriage . . . She felt that I wouldn't have to, not if I really cared for Chris and could understand how important sex was for most men . . . And then she said something I'll never forget in my

196

whole life because it tied everything together. She said that for the past ten months she and Dave had been swinging.

INT.: *Weren't you prepared for this?*

MELISSA: No. Oh, no! I just never could think of my mother doing anything like that . . . I cried.

INT.: *You thought that she was doing something wrong?*

MELISSA: You don't understand! I cried because I believed her. I believed that she loved Dave and this thing she was doing with him was only helping the love they had for each other. But I was startled, surprised. Damnit, tell me how many mothers would ever be willing to talk that way to a daughter? How many, really? I'm yelling now, aren't I?

INT.: *That's okay.*

MELISSA: I'm sorry. But this was a very special night in my life and in my mother's, too.

INT.: *Did you feel that she was, in a way, encouraging you to swing with Chris?*

MELISSA: No words were said about it, but that was the feeling I got . . . And then we just sat there in silence, not even aware of the fireplace anymore. I think the only thing I was aware of was the buzzing in my ears . . . When a room becomes so silent it almost becomes deafening in a way. And I could see tears in my mother's eyes, and maybe she was worried about what she had said. I don't know. That perhaps she had gone too far . . . Well, I just put my arms around her and put my head on her chest like I had done so many times in all those years I was growing up. It was a real weirdo feeling. Like I was resting my head on my mother's softness, and her sweet-smelling odors. Feeling it at age five, age seven, and now . . . I don't think I ever felt closer to my mother before or since . . .

(At this point, Melissa felt "wiped out" so we took a break. She went into the kitchen, poured herself a soft drink, then went into the backyard to turn the sprinklers on. Almost a half-hour later we continued the interview.)

INT.: *Do you remember where we left off?*

MELISSA: That night . . . Yes, the next morning is a good place to start. My mother must have told my stepfather because

197

both of them were very solicitous of me when I told them that I was going to try swinging with Chris . . . But I still had some hangups. It wasn't a fear of pregnancy because I had an I.U.D. put in a few years before. Mainly, I was worried about my body. I have a tendency to put on extra pounds, and I have freckles and occasionally my face breaks out. I was worried about that, too. I mean, my skin wasn't bad, but it wasn't like in all those beauty ads. How would I measure up to the other girls who were swinging? Would Chris start making comparisons? I think what saved the day, again, was the fact that my mother, at forty-five, had gone through those same anxieties. Now it was my turn . . .

INT.: *When did your first swinging occur?*

MELISSA: About two or three weeks later. It was at a house up in the hills . . . I remember my mom kissing me and insisting that no matter what time I came in, no matter how late it was, I had to wake her up. And my stepfather made me feel I was a raving beauty. The main thing he said was that I shouldn't do anything I didn't want to.

INT.: *How did Chris take all this?*

MELISSA: By now he knew about the stamp of approval from the "old folks" at home, and I think he felt better . . . But when we were driving up I was plain scared. He knew it, and neither of us did much talking . . . When we got there people were arriving, talking to each other. It was just like a cocktail party until that one bitch showed up.

INT.: *Did she have a name?*

MELISSA: To this day I don't know her name . . . But Chris knew her, and she was attractive. After some amenities he walked off with her and my heart started going flip-flop. I mean, I was alone, and I didn't like the idea. All I could think of was: what was *that* girl doing with *my* guy? I must have been out of my mind to come here in the first place . . . Well, I needed a drink. Something strong. There was an open bar outside on the terrace near a large Olympic pool, and that's where I met this other fellow. We started talking, God knows about what, because my mind was still racing, and I was drinking and looking around for Chris . . . I finally caught a glimpse of him through one of the windows facing the terrace, a flash of him undressed. Just about then this guy, who shall remain nameless because I just plain don't remember his name, invited me into the pool . . . That did it. I put down the glass and never undressed so fast in my life. And suddenly we were skinny-dipping . . . There I was nude and so was the guy, and he was kissing me and I was saying to myself, "Well, what the hell, enjoy it, go ahead since you're already here." And after a while I was enjoying it . . .

INT.: *Did that surprise you?*

MELISSA: I guess so, at the time. I can't really sort out the sequence of events, but I know after the pool I ended up in one of the bedrooms with the same guy . . . And afterwards, I do remember there was a difficulty about saying "no." I had sex with more men than I wanted to. Little by little I was getting drunk on sex. I think I must have swung with three or four men.

INT.: *Did you have any problems being satisfied?*

MELISSA: I thought I would. Oh, boy, did I worry about that! But it was the other way around. I climaxed for the first time in my life. I had never come like that before, and I feel it had a lot to do with the general mood of the evening. Some people call it "vibrations." Whatever it was, I mean, you could smell sexuality everywhere you went. The odors, the colognes, and the sounds of sex, too, it was incredible . . . My first climax was exhausting because it was violent. Very violent. I felt myself rising up and down, screaming out, and that wasn't like me. I was afraid of what that meant, and yet exhilarated by the release of it . . . I had this crazy feeling that I was pushing myself off the ceiling. I must have come, I told myself, because there were three guys bending over me hugging me, and I was perspiring. I even cried during that climax. I mean, it was something I had never done before, and it was so stored up in me.

INT.: *And then?*

MELISSA: I slept for a while. When I got up I had to find Chris and tell him what had happened, and I did. He was so happy for me . . . We didn't stay too late. When Chris took me home, on the drive back I didn't feel like talking much, but I wanted to be close to him. I didn't want anything physical

199

with him. I don't know why. Maybe I was afraid it would be less than perfect and that would ruin the feeling of all the good things that happened.

INT.: *Did Chris understand?*

MELISSA: Yes . . . I think he wanted to make love, but he didn't make an issue of it . . . The moment I got home I ran upstairs and woke up my mother and stepfather, who sort of grumbled with a broken-sleep smile . . . Mom and I went downstairs and we talked it all out, how her one and only daughter had become a second-generation swinger.

INT.: *And you've been swinging since then.*

MELISSA: Oh, yes . . . On weekends mostly. It's changed my life.

INT.: *There's another area I'd like to discuss with you, if you're willing.*

MELISSA: I'm ahead of you. I'll bet it's, "Have I ever gone to swinging parties with my parents?"

INT.: *Now that you've asked the question . . .*

MELISSA: Yes, of course . . . We talked about it after my first experience, but made no plans. About a month later Chris and I were at a party—we had been there for about an hour, everyone was undressed and all that—and I was walking down a hallway toward the kitchen when I saw my mother coming out of one of the bedrooms . . . We nearly screamed in whispers when we saw each other—you know, flash-look, "What are you doing here?" Flash-look, we knew what we were doing here, but by accident we were doing it at the same place . . . Anyway, we found a washroom, locked ourselves in and tried to figure out what to do. My mom didn't know how the other people might react to a mother and daughter at the same party, so she suggested that I call her by her first name, Diana.

INT.: *I think that's the first time you ever mentioned your mother's name.*

MELISSA: That's what I mean: I always call her Mom or Mother. You'd better believe it was difficult walking around that night forcing myself to say "Diana" . . . And then there was the problem of telling Dave, my stepfather, and Chris, and getting them to go along with the name routine.

INT.: *Was it complicated?*

200

MELISSA: Yes, for a while until we got used to it.

INT.: *Was this the first time that you and Chris and your mother and stepfather had been in the nude together?*

MELISSA: Yes.

INT.: *Was there any awkwardness about that?*

MELISSA: A little curiosity, I guess . . . But there were so many people that even with the special feeling I had about my mother and stepfather I don't think it really mattered. Anyway, there wasn't much swinging at that party. My mother did, and my father did and also Chris, but I didn't . . .

INT.: *Any reason why?*

MELISSA: I think I was probably a little uptight about it all . . . I wanted to see how I felt being at a swinging party with my parents for the first time.

INT.: *Well?*

MELISSA: Mixed. I still can't, to this day, sort out the different feelings I had.

INT.: *Did you all get together afterward and talk it out?*

MELISSA: No, that's a funny thing. We never did. Sometimes it's better if you don't talk out something that's bothering you, at least not right away. It's better to let it settle in your mind before you go running off at the mouth . . . In this instance it resolved itself without formal discussion. The next weekend all four of us were invited to the same party, and we drove up together . . . It was a big affair, and after we got there we sort of lost each other . . . Later I remember being in a bed—no, it was a king-size mattress on the floor—and there was my mother two or three couples away. I wasn't there to watch her and I am sure she wasn't there to watch me, either, but that's the way things happen when you swing, especially in a group thing. There are a lot of bodies all together, and if I happen to see my mom and dad as parts of it, well, it happens. I don't dwell on it. I'm not embarrassed about it any more . . . In fact, my mom and I have had some funny experiences swinging together. In the beginning, as I said before, she wanted me to call her Diana. Well, at one party we were both undressing and I was bending over to pick up something when she said, "Melissa, you're breaking out all over . . ." She was looking at my rear end. And I said, "Oh,

201

shit, mother . . ." It slipped out. I wanted to tell her that this wasn't the time to go into that. Anyway, it was only a heat rash. Well, after that it was just mom or mother or Melissa or honey, just like it used to be around the house . . . Our swinging friends got to know us as mother and daughter. And it worked for us, too . . . One time my mom and I were in a pool with a few other couples, and a guy kept bugging her. He was around forty, but no matter how many times mom said "no"—and she was very polite about it—he kept swimming back to her and trying to get her to change her mind. Finally, I swam over, and he tried to make it with me. There was some light chatter about mother and daughter—starting with one and having dessert with the other. Neither of us liked that coarse approach, not one bit. I finally told him I had awful exams coming up on Monday. I said I was afraid I was going to fail, and how good was he in chemistry and advanced trig? I sure needed help, and I started bugging him. He smiled weakly and paddled off into the sunset . . . There have been other times when we have helped each other out of situations when one of us didn't dig a guy who was digging us.

INT.: *What about competition and jealousy?*

MELISSA: You mean between my mother and me over a guy?

INT.: *Yes.*

MELISSA: (smiling) Oh, no . . . Never. Neither one of us babysits for the other. Sure, we swing at some parties together, but our tastes in men are different. She and Dave tend to go with an older crowd. I don't like to swing with middle-aged men. It's kind of creepy. Maybe Mom and I are having a good time at a party and, riding back in the car or on the phone the next day, we'll talk about some of the men we've been to bed with, just like you're remembering a good time you had at a dance or a party or a weekend at the beach . . . Maybe we did go to bed with the same man at this party or that, but it wasn't a planned thing. Sometimes we don't even know this happened until a couple of weeks later when we're talking about a guy who was something special. Then it may come out: "Well, wow, I know who you're talking about! Oh, yes, that guy *was* super . . ."

INT.: *This leads to another obvious question if you won't find it offensive.*

MELISSA: There you go! Stop apologizing in advance.

INT.: *Was there ever a problem about Chris wanting to swing with your mother, and you maybe having the same feeling for your stepfather?*

MELISSA: For me, anything like that would be sick . . . I don't think it's necessary to resort to the family for sexual satisfaction. Our relationships create the "family"—that's why it's called a family. And that should be reserved for family things. Otherwise we would be in a constant "swinging state!" I don't think anyone could handle that . . . Swinging should not destroy families, and families should not destroy it!

INT.: *How does swinging affect your other close relationships outside of the family?*

MELISSA: Are you talking about friends?

INT.: *Yes.*

MELISSA: We separate the haves from the have-nots . . . We *have* swung with our swinging friends, and we have *not* with our nonswinging friends. I feel very strongly about this, too . . . There's a big difference between meeting people on swinging terms and meeting them "outside." To bring four very close people who have developed a relationship completely outside the swinging scene into it could bring about serious conflicts . . . For example, how will they know that we weren't trying to seduce them and use our friendship to move it into the sexual area? If we have something good going with nonswinging friends, and we have, I don't want to risk hurting those relationships.

INT: *Well, suppose a nonswinging couple willingly consented to do this?*

MELISSA: If we met them, to begin with, in the swinging scene, that would be a different story. I don't want to have the responsibility—I guess that's it—of turning nonswinging friends into swingers . . . I can explain it this way: I had an experience once, when I invited a girlfriend of mine, as a single, to a party. She had told me that she was frustrated sexually. Sex for her in the straight world hadn't been much fun. Okay. So, wow, I'm a real friend, very understanding, and right off when we get to the party she wants to go to bed with Chris. I told her I didn't want her to do that. She sort of nodded like, "Yeah, I'll cool it"—and then she did go to bed with Chris. Well, I didn't like any part of it . . .

INT.: *With all the choice of sexual partners, why did it bother you to share your guy with her?*

MELISSA: It was just something I felt about her and my guy. And that's not asking too much, to ask one person not to have intercourse with one particular other person. Maybe I was getting negative vibrations. Or call it a personal hangup . . . There has to be a special kind of consideration between a couple in the swinging scene . . . You need approval in swinging. That's very important.

INT.: *Are you insisting on mutual consent as a prerequisite to select a new bed partner?*

MELISSA: In that instance, certainly. But not always. I mean, there are things that happen when a party is really going well. I could be in another part of the house, maybe not even knowing where Chris is . . . Well, if there's a fellow I'm with and he is turning me on, sure, I'll have sex with him without clearing it with Chris first . . . And I would understand Chris doing the same thing. If later Chris or I find out we had some negative vibes about those people, well, it's too late, isn't it? . . . I'm just talking about situations where Chris and I know before it happens that we don't like someone. Those feelings should be respected.

INT.: *Let's stay with this issue of selectivity: Are you saying that for you it can't be sex without love?*

MELISSA: Wow, you keep complicating things, don't you? It's so hard to weigh your feelings on a scale and say "I love him, I love him not, I like him a little, I like him not so much . . ." Personally, I don't swing with a man just because he's a man. But I do have a desire, a need to be satisfied sexually, and I would much rather spend time doing it with one man instead of several. At that moment that man is the most important person to me.

INT.: *You're still a romantic at the core.*

MELISSA: Hallelujah! I hope that part of me never changes.

INT.: *What has changed for you since you started swinging?*

MELISSA: There's been one change right off in sex. I thought it was something that should only be shared in the privacy and secrecy of a bedroom with the door locked. I don't feel this way at all. I'm not afraid of showing my body anywhere. If something happens between me and a guy, I don't have to run off and hide in a special room or anything. We can do it wherever we are. I don't even care if people are watching.

INT.: *Are you getting back to your personal need for approval, maybe group approval?*

MELISSA: No. I'm telling you I don't particularly notice who's there and who isn't. All I want when it comes to approval is Chris' okay, because there is much more to our relationship than just swinging.

INT.: *Is there a danger that sexual variety could hurt your relationship with Chris?*

MELISSA: No. It's only strengthening it. Now we know each other so much better. A true swinger is one who adjusts to people, not just sexually, but to people. I've noticed my own feelings to other people in school, my classes. I'm working on seminars in personal social adjustment, and I've talked to other students in class about swinging. They were surprisingly open about the idea. The main thing I stressed was the relationship I have with my swinging friends, how most of them are friendly in the best sense of the word—not hostile.

INT.: *You don't conceal the fact that you are swinging from nonswingers?*

MELISSA: Why should I? It isn't against the law, is it?

INT.: *It isn't if you're over eighteen and doing it with another consenting adult. At least in this state it's okay under those circumstances.*

MELISSA: (laughing) Anyway, I'm not ashamed of what I'm doing.

INT.: *How does it affect the mainstream of your nonswinging life?*

MELISSA: Right now it's graduate school . . . I was always a B student—A's only in courses I really dug, like trig and some psych classes, if the teacher was really super. That hasn't changed much except that swinging *has* forced me to become more organized about studying and prepping for exams. Chris and I both have to get that stuff out of the way if we want to go on a swinging weekend.

INT.: *Melissa, as a second-generation swinger who seems to be benefiting from the discovery that her parents are also swinging, would you advise other couples to tell their children about what they're doing?*

MELISSA: (For a moment she is silent) You do have to teach a child that he or she lives in a world with many, many double standards. There is a world at home and there is a world outside. It's too bad we have this condition, but it's worse yet to deny it doesn't exist . . . It comes down to being considerate of the child's capacity to understand. When is he ready to accept these different standards? I was told about the fact that my parents were swinging when I was old enough to handle it . . . But if you tell a child that his parents are practicing what he's been taught is "infidelity," and he has to go back out there with other children who pick things up and talk, well, if your child's mind is not capable of handling this new information it could be very harmful to his psyche, his growth.

INT.: *What's a good age then?*

MELISSA: When he's ready: for some kids, when they reach puberty, when they know about the birds and the bees; for others, including some that I know, I would say never.

INT.: *Who's to decide?*

MELISSA: Ideally, I'd like to see studies made on this. I would like to hear what qualified people think. But until that time comes it's going to have to be the parent's responsibility.

INT.: *We have asked this question of most swingers: Do you feel it's necessary to be on drugs to be better sexually?*

MELISSA: No. Not at all. Drugs or alcohol, to me, are quite artificially stimulating to open up your mind or loosen you up. If someone needs drugs or alcohol in extreme amounts in order to swing, they should not be swinging at all. Swinging, when it's good, is an experience that should free a person from the need of crutches to lean on. I get my "high" on people.

INT.: *You've been "high" on Chris for quite some time. How do you feel about marrying him?*

206

MELISSA: Probably it'll happen one of these days . . . But if I do marry I'd want kids, and then I'd stop swinging for a while. Afterward I don't think I could play it straight for the rest of my life.

22

Some Observations About the Children of Swingers

Almost sixty percent of the twenty-eight children (aged twelve to twenty-one) interviewed in this sampling had been repeatedly exposed to the nudist scene, either in family gatherings or in their homes. Most of the children liked it. It seemed to satisfy many of their basic curiosities about the body differences between the sexes. Generally, they found it to be a reassuring and natural way of behaving with their brothers, sisters, and other immediate members of their family as well as with friends and their families. Children who had not been involved in the nudist scene during their maturation seemed more awkward about discussing nudity and more protective and secretive about their parents' groupsex encounters.

Almost ninety-five percent of the children indicated a great reluctance to discuss either their nudist activities or their parents' swinging activities with nonswinging friends. They did not want to defend what they felt was a minority behavior on the part of their parents, nor risk abuse and criticism. More than seventy percent of the girls did not have strong positive feelings about the sex act. They had been aware of their parents indulging in sex behind closed doors, and the sounds of sex and the general feelings connected with it were that the mother was suffering pain, not pleasure, that sex was evil, not good. Sex was also for making babies—an activity that is only pursued with one person.

Almost all the boys appeared to be less mature and less sophisticated than girls of the same age. They were shyer about discussing the sex act and their inarticulate feelings seemed to carry out the stereotype that the male was the initiator, the aggressor, quite superior and prolific in handling the act. There seemed to be little concern over how the woman felt, or an understanding, for that matter, of how she should feel. Inferentially, this could give a boy a simple yardstick to gauge his performance. Certainly, sex becomes less challenging that way.

One of the thorniest issues to understand was how the children felt when they found out their parents were involved in groupsex. Approximately twenty percent of the children discovered this by accident, usually through a revelation by swinging friends of their parents or a knowlegeable child or children of swinging parents. Or, at times, by just coming back home a little too early and discovering a swinging party in progress.

Almost sixty-five percent of *these* children appeared to evidence a basic resentment of their parents' involvement in groupsex. They seemed to reflect a shame and a guilt about it, not only for their parents, but also for themselves. It was almost as if it had to be something bad because their parents were afraid to tell them about it, and it did not seem to enhance their own self-image and self-esteem. After the discovery, they tended to avoid comment. The best they could say was, "Well, if that's what they want to do, it's okay by me . . . They're old enough, aren't they . . .?"

The approximately eighty percent of our sampling who were told by their mothers and fathers at varying times in a planned way about the parental involvement in groupsex seemed to be quite relieved and rather nonjudgmental. Their comments were more upbeat and optimistic. ("It *must* be all right if they're doing it . . .") than the other group of children who, in essence, accepted reality without any great enthusiasm. Many of the children who were introduced to this knowledge by their parents said it made them feel much closer to them because they had been told "the big truth." They felt the revelation was a sign that their parents trusted them and they would never betray this trust.

We realize, especially in discussions with younger children, that what they say does not always reflect how they feel. We think that our information is not complete enough to allow final conclusions. For example, we still wonder how normal feelings of jealousy and competition between children and their parents are affected by this new sexual realignment.

Children aged twelve to fifteen did appear to be drawn closer to their immediate family, but they grew estranged from their peer group at school and in the neighborhood. They tended to stay home more often, read a lot, listened to music and preferred other noncommunicative solo endeavors. Perhaps at this early age this kind of revelation and the ensuing isolation might rob some of these children of a natural tendency to engage in nonsexual activities with their contemporaries. They tended to rationalize this decision to keep silent by saying they were afraid that their parents could be hurt by these disclosures. As a group, the children clearly seemed to be even more sensitive than the parents about their position as a minority in a rather hostile, nonswinging world.

About forty-five percent of the children knew other children of swinging parents and indicated they got along much better in this group than they did with nonswinging friends. It appeared that children of swinging parents also need a form of group approval, an inner bolstering and therefore tended to form dependent attachments to other children who shared this need.

Children who were unable to find friends to share these feelings with tended to draw much closer to their parents. Over and over we heard how much more honest they could be with mother or father, how much closer they felt, how their parents' liberal sexual attitudes led to freer discussions on other issues. There was more understanding and a tightening of family bonds.

We tried to get some insights into how the children of swinging parents felt about sex before they discovered that their parents were involved in groupsex. There appeared to be a sharp shift in attitude among young people aged fifteen to twenty-one, especially the girls. Almost uniformly, they seemed quite happy with the knowledge of what their parents were up to and able to cope with it. They even took delight in the secrecy and gamesmanship that was required of them to be able to interact with nonswingers on many levels. Most of them felt they had acquired new, superior knowledge that would work for them in many of their relationships outside the family. The boys seemed to exhibit the same tendencies, but, again, were less articulate about it.

We found it awkward to ask these children directly how they felt about eventually becoming swingers themselves. Fortunately, during the course of interviews, the children almost invariably raised this question themselves. Almost sixty-eight percent of boys as well as girls adopted a wait-and-see attitude. Thirty-two percent thought it was a good thing for frustrated married couples, but not for them; they said they would never swing. Further probing indicated that seventy-eight percent felt they were benefiting from their parents' swinging. They thought it would enable them to be freer about sexual relationships later on. And with that freedom it would not become necessary to participate in swinging.

The overwhelming majority of these boys and girls felt very strongly about wanting to marry, have children and carry on a more viable monogamous relationship than preceding generations. However, a number of them brought up concerns about raising children in the world as it exists today.

PART V

The Groupsex Phenomenon

---

23 DR. X.:

A Psychiatrist Defends Swinging

Dr. X. is a psychiatrist in the Midwest. He is middle-aged, married, has two children and three grandchildren. Dr. X. and his wife have been swinging for the past ten years.

He received his medical degree at a leading university and continued with additional psychiatric training there. He spent several years in private practice, and then became a professor in in the Department of Psychiatry at one of the leading universities in the Midwest. He still has his practice, but has called in other associates to help lessen the case load because of his responsibilities as an instructor, author, and consulting psychiatrist at a hospital close to the university.

Of all the interviews we conducted, this proved to be the most trying.

First, there was the question of Dr. X.'s anonymity. Under no condition would he have allowed the interview to be taped had we not agreed upon certain ground rules before we began. Every possible precaution had to be taken to make sure that we did not accidentally disclose his identity to the public.

Most people consider swinging a challenge to traditions of Western society, and even though he didn't agree, he respected those feelings. Furthermore, he was keenly concerned about his responsibilities to the people he treated. He did not wish anything that he said or did to have any unfavorable bearing on the patient/ doctor relationship. His views about swinging and his own experiences as a swinger could not be interpreted as an endorsement for everyone.

Dr. X. met us on a Sunday afternoon at his suburban home. We were led to the back of the home by his housekeeper. The doctor was spreading out breadcrumbs on the lawn and watching with amusement as the robins came down from the trees for an unexpected but pleasant, late afternoon feeding. The lawn in the back is seemingly endless.

"It's such a nice day, why don't we talk outside on the patio," he said. "There's a wall socket over there for your tape recorder. No, behind the lounge; that's it. Good."

His warm smile and soft-spoken manner put us at ease. The doctor is distinguished looking, round-faced; he wears glasses only when he remembers to bring them along. They're used for reading when his eyes tire. He reminds us of everyone's favorite uncle.

Dr. X. is not heavy-set; he is of average build and height. The pace he keeps up during the days and nights burn off a lot of intake so weight watching really is more "in my mind than anywhere else."

Because of his schedule, which even on Sunday can change at the last minute, we agreed to talk no longer than an hour and a half, but the dialog continued to flow with relative ease. When we finally reached the last point we all were a little surprised to see that we had been talking for three hours.

INTERVIEWER: *Doctor, why do you think swinging is gaining such popularity?*

DR.X.: I would say because it's a natural thing to do. I don't believe it's the nature of human beings to be totally monogamous. Absolute monogamy forces a person to react as if he were imprisoned. And when a person is forced to adhere to a certain standard, that automatically induces a desire to break away from it. If a man and wife don't feel compelled to restrict themselves sexually just to each other, then their marriage doesn't imprison them. They can walk away, figuratively, to someone else and feel free to do so. Not to feel confined is a state that is pleasing to a human being.

INT.: *Can you explain this further?*

DR.X.: It's simply a fact that men and women do desire a variety of sexual relationships, particularly if they're not allowed to have them. Whenever there is a standard of absolute monogamy in a culture, the culture must constantly go to great efforts to enforce it. There are no laws that force us to breathe because breathing is a natural occurence . . . But we have to make rules to enforce monogamy because it's not a natural state. One of the values of swinging for a married couple is this fact. Once a man and wife permit each other to swing, quite aside from the sexual pleasure that is produced by swinging, they're not possessing each other as property. They're not domestic animals. If a married couple does not restrict each other, they don't need to escape from each other. Therefore, swinging acts as an equalizer for the sexes as much as it provides sexual release. It's important to note that most married swingers enjoy sex more with their own partners than they do with the spouses of other married couples. Most of them feel their spouses are, in fact, the best in bed.

INT.: *Then why the need to go beyond the marriage unit?*

DR.X.: The greatest value that swinging can offer married couples is the feeling that they can have extramarital relationships with other married couples openly and thereby eliminate the feeling of confinement which is inherent in all marriages. When a married couple swings and still feels jealous or suffers from a lack of self-confidence when they see their spouse having sex with another partner, then swinging is not good for them.

INT.: *Recently I read an article in* Look *magazine entitled "A Look Into the Seventies: Why We Need A New Sexuality." I am quoting from the last paragraph: ". . . New sexuality leads eventually to the creation of a family as wide as all mankind that can weep together, laugh together and can share*

214

the common ecstacies . . ." Is this what swinging may lead to —group participation in other social functions?

DR.X.: It certainly could, and I'm sure that in some instances of swinging it does. However, at this point, I can't say to what degree. A system in which something, whether it's an action or an article, an item of some sort, is possessed only by an individual or an individual and his immediate family, and others are banned from possessing it, this exclusivity automatically presents a situation of competition. The goal is to possess as much as possible, to be as wealthy as possible, and not merely in material goods ("This is mine and not yours") which means the hope of having more than anybody else. To have more status, more property than others is to be better off than others, regardless of how much this means. In one culture, owning a horse may be unusual and, therefore, an item of wealth; in another culture where a man has five horses, owning one horse is considered to be poor, so it's always a matter of having more than the other guy has. It's a feeling of competition, and competition always has implicit in it some element of hostility. A strong sense of property rights is created by the isolation of one man and his family or one woman from others. But when there is some flow of goods in services or activities, where one family doesn't insist on total possession, there's no need for the same degree of competition.

INT.: *Will this challenge some of the traditional cultural standards of our present-day society?*

DR.X.: Yes. I see sexual restraints as part of possessiveness. The man owns his wife—that's been traditional. A partial step to equality comes when the wife also owns the man. In reality that means that neither owns the other. I would say the need to possess human beings as if they were property is the bad side of capitalism. In the past, a man owned his horse and his ox and his wife and his dog and his saddle; the wife was considered a material possession. The man had exclusive rights to determine her actions, her uses, to what degree he would or would not loan her, the same way in which he would loan his horse to another or not. This was a property

215

right and this applied to his accumulated goods and everything else, providing him with an exclusivity of ownership. In this setting there was, and in certain instances there is still today, a wall surrounding each family, shutting them off from others.

INT.: *Are you talking about a genuine revolution in the sexual scene or is this more of an evolutionary process?*

DR.X.: In any given stage in any given culture and also in any given individual, there has to be some kind of compromise between the desire for security and familiarity, on the one hand, and the desire to make things better, on the other hand. Evolution, then, is the striving for a better life. But since evolution has to overcome resistance, which is brought about by mankind's desire for constancy, at some point we have revolution because revolution implies bringing about a change that somebody opposes, and the tactics employed in a revolution take on the forms of either a struggle or a fight. I suggest that swinging is both a sexual evolution and a sexual revolution because one follows the other—evolution being the seed of change and revolution being the act of change.

INT.: *Is it due, in part, to a greater awareness of sexuality?*

DR.X.: I assume you are referring to the fact that there are all kinds of sexual activity which are well publicized now, while in the past it wasn't so much that sex wasn't being practiced but was more secret. There hasn't been as much a change in sexual activity as in sexual attitudes. This brings up one of the big stumbling blocks: morals are mostly a matter of appearance. A moralistic man may not want to be among a group of people who are naked, but a moralist obviously is not saying that there is anything wrong with having genitals or legs or arms or breasts. So when a moralist is objecting to a particular kind of behavior that he cannot accept, what he really is saying is, "I can't let people *see* me doing it," or "You don't have to be so open about it." For the moralist, the most emotional part of his objection to a particular act will be about the visibility of the act rather than the act itself.

INT.: *What about married couples who don't have enough ego*

216

strength to handle the sharing aspects of swinging? Can they
suffer emotionally from such encounters?

DR.X.: Yes . . . People who have some reservations can develop
feelings of guilt . . . It is important to understand that not
everybody who participates in swinging or in any other activity
participates altogether. Participation requires more than just
going through the physical act; that is absolutely essential,
but it does not alone accomplish it. I have to fall back on
the standard statement: you have to participate in spirit also.
Sometimes in a swinging situation this is rather important. In
the atmosphere of swinging, it's much easier to criticize a
swinger for not participating in spirit, because swinging frees
people to be open and honest with each other; nonswinging
people feel that criticism of another person may be misin-
terpreted as an insult and that sometimes the extreme of
politeness is really a euphemism for phoniness. The very fact
that swinging is a kind of loving situation makes it easier to
change. The exclusive situation of property and the feeling
of "everybody keep his hands off what's mine" (which is
the antiswinging attitude) also creates intolerance. The
minute you don't have to present a false front anymore, in
any sense at all, you're accepting yourself. If you have to hide
yourself, you're not accepting yourself. In a sense, you're not
accepting mankind. For one thing, you use other people to
blame them for what you feel are your own defects which
you want to deny, and this creates hostile criticism. If you
have traits that you want to deny having, but you have them
anyway, you have to account for them by finding them in
other people. You have to project. In swinging, this is not
the case because swingers accept each other as total human
beings. They're tolerant of each other. If they feel the need
to criticize, they will do so without feeling that the person
who receives the criticism will be hurt or insulted.

INT.: *Doctor, you've been swinging for quite a few years. How*
would you sum up the experience for yourself?

DR.X.: A happy anticipation, without fear, the feeling of sharing
enjoyment with somebody else, much like enjoying a concert
because each one enjoys it more knowing the other is sharing

217

in the enjoyment, too. At a swinging party, people share the same activity. They are happier because they are sharing together as equals, and this feeling of mutual enjoyment can be continued even after experiencing groupsex. That's the condition of absolute arrival.

INT.: *We've interviewed some swinging married couples who've indicated that they would have no objection if their children watched them have sexual intercourse. What do you think about that attitude?*

DR.X.: The need to encourage children to watch their parents have intercourse or, when a child becomes older, encouraging him or her to swing, implies that there is still a feeling of resistance to swinging on the part of the parents. Any parent who has to encourage his child to swing is, in a sense, reinforcing his own reasons to swing. Why should a parent encourage his child to swing? . . . This indicates, to me at least, that as an adult he is not yet fully accepting swinging. A child's business in life is to find out from the adults in his "world" —which principally means his parents—what life consists of, how one lives. We're talking here about a system of values, a standard of ethics, moral reflections . . . There is no need to instruct a child in those attitudes. He learns from observing what occurs in the realities around him and from his feeling response to those happings.

INT.: *Almost all swingers we've interviewed—particularly the married couples—say they can separate love from sex. How do you feel about that?*

DR.X.: Swinging can be a pleasure to both partners without having the kind of love that a husband and wife have for each other. But there also has to be some element of what a swinging married couple has for each other as husband and wife which carries over into swinging relationships with other people. As for distinguishing between love and sex, I would say simply that, if you have a good sexual reaction to each other, there's some element of love, too. It simply doesn't include all the aspects of feeling that married people have for each other. You don't need to be in love with each other, in the sense that a married or engaged couple needs love, in order to have sex. Nevertheless sex has to have with it some feeling

218

for the other person; otherwise there wouldn't be a difference between that and masturbation. Another person is there and you react to that person. It's an emotional reaction and attraction to someone, so an element of love is there.

INT.: *Do you feel that swinging is a way for a man to justify having sexual relations with someone other than his wife?*

DR.X.: Well, she has less basis for objecting if she also participates. I don't doubt that that's the reason for some husbands to seek out a swinging situation, but I think they're kidding themselves. If their real interest is to get extramarital sex, the probability is that they won't tolerate their wives doing it, because I imagine this type of a person would believe in the double standard. The man who can feel free, who can accept his wife's swinging as an equal, is not the kind of man who needs to make excuses to justify his own swinging. Justification is required when a person wants to do something he feels is wrong. If he feels it's wrong, he certainly isn't going to be liberal about it. When a person wants to do something but considers it wrong, he has to make a compromise. That involves two people. The compromise is going to involve an idea that, "I want it, but I also think it's wrong. So for me, it will be the coming out of the desire; for you, it will be the conformity with what's life." And this takes many forms. Take a boy who has intercourse with a girl and holds her in disdain. She's "nasty" because she had sex. Then for himself, the boy assumes the role of a man who had a successful sexual encounter, which becomes his victory and her defeat. So he gets his jollies and is thereby able to project the guilt on somebody else.

INT.: *Some swingers claim that it's often the woman who is the precipitating force in continuing to swing. Does this suggest that women are taking a more active role in sex, the role which was primarily considered to be the man's in "A Man's World?"*

DR.X.: I'm not at all surprised, because for the woman, swinging is restoring a state of equality for her. For the man, swinging is giving up his right to initiate, giving up his usual superiority, the attitude, "It's right for me and wrong for you." Swinging is a great leveler between the sexes. The age-old notion which seemed to allow the man to have both a wife and mistress but which demanded absolute fidelity from the wife, no longer exists.

INT.: *Swingers pride themselves on the fact that they're quite open and liberal in their thinking. Why aren't there a greater number of blacks who swing with white people?*

DR.X: I think it's fear.

INT.: *Who fears whom?*

DR.X.: Mainly, the blacks. I think black people who are upward-bound, trying to achieve their share of success, are extremely prudish. Black people feel constantly threatened, fear the loss of gains and status which they've achieved. Therefore, the black person will watch every little move he makes and won't dare venture out of the area he feels might jeopardize his achievements. There are too many white voices wanting to pull him down again. So the black man bends over backward to avoid any hint of savagery, primitiveness and animal sexuality, because, unfortunately, throughout history this was the white man's image of the black man. The black man and woman strive for propriety far more than whites do because whites happen to be in a better position in this world, and they can afford not to try so hard to be "proper."

INT.: *Is it true that more black men swing than black women?*

DR.X.: Yes, I would say so.

INT.: *Why?*

DrX.: The thought that pops into mind, because I don't have much specific data on this subject, is that the black woman conforms to ordinary standards because she has a little more status in white society. The black woman in the past has always been more employable. She was the one who was considered to be the head of the family. She supported the family and raised the children. The black male then felt discouraged and depressed, an object of scorn not only from whites but also his wife. So you might say, in a sense, that the black woman is more middle class than the black man. She has a certain position in life and perhaps feels she has something to lose if she ventures out into an area that doesn't conform to middle-class standards. The black man feels he has less to lose if he ventures into that same area.

INT.: *Are you saying that a black man swings because this is a way for him to share some of the white man's status?*

DR.X.: What I'm saying is this: what a person sees in any kind of relationship with another is a certain element of completion of himself. In others we hope to find what we lack in ourselves. There's no point in duplicating what we already have. What we seek are opposites.

INT.: *What is the need for "opposites" in sex? Is it purely animalistic?*

DR.X.: It's a very obvious fact that humans function to a degree like animals of a lower order. We eat food—eating is animalistic; we breathe—breathing is animalistic. But I don't think it's necessary to justify sexuality in a swinging sense by saying one is or one is not animalistic because, really, this is not the issue. Sex *is* a natural desire and so we don't have to ascribe that feeling to another condition.

INT.: *If the need for sexual variety is so instinctual, why do so many of the swingers that we've interviewed feel so secretive?*

DR.X.: First of all, they *are* a minority. This is an understandable feeling for any people who follow a way of life that departs from the particular culture in which they are living. The reverse is also true wherever a more liberal, promiscuous sexual behavior is evident and considered part of the norm. In certain cases, swingers are revealing their own doubts about the "rightness" of swinging.

INT.: *What about the need to have sex talk, or what some swingers call "fuck talk," to stimulate them during a groupsex encounter?*

DR.X.: I feel this kind of communication—having to verbalize the act that swingers are engaged in—is almost a ritualistic thing they have to do in order to break through the restrictions and barriers that some swingers feel. I'll give you an example that is in no way a comparison. In warlike cultures, to break the resistance of going to war, the warriors need to participate in war dances or rituals of war led by a chieftain or a group of people. In swinging, sometimes certain swingers feel a procedure is necessary, almost like a pep talk or a selling job to get themselves in the frame of mind, to get themselves into the activity.

INT.: *Does swinging take a lot of preoccupation out of sex?*

DR.X.: I think so.

INT.: *How?*

DR.X.: In general what a person has, he needn't yearn after. You can quote someone as saying that the reason for swinging is that it translates a fantasy into a reality. When something is part of a human need but is lacking or insufficient, it results in a greater preoccupation with that thing, even concrete things. We don't worry a great deal about getting enough to eat, but, as we know, in some parts of the world when a man wakes up in the morning, the first thing that pops into his head is: how in the world is he going to find enough to eat for himself and his family that day? So in that culture, food is a pressing need. In other cultures, other pressures predominate. In our affluent society, sex is often repressed and, therefore, constantly intruding itself into other things. It will come unbidden to mind, contaminating everything. The businessman sees his secretary come in; he wants to dictate something, but it's hard to keep his thoughts straight because he's looking at her crossed legs. He starts thinking of her in sexual terms. The thought gets in his way. It's there, demanding recognition, attention and fulfillment. But he's struggling not to express it because he feels he can't do it in the natural way. Whatever feeling you have and don't express is going to nag you; it's going to haunt you, to keep pulling at you and say, "recognize me."

INT.: *How does swinging affect man's need for sexual fantasies?*

DR.X.: When a person fantasizes, it's a part of his being. Whatever is a part of one's nature, of one's needs, must take on a form of expression . . . Expression is a part of human nature; it will inevitably have some kind of outlet. If it's not a natural one, it'll be a devious one, which is unnatural and will lead to something basically unwholesome. Fantasy is one natural way to let an expression out, I suppose, but it's seldom adequate. Therefore, it is much healthier if fantasies that are obviously not injurious to other people can be acted out rather than repressed . . . Though swinging eliminates a preoccupation with sex, it hardly eliminates thoughts of sex. We think of food even though we're not in danger of starving. Preoc-

222

cupation implies an *inordinate* amount of thought about a subject and is significantly involuntary. A person unavoidably thinks about sex whether he wants to or not. When you deny having a quality or a trait or a drive, you, in one sense, eliminate it; you cease to be consciously aware that you want to do such a thing. But once you've blocked it out, you've also lost control of it. Going back to the situation between the man and his secretary and her legs, he forgets what he was going to say when he was dictating to her and he may begin to stammer. His preoccupation becomes unvented because he doesn't have any control over its manifestation. He relinquishes it by denying its presence.

INT.: *Would you recommend swinging as therapy for some people who have sexual problems?*

DR.X.: You're being much too general. For some people and some problems, yes. For others, no. Swinging should never be recommended unless the person is fully aware of why he is swinging. He should fully recognize that he has a sexual problem of some sort. Ordinarily, I think the problem would be some sort of inhibition since swinging is certainly an enormous step forward . . . If a person who entertains the idea of swinging is not fully aware of the possible consequences of his actions, then swinging might not be good therapy for him. But an insightful person who is able to comprehend what swinging means and not have any significant concerns about it, could conceivably benefit from swinging.

INT.: *Could swinging be helpful for an impotent male?*

DR.X.: I think there are a number of men for whom the swinging setting would be the most impotency-*inducing* situation possible. For example, any man who is afraid of being sexual might discover that swinging could scare him into the particular kind of impotency that he is trying to rid himself of. We have to deal with the particular case. The kind of man who has difficulty functioning sexually without adequate permission might be helped because a swinging situation provides the most effective kind of permission possible. And the woman who swings wouldn't be afraid of being aggressive. She wouldn't have the need to submit as so many women do. And a woman who merely submits is a woman who is asserting her innocence. She is thinking, "A man is doing it to me; I'm merely the victim." The woman who takes an active, joyous part in the swinging process does not find it necessary to dump the responsibility for the sex act on the man. Such a woman can relieve a man who is impotent from all the guilty blocks he has to functioning sexually. In this case, obviously, swinging can be of great therapeutic value.

INT.: *Many swingers who talk about women giving pleasure to other women say this is not lesbianism or even being bisexual.*

DR.X.: There is a lot of truth to that. It's common for a woman in a groupsex situation to watch another couple have intercourse and go to them and add stimulation to the woman who is having sex with the man at that particular time. She may rub the woman's arms or her breasts and augment the sensation that the woman who is having intercourse is experiencing. Whether that is lesbianism or not, I think is a matter of definition. If a sexual caress between two women is what the definition of lesbianism is, then it's lesbianism. Swinging women try to avoid the judgmental term since homosexuality or lesbianism is considered by this society to be a "bad" thing. If a woman considers herself not to be a lesbian, then caressing another woman is not a homosexual act. I think what we're talking about is a confusion of semantics. Homosexuality is a part of every person—this is a fact. And since it exists, it will be manifest in some way or another—if not overtly, then in some other way. One way for unadmitted homosexuality to manifest itself is by extreme intolerance of it. A man who hates queers will, if he sees one, have the feeling that he wants to "go and beat him up." This man is expressing his own homosexuality. It's not a question of whether a person is homosexual or heterosexual, but how much of each he or she is. I think when swingers talk about women having relationships with other women in a groupsex encounter and say it's not homosexual, they mean this is not what the woman does *instead* of having sex with a man. It's not the main part of her sexuality. To deny vigorously that there is anything homosexual about this is tantamount to saying, "I'm purely heterosexual," which is absurd. Unfortunately, most people cannot be comfortable with what little

224

homosexuality they have. So when women give pleasure to other women it's homosexual!" So what? Does that make it bad? Where do you draw the line? If any degree of homosexuality makes a person bad, then all people are bad.

INT.: *To what degree, if any, can swinging cause basic changes in the people who practice it?*

DR.X.: In general people are prepackaged. We're made in a certain way with a certain nature. None of us was consulted during the engineering state, during the planning. And none of us has the power of reconstructing human nature. Nevertheless, man is forever trying to reconstruct human nature because of his vanity. Whatever we try to block, we succeed only in diverting. Diverting a drive into a different direction is synonymous with perverting it. You know "pervert" comes from a word that means "to turn." So we turn a drive out of its natural path into an unnatural one. It's going to show up some way. There is no way in the world to get rid of a character fault or a neurosis or however you describe a personal flaw, except by converting it into what it was supposed to have been. A defect is simply a trait gone wrong. It cannot be erased; it cannot be eliminated. All you can do is pull out what was supposed to have come out in the first place . . . You just have to attack the neurosis in its right place. This is a problem every tyrant runs into, trying to mold his people into his idea of what he wants them to be. Every time he pushes his subjects' feelings down in one place, their suppression pops up someplace else. Swingers see sexuality exactly for what it's worth and what it's for . . . The truly free swinger is not bothered by society's prohibitions. The only taboo that is meaningful is a taboo which one places on oneself. Today it's possible for swingers to swing, if they're consenting adults, without fear of prosecution. Therefore, the opposition to it comes from within. But there *are* a lot of swingers who function without being militant about it. That is where the real gratification lies.

INT.: *When swinging is experienced under those rather idealistic conditions, does it encourage the breaking down of other social barriers?*

DR.X.: Some of what I have said is in a way off the point of

225

swinging. Yet unless this can be understood, we will be presuming that swinging or sex can somehow be neatly separated from the total human endeavor. This is not possible. The important issue here is that sex has to be regarded as a part of the human makeup, like everything else. I would rather see sexual desires and the regulation of those desires handled in a nonjudgmental way.

INT.: *Are you saying that if sex taboos were eliminated, there would be no need to swing?*

DR.X.: No, but I imagine it would take a somewhat different form.

INT.: *How would it be different?*

DR.X.: I imagine swinging would occur casually. It would be less planned, with less effort to set it up. I would expect it to occur more when people happen to be together, without consciously making a deliberate effort to organize a swinging party, without having to plan an agenda. To me the ultimate would be: no swinging parties, just people getting together and sex developing at any point between anybody. Then there would no longer be a need for "swinging." Spontaneous feelings would just happen in a free-flowing, open and fulfilling manner.

24

A Symposium of Male Swingers

After reviewing our taped interviews we felt there was a need to focus in more depth on a number of important questions that had been raised by many of our nonswinging friends about the swinging subculture.

We discussed this with swingers who had been particularly helpful in the past and concluded that it might be beneficial to bring together a group of them for a symposium on specific issues that remained unsettled in our minds.

The symposium began at seven o'clock one Saturday night at the home of a married swinging couple in an exclusive California suburb, a community of homes in the $50,000-plus bracket.

The participants were:

ANGELO: Fifty-six, a professor of history. He and his wife have been married for twenty-three years. They've been swinging for the past ten. They have two children—a daughter who is twenty and a son going on seventeen. Angelo looks much younger than his years. He is tall, strong in manner and in excellent physical shape. His heavy-lidded eyes are set back, which gives him a brooding look at times. Yet his voice is soft, almost soothing. When he talks, the whole room listens. Most of his interests center around the college campus. Because of his own workload at the university, he has little time to relax on weekdays. But when he has the chance, he takes advantage of the tennis courts which are on campus. Usually, though, his free periods are spent with his students, in informal rap sessions either in his office or the student lounge or outdoors on a grassy knoll overlooking his office.

EARL: Thirty-three, has been married for ten years, has two boys, one seven, the other five. He and his wife have been swinging for five years. Earl is the kind of person who is hard not to like. Even before you have a chance to talk to him, the devilish smile on his face is inviting. In conversation, he is a provacateur. He handles the role well, almost like a straight-man, leaning forward, looking into his protagonists' eyes like a sober hanging judge, who then comes forth with side-splitting jokes. Although he and his wife had flown in from the East that morning, Earl was fresh, very much a vital contributor to the symposium.

MIKE: Twenty-seven, the bachelor. Mike has been swinging for over three years. He majored in business and finance at an Eastern university where he received his B.A. degree. He collects antiques. And, as Mike admits, with that kind of hobby, he can't afford much else. He has a quickness about him that emphasizes his directness and spontaneity. Sometimes he would sit back on the sofa and carefully study what the others were saying. Then, unexpectedly, he'd spring away with a barrage of crosscuts and earthiness. Mike also kept commenting about the meager buffet we had supplied, perhaps because he considers himself a connoisseur. He runs a successful business in Ohio. Mike is a ladies' man—maybe not as soft as some, but he possesses a masculine kindness that most women like.

LARRY: He is a bit prematurely gray. His dry wit makes it impossible to take him literally all the time, yet he is the picture of a conservative businessman. At forty-two, he is just that— the president of an expanding company. He has been married

228

for fifteen years. He and his wife have been swinging for seven. They have three children—two daughters and a son. The girls are thirteen and eleven, and the boy is eight. Larry studied music seriously and for a time considered becoming a professional. He still plays the piano, and with a few glasses of wine and some encouragement, he will offer a private concert. Once he stops "goofing around," which unnerves his wife, and gets down to serious playing, the years of his training become evident.

Jealousy, Ego and Competition

The interviewer began by asking how swingers feel when they witness their partners having sex with outsiders and when they themselves become involved with third parties.

ANGELO: I think when you first begin to swing, there is often a great deal of insecurity . . . It affects both partners, whether they're married or not. As long as there's a deep relationship between a couple, neither one really knows how the other is going to react, how far they can go. Certainly, for me, there definitely was an element of jealousy whenever the competition was too strong, if there were guys like Mike around who can keep it up for hours and come and come and come . . . But once a couple gets swinging, they become secure in their own individual relationship and the jealousy gradually fades away.

EARL: Yes, but I think this applies to men more than to women. The girls are more uptight about getting involved in swinging initially. I've known guys who've had to work on their wives for months to convince them to give it a try. Then, when they get into it and the girl blows her mind, the man is shaken up because she's having such a great time.

INT.: *What causes this reaction?*

EARL: For the most part, a woman is an easier swinger, but her man doesn't like to believe this. It's the Playboy image. Actually, once a woman breaks the ice, she can go to a party, get turned on much faster, and some of them never stop. That's not so good for a man's ego.

INT.: *Why? Is he afraid of losing his woman to someone else?*

EARL: That would be the last thought in my mind. I'd be thinking about the sex part, rather than the love part. I mean, if another guy were pleasing her more than I could, that would bother me. But I love my wife, she's my wife, and we're grooving on that. I don't think, my God, I'm gonna lose her next week because this guy is much better in bed than I am.

ANGELO: It's our upbringing that says, "If anyone screws my wife, I'll kill him."

EARL: Right. It's pounded into you for most of your life.

MIKE: Bachelors don't have those problems. If someone turns my girl on or I can't turn on a girl I'm with, I don't take it personally. I don't have that much going with anyone.

ANGELO: We're confusing two issues here: one is jealousy, and I think that ties in with your ego. In other words, someone else is a better lover for my wife, which hurts my image, my feeling of my own competence. But apart from this, there's also a cultural taboo against another man making it with my wife.

EARL: In America, once you get married, you feel you have an instant sex partner guaranteed, unless the marriage falls apart.

LARRY: Even if it turns sour, as long as there's a legal knot there's the concept that you can still ball your old lady, even if she hates your guts.

(Group laughter)

INT.: *You know that old joke about the married man who comes home and finds his best friend in bed with his wife. He stares at him unbelievingly—"Henry, I have to, but you . . . ?"* (More laughter) *There are many sexual jokes like that which intimate that the "straight" married woman isn't very good in bed. That's also a cultural concept, part of our Puritan background.*

LARRY: Most square men don't believe their wives have deep sexual desires or the capacity to fulfill them.

INT.: *This goes back to the belief that sex is love, and you can't separate the two. If a man and wife aren't really in love with each other, they can't have a good sex life.*

230

MIKE: That's a bullshit concept. We know that from the swinging scene.

LARRY: Once a married couple experiences variety, it actually takes the jealousy out of sex, takes the threat out of it. The fact that my wife can go to bed with lots of other men is the best way to keep her from leaving me.

INT.: *I don't quite follow that.*

LARRY: Look, before we started swinging, there was a desperate need to have sex. If I didn't get enough, I was mad as hell. And you know all the excuses a wife can come up with. The swinging scene really puts it on the line for a marriage. You've got to have much more than sex going for you to make it work.

MIKE: I think that can be very, very threatening to the squares because lots of guys like it the way it is. They can play around outside of marriage most of the time, and still have the wife back home taking care of the kids, the diapers and other cruddy problems. But if he gives her the same freedom he's got she's liable to turn to him one day and say: "We can't afford a babysitter tonight, so why don't you take care of the kids while I go out and . . ." (Laughter) I mean, right now most of the men can have it all their way. Why should they start sharing?

ANGELO: For one thing, swingers are better lovers; they enjoy it more.

INT.: *Are you separating sex from love?*

ANGELO: Sex is sex, and most of the time it doesn't have much to do with loving the person you're fucking. But I think most married swingers will agree that we have the best sex with our own mates.

MIKE: I don't agree. I think at a given time I can please your wife better than you can.

EARL: Hey, now, don't get personal!

ANGELO: No, it's all right. For argument's sake, let's say you can. What I'm saying is that sex is just a physical act. So she has a great release—that doesn't bother me, because swinging is a joint pleasure and if both of us are in love and have faith in each other, then I'm happy for her . . . Once in a while it's nice to have variety. Swinging is a communication. Instead of just knowing one person, your wife, very intimately,

231

you grow to know a variety of people very intimately, and that's better for you and your wife.

INT.: *And it leads to better sex with her? I still don't understand why.*

LARRY: It just does! Try it.

INT.: *Remember I'm one of those squares.*

EARL: That's your problem.

ANGELO: In a way, it becomes a personal competition. Maybe at a party I'll meet an absolutely charming young lady. We'll have a wonderful thing. Then when Gina and I get home, we talk about it, about her experiences also, and that turns us on to each other . . . I admit I'm trying to prove to her and to myself that I'm still pretty good in bed, and there are special private little things she prefers in sex that a guy at a party doesn't know about, so that knowledge is working for me. More often than not, our sex together is better.

MIKE: I'm beginning to feel left out of this super-swinging married state. What about nonswinging married couples who agree to go out with other partners, separately? That can be just as satisfying.

LARRY: Doing it separately is not the same as doing it together. It seems to me that would lead to jealousy and fears of losing your mate, a double jeopardy, because neither partner would really know what the other one is up to, and that fear of the unknown can cause all kinds of trouble.

MIKE: You're saying that swinging is paradise, that there's no hope for anyone unless they do it. But most people don't swing.

ANGELO: Sure, but according to the available sex research, about forty-five million Americans are sexually inadequate.

MIKE: We know that. We also know that for lots of married couples who try swinging it's a disaster.

ANGELO: Let's get back to definitions. I think a married couple must have individual stability to make a go of the swinging scene. Both partners have to have strong egos. Sure, lots of couples try swinging and then pull out. Well, they were vulnerable to begin with. That just points up another value of swinging; it has a way of sorting out those people who can't handle it.

Does Swinging take the Challenge Out of Sex?

The interviewer raised several questions about how a woman turns on a man (and vice versa) in swinging, as opposed to non-swinging situations.

EARL: Sure, there was a different challenge for me when I was trying to pick up a girl at a cocktail party. It was an ego thing if I was successful. And there was much more anxiety about whether I'd make it with that straight girl in a straight situation. In swinging, it's instant sex, no doubt about it. You know that you don't have to work too hard to score.

ANGELO: I disagree with that very much. Maybe I'm taking this personally now, as an older man, but at almost any party most of the men are a lot younger than I am. If I have my eye on a particular woman, I have all those men to compete with, and that's certainly a challenge.

EARL: But the point is, Angelo, when you walk through that front door, one thing is sure: the girls inside have come there to go to bed with someone; maybe not with you, but very seldom will they sit around all evening with their legs crossed.

LARRY: I grant you that. But there's still that individual challenge for a particular man to get a particular woman to say yes, regardless of age.

MIKE: And if she doesn't, to eliminate her and move on to the next one.

EARL: The point I'm still trying to make is that in a swinging situation, there's a general assumption that everyone is there to swing. You don't have that going for you when you walk into a square dinner party.

LARRY: Sure, that's a different ball game: the feeling around, testing, the phony romancing, all as a buildup to the act of copulation. And if you're married, there's the lying and the planning. What it all comes to, even if it works, is a great deal of dishonesty. What kind of challenge is that, really?

233

ANGELO: Yes, it's a phony game, because you're playing it according to the standards of the straight world. Even if the girl has decided to give in, she has to play at being coy, unsure about doing it and—this is what disturbs me most—when it finally does happen, she has to make you feel she lost control. You "overwhelmed" her. It was just an uncontrollable "accident." I suggest that this kind of challenge is not conducive to a healthy, mature, man/woman sex relationship.

INT.: *And swinging is? What replaces the so-called challenge of seduction?*

ANGELO: I think I could call it something like an anticipation of discovery. What will relating to a new and different human being lead to? The nuances and the complicated symbolism that exists in this scene is cleaner and healthier than in a straight situation.

INT.: *I think you're stacking the deck. Don't you ever go to a swinging party where there is no woman you want to "anticipate discovery" with?*

LARRY: Oh, I've been at many parties over a period of years where Barbara dug some guy and I didn't dig any of the girls, or vice versa. So while I was talking or drinking or sometimes just being plain bored, she'd go and have a big romance.

INT.: *Were you upset?*

LARRY: No, but if she were at a straight party, making a date with a guy outside the swinging scene and not tell me about it, then I'd be mad as hell.

INT.: *Suppose she told you.*

LARRY: Before or afterward?

ANGELO: That has nothing to do with it. Most swinging couples don't do that. That's part of our code of ethics. Gina and I have a very definite agreement that I won't swing with anybody that she dislikes or vice versa.

INT.: *Is that a general rule?*

EARL: Not that I know of.

LARRY: I think it's an individual decision.

EARL: Well, Susan and I don't have that kind of understanding, and I'd like to pursue this a little further with Angelo. Suppose you and Gina are swinging and she says, "Look, I really dig this guy and I want to go to bed with him." Hasn't that ever happened?

234

ANGELO: Not that I recall.

EARL: Suppose it did. What would you do?

MIKE: You'd be a rotten bastard if you said no, Angelo.

ANGELO: It's difficult for me to answer in advance because it's never come to that.

LARRY: I'd take into consideration the fact that my wife, whom I love and respect, has good taste. I'd go along with her desires.

ANGELO: Even if you didn't like the guy she wanted, if you really were disgusted by him? I don't know. I think the love between a husband and wife is more important than swinging.

EARL: But, Angelo, aren't you then, in effect, putting restrictions on swinging and the freedom we find in it?

ANGELO: You're making too much of this. If there's a guy I absolutely dislike, I think I'd say to my wife, "Look, do me a favor. There are fourteen other guys here, you've got thirteen other choices." I think that my wife would go along with that restriction.

MIKE: You can be subtler about it, you know—take her aside and whisper very quietly, "I hear that guy never gets an erection."

EARL: This gets back to why we enter the swinging scene. For me, it's always been a search for total freedom.

ANGELO: There's no such thing, even vaguely, as the concept of total freedom anywhere. In swinging we are replacing one set of cultural rules with a new set of values that are more advanced but still very definite. There have to be standards in any human encounter. What do you mean when you talk about total freedom? The freedom to murder somebody?

EARL: You're taking it too far, ridiculing it.

ANGELO: I'm not trying to do that.

EARL: I'm talking about the freedom to fornicate within the group scene, without any restrictions on you or your wife, whether you like who she's fucking or not. We're separating sex from love, and it seems to me you're putting emotions right back into it.

ANGELO: Not really. I'm just saying there *is* a reality. While the emphasis is on sex and the physical act, I don't have to go to bed with every woman at every party.

MIKE: I beg to differ. I always try to ball every chick at every party.

235

EARL: That's why you'll die at an early age, but it'll happen slowly. You'll just peter out.

ANGELO: Let's be serious—this is an important issue. I'm talking about growth. Any freedom is counterbalanced by a limit. In the swinging scene, we're not talking about freedom to hurt or to be cruel. We're talking about a freedom based on a loving principle, kindness, cooperation. And that freedom is balanced, because in order to share these feelings, you have to take into consideration the feelings of others: your wife, your girlfriend, whoever you're having sex with. There is a balance of considerations in swinging. That's what makes it work. When it's missing, swinging can leave you with a bad taste.

LARRY: (After a pause) Touché.

INT.: *From the way you've been talking, it appears that married couples are the dominant force in the swinging scene.*

MIKE: It wasn't that way in the beginning, years ago . . . The pill freed women from the fear of having children. Now, certainly in my circles, most swingers are married couples—middle-class marrieds, I might add.

INT.: *Does that bother you, Mike?*

MIKE: Why should it? My only judgment concerns the individual girl: does she turn me on or not?

EARL: Aw, come off it! The moment you walk in the door, it's off with the clothes and where are the broads?

MIKE: I'm still selective.

ANGELO: You said earlier you go after every chick.

MIKE: Because the parties I attend only serve up luscious ones.

LARRY: I agree with Mike in one sense. Most swingers, married or single, do it for sex, period—the variety of it.

ANGELO: I, for one, feel a lot of friendships grow out of the swinging scene. I'll grant you sex starts it off because "The grass is greener . . ." but after you find out that the grass is really not that much greener, you move on to other things. You find more rapport with this couple or that. You end up going to other parties with them and a real friendship develops which is more permanent that you expected, a sort of love feeling that spreads out and gives you a feeling of living in a separate world with new friends. You can't find that openness with friends in the straight world.

EARL: There's something to that, definitely. Susan and I still keep asking ourselves why we swing. More and more, sex becomes "the frosting on the cake," because our friends, the ones we can identify with, are swingers. I mean, when you fuck someone else's wife with the consent of the husband and watch your own wife enjoying it with that same guy, it opens the doors to a new kind of intimacy that you can't ignore . . . I think it's just a minority of swingers who want sex, sex, sex. Most swingers do look for lasting relationships.

INT.: *And when you find them?*

EARL: It's more fun to do straight things with them, to go on camping trips or a weekend of skiing.

INT.: *Don't you tend to get cliquish with these friends you feel close to?*

MIKE: Do you mean at parties?

INT.: *Exactly.*

ANGELO: It depends on the number of people there. At a big one, say with thirty or forty couples, yes. I've observed a lot of cliquishness, especially among married couples.

LARRY: But it's not the same thing that happens at a straight cocktail party. There the subgrouping is dictated by snobbery and status. At our parties, it's a natural reaction to all the new bodies. Until you get to know your way around, you tend to stay with your old friends.

EARL: Just like the squares.

ANGELO: The situation conditions it. Anytime you have more than fifty people, well, the beds are only so big.

MIKE: Right. A king-sized bed holds four couples if you're lucky.

EARL: Six, if they're highstrung and underweight.

ANGELO: But don't forget that this subgrouping breaks up quickly. The purpose is to get to know new people. There are no barriers or boundaries. You switch back and forth from one group to another and pair off.

INT.: *Who directs traffic?*

LARRY: The host and hostess.

INT.: *And they invite the guests?*

ANGELO: (Nodding) It's like planning any party. There's a very careful process of selection, though, in deciding who and who not to invite to put together a successful party.

INT.: *And there's no snobbery, no hint of status?*

ANGELO: (Laughing) The decision-making process is different . . .

237

In the swinging scene you try to arrange a successful evening. It's a much more loving decision.

INT.: *What happens to gate-crashers—friends of friends who're not so loving?*

LARRY: There are bad scenes but not too often. Usually it's a newcomer—mostly a man—who may offend a girl. The host or hostess or some of the other men talk to him and see to it that he calms down or leaves. There are not many occasions when a man or a woman gets drunk, paws over someone and a fight starts. Things usually don't get out of hand.

MIKE: The controlling factor is the atmosphere. The emphasis is less on drinking because most of the guys know that this can affect their ability to perform. There's much less anger and hostility at a swinging party, less of a frustration gap.

INT.: *Are you saying that open sex tends to curb violence?*

MIKE: You're getting philosophical now. All I know from my swinging experiences, especially in the group scene, is that the need is to screw and be screwed and you keep other feelings under wraps. When you're really going good, you couldn't care less about arguing or almost anything else.

EARL: Absolutely. Most swingers, even if they have difficulties getting it up or problems with their wives or girlfriends, cool it.

INT.: *That sounds as if they're holding in a lot of frustration.*

EARL: Oh, sure, swinging couples have fights. I certainly don't think that fucking is a cure-all, but when you take the sex out of the argument, somehow it's not so bitter. It's more objective and you can get it over with by making up in bed. At least, that's the way it is with Susan and me.

Inhibiting Factors in the Swinging Scene

The interviewer tried to examine sexual hangups that swingers may still have, as well as initial inhibitions and how they were overcome.

ANGELO: The do's and don'ts for swingers are as wide and varied as people themselves. Generally, swinging people are much more interested in experimentation when it comes to positions and techniques, but there are varying degrees of looseness. Many swingers still have hangups about male-to-male relationships and anal stimulation.

INT.: *Why do you call these limits hangups?*

ANGELO: Perhaps I shouldn't. At any rate, those appear to be, from my observation, the most inhibiting areas even for swingers. On the other hand, there is a great deal of openness about women pleasuring women and, most of all, oral sex of all kinds; that's quite popular.

INT.: *Why?*

ANGELO: Superficially at least, I'd say oral gratification is easier to achieve.

EARL: And I think a lot of women are more bisexual than men.

INT.: *Is it inhibiting for some men to see a woman pleasuring another woman?*

EARL: Most of the time it's a turn-on. But mainly, if I'm tired and a little anxious, I like it when a girl takes over because it takes pressure off me.

INT.: *Do these pressures sometimes lead to impotence?*

ANGELO: Sometimes in a group situation the presence of a lot of new people can inhibit some men for a while.

MIKE: Really?

(Laughter)

ANGELO: I've seen it happen and it's happened to me on occasions when I felt compelled to perform, rather than letting the desire come more naturally.

MIKE: Yes, but just think of how great you feel when somehow or other you do perform as expected.

EARL: And remember how bad you feel when you don't! (Laughter) We've all been there. We've gone to swinging parties and couldn't get it up, no matter how much we wanted to. I remember once feeling hornier than hell, but I just couldn't.

ANGELO: Sometimes it's because of a bad day that you've just been through, or maybe you've had too much to drink. Or a series of things happen at a particular party that start you on a bad trip.

MIKE: That's about the size of it.

EARL: Or the lack of size.

ANGELO: I think the biggest problem with swingers who now and then can't get an erection is what we talked about earlier. A swinger develops his own reputation, like the old gunslinger in the West. It follows him around and, at times, he just isn't quite with it and can't match what he's done in the past. I'd say that this leads to the greatest percentage of temporary impotence among swingers.

EARL: Temporary or not, those moments are the most agonizing times—when I'm expected to get it up and can't.

ANGELO: One of the nice things about swinging women is that most of the time they're very cool about this situation. They know that even when it happens, just by waiting an hour or so the patient can be cured. And when a man is most vulnerable psychologically, they tend to be understanding.

MIKE: Don't make madonnas out of those ladies. Another plus about swinging works for you when this happens: a chick has many other alternatives.

INT.: *Doesn't the availability of so many alternatives sometimes turn you off?*

ANGELO: Once you begin to accept sex as a natural thing, the more sex you get, the more you need. The less sex you get, the less you need.

EARL: I'll argue with you on that. When my wife and I first started swinging we'd go to parties three times a week, and we always had to get laid. After a while, we turned to ourselves and said, "What's this all about? What do we really want out of the swinging scene?"

MIKE: The novelty wore off.

EARL: Yes, the novelty of just scoring. At that point we didn't know what else we wanted, so we didn't swing for three or four months. And then we got horny again.

ANGELO: I know what you mean. I think this *is* true with almost any kind of activity. It turns you on in the beginning and you tend to overdo it for a while. Then you slack off for a while.

240

INT.: *So swinging is literally swinging: dropping in, dropping out.*

LARRY: Barbara and myself had to drop out of swinging because of a physical impairment. Afterwards, we didn't rush back in. Our relationship had changed. We hadn't had sex in a sharing way with others in quite a while, so it was almost a new thing for us to get back into the swing of things, so to speak. And this feeling about moving in and out of the swinging scene changes—sometimes week by week, or, if the mood strikes you, day by day.

MIKE: Just keep us informed, Larry!

INT.: *Is it difficult to "drop in" again once you've been out for a while?*

LARRY: Not really.

ANGELO: Sometimes you don't drop out completely. Gina and I still went to some nudist gatherings, maybe for a picnic to meet old friends. We kept in touch.

INT.: *Is nudity a must at swinging parties?*

EARL: You better believe it. But getting a couple to take off their clothes is also the biggest inhibiting factor. People are so self-conscious about it; they hide behind the image that clothes give them.

ANGELO: I've seen this happen with experienced swingers, too: at parties they go into the bedrooms, take off their clothes, have sex, share their bodies with many others, all nude, and then come out with a towel carefully wrapped around them . . . As a nudist I'm very aware how funny that is.

LARRY: Not every swinger is a nudist.

INT.: *Do you think this happens because people are so concerned about their bodies—how they look, how attractive they are?*

ANGELO: Maybe. That's another inhibition one faces in swinging. You don't have to be an Adonis or a Helen of Troy, but swingers *are* fairly attractive people.

MIKE: That's a plus. Incidentally, swinging is one of the cheapest ways to instill a tremendous willpower for losing weight and staying healthy.

INT.: *Doesn't all this nudity become boring after a while?*

LARRY: No.

ANGELO: The desire for and the response to a woman's body is instinctive in any healthy male.

LARRY: I think the biggest problem with nudism relates to people with children, when parents don't think their kids can cope with it.

EARL: Nudism the kids can cope with, but the sex action is something else again. Explaining it to them can be very rough.

ANGELO: Do straight people tell their children everything? It's just a matter of withholding certain information until you feel your kids can handle it.

MIKE: I think kids can handle a lot more than they're given credit for. It's the parents' problem. You also have to understand it's a new thing, so the mature parent is concerned not so much about his own shame or guilt but rather about how a young adolescent will handle this—let's face it—startling information with his nonswinging friends.

INT.: *It seems to me that if swinging is on the increase, swingers will have to face this problem much more realistically.*

Swingers and the Straight World

The interviewer asked how the swinging minority lives in the nonswinging world. Do they feel threatened, persecuted? How secretive are they about their sex life with nonswinging friends, at work and in various other situations?

MIKE: It's like leading a double life, in a way, which makes it very interesting.

LARRY: I don't connect the two.

ANGELO: I think it depends on what you do for a living. If you're a banker or running a Sunday school and are swinging, then you're in a lot of trouble if they ever catch on.

EARL: It's two separate worlds for me. Absolutely. And the square scene bothers me because it seems that the only way guys can get their jollies out there is to get smashed first.

MIKE: You have to hold back and calculate everything you say so much more. It's a lack of honesty.

EARL: But you can't say that swinging is the epitome of honesty. It's just that dishonesty is more emphasized in the square world.

ANGELO: I think the most rewarding factor in swinging is the closeness it creates between husband and wife. The complete openness about sexual feelings carries over into other areas.

EARL: For my wife and me, it's really broken down our hangups. We're totally honest with each other, and she'd better be!

(Much laughter)

INT.: *Does this deeper sense of perception lead to a keener awareness of the square world?*

MIKE: It makes me sick every time I go to work.

ANGELO: Square living is debilitating. Most men indulge in so much sexual daydreaming, watching their secretaries go by— all those fresh, young bodies on the street, in cars and wherever—and they very rarely fulfill their fantasies.

INT.: *If swingers do, does this help in day-to-day activities?*

ANGELO: I have no problem fitting into the square world with all its pettiness, because I started out as a square. That's how I was raised—very square and very Puritan.

EARL: But we're in a better position to analyze what squares are up to.

MIKE: It's like those people are only seeing half a city . . . shutting off a half view of everything . . . But it really doesn't give me an edge in my business.

EARL: From a personality standpoint?

MIKE: (shaking head) I deal only with men. But, I do understand things better and I'm more open. Swinging broadens my total understanding and awareness.

ANGELO: Once you break a cultural taboo, you're through a wall and you realize how artificial and unnecessary the barrier was. You see people and ideas boxed in all around you. Many times you're able to discover doors in walls that are not visible to others, and answers to questions and problems as well.

INT.: *Isn't the fact that you're a swinger also a problem in the straight world?*

MIKE: How?

INT.: *For example, a lot of your sexual acts are illegal.*

ANGELO: That's changing.

INT.: *Granted, but in many states you're still breaking the law. Doesn't that give you a feeling of anxiety, jeopardy, that might affect the quality of what you're doing?*

LARRY: I certainly don't go around telling my employees that I'm a swinger. Is that what you mean?

INT.: *Yes. Would you tell them if it were legal?*

LARRY: I'd have to think about that when it happens.

MIKE: I don't care. When I'm making love to a woman, I'm not worried about what's legal. Anyway, there are so many laws on the books that people are constantly breaking. I took a course in that once. Did you know that in several states there's still a law against shooting deer from stagecoaches, and that there has to be a foot of daylight between dancing couples?

EARL: You're kidding.

MIKE: It's the law. The point is no one goes around enforcing it.

INT.: *Do you think authorities are becoming lenient about swinging?*

ANGELO: I'm sure in some places they are. But I think you'd be courting trouble anywhere if you become involved with under-age girls or hard drugs. The groups I know don't go in for freaky things like that, or bestiality, whippings, etc.

INT.: *Are we getting back to inhibitions?*

ANGELO: Realistic inhibitions. There have to be limits.

EARL: Here we go again: pick your limits! It's like Christianity, saying that you can't commit adultery and that your wife is your possession.

INT.: *Do you think the Ten Commandments have just about had it?*

ANGELO: For me, the one I take most personally is "Thou Shalt Not Covet Thy Neighbor's Wife."

INT.: *How did some of you break basic taboos?*

ANGELO: For me, it was my experiences in World War II: being in constant danger because I was working with the under-ground, believing in a cause and yet seeing the basic im-

244

morality of war, even one I believed in. In a sense I became disillusioned with the whole Christian ethic.

MIKE: I was never conscious of breaking any taboos. I just fell into it. It was an individual thing. I don't harm anyone doing it. I give pleasure and joy myself, and I think it's right.

INT.: *Right by what moral standards?*

MIKE: My own—swingers have a strong moral sense.

ANGELO: The Judeo-Christian religion contains nothing specific against swinging, but the double standard has been maintained for over 2,000 years in countries dominated by religious values. Swinging was allowed for men because they did not get pregnant, and that is why women were excluded from the practice. If you check the Bible, you'll see that adultery was only applicable to women. To this day a prostitute is arrested, but the male client is not . . . There's a controversy about this, but many authorities feel that sexual problems started with St. Augustine. Priests were allowed to marry until the thirteenth century.

INT.: *Do you think, Angelo, that any religious leaders would condone swinging today?*

ANGELO: Probably not today. But how many of them would have condoned the pill or premarital sex fifty years ago? Look at the changes that are happening with regard to sexual mores. No church, no authority, can be totally oblivious to this.

EARL: I think we have to relate to these changes rather than to the philosophical origins of Christianity, because we're all influenced by the practical application of these philosophical concepts.

ANGELO: There are two separate issues here: culture and religion. Culture varies in all countries. For example, if you go to Spain, it's un-Christian for a girl to walk around in a bikini. These are cultural values which often reflect religious dogmas, but, conversely, cultural pressures can also force social change. Inevitably, you see religion going along in some way with the temper of the time.

INT.: *Are you saying that a person responding to cultural change can swing without guilt and still be religious?*

ANGELO: Definitely. I'm a religious person and I swing.

INT.: *I'm talking about someone who believes in God.*

ANGELO: I do. But I don't believe in a God who is cruel or punishing or vengeful. God gave us the urge for sex, put it into our bodies, our systems, because he meant for us to use it, to satisfy ourselves and other people close to us. Sex to me can be a very spiritual, elevating experience.

25

A Symposium of Female Swingers

The female symposium is the second session of interviews taped the same night as the male symposium. One of the women suggested that the meeting be held in the master bedroom. The other ladies agreed. It seemed to be the most appropriate place to talk about swinging. The door to the room was left open.

Another panelist suggested that the tape recorder be placed in the middle of the massive bed and that everybody then sit around it and talk. After some discussion, a compromise was reached. A small table was scooted toward the middle of the room. Those who wanted to make themselves comfortable on the bed, could; the others had three overstuffed chairs and a large sofa to choose from. One chose the bed. Two others, the chairs. The fourth sat on the couch with the interviewer.

The participants were:

GINA: Angelo's wife, forty-two years old but looking much younger. Honey-blonde hair pulled back in a ponytail. Soft, green eyes. A few freckles sprinkled over clear, sunburned skin. One reason why Gina looks so young is that she made a vow to her husband: "I was eighteen years old when I married Angelo, and I told him that after I was thirty-five, we'd stop celebrating my birthday." He said, "Okay, providing you stay thirty-five." She did. Gina lookes like a graduate student—bright and cheery. Slightly thin, but well-rounded lips. Her sometimes vague, searching expression is not a reflection of incompleteness or ambiguity. It's a veil of innocence and hides surprises waiting to catch you at the least unexpected moment. She divides her time working with Angelo and taking care of their home. She does all the housekeeping herself ("It's good exercise"). Recently, she redecorated their home, choosing new colors and fabrics and then designing two living-room chairs which were custom-built by an upholsterer: "I'll let you in on a little secret, though, I did get help from my children and from Angelo. Supervisory. But my daughter helped me cut out the pattern for the drapes, select the material and then sew and pleat the fabric together. And my son wanted a special kind of desk for his room, so he and Angelo spent about three weekends with an electric saw, sandpaper, varnish, glue, nails, assembling his desk."

SUSAN: Earl's wife. Twenty-eight years old. Pert, bouncy. She has high cheekbones, dancing eyes. A sometimes pouty mouth and almost perfectly shaped lips which on occasion break into a warm, enveloping smile. Like her husband, Susan provokes and then withdraws and waits. Sometimes testing. Sometimes watching. Then, like a little girl dying to reveal a secret, she catches us all off guard—and reacts as if she, too, is surprised over what has come out. Her two sons keep her going most of the day. "Fortunately, they're both in school now, so I do have more time to devote to other things." One project is a special program in which she is being trained to work at a hospital. There is also the PTA, and other community organizations. Susan spent some time in college but then left after she married Earl. She plans on finishing her undergraduate work fulltime next year when her youngest son enters the first grade. She has already been accepted and plans to complete her major in sociology.

BARBARA: Larry's wife. Thirty-six years old. Patient. Extremely cooperative. Soft spoken. A beautiful woman. Long, black hair that flows gracefully down to her shoulders. A deep, all-year tan. Blue eyes. A small, clipped nose. And exectly the dimensions Larry described—38-24-36. She doesn't hide her natural endowments. She wore a red blouse open at the neck and a simple blue miniskirt. No nylons. Her legs shaped like a dancer's. Early in the evening she wiggled out of her sandals and sat curled in the corner of the couch, resting her chin intermittently on a throw pillow. Her three children keep her active. "Our little eight-year-old son is something else. You'd think with two sisters he'd have a heck of a time. But he has made the adjustment beautifully. He's all boy, and he does get a kick out of having two older sisters." Although Barbara does have help five days a week, she manages the household—planning the meals, getting up with the children, making sure they're on the way, with the lunch money and the weekly reader money and the notes from home giving permission for field trips, special projects, which seem, as Barbara sighs, never ending. Three days a week, she is assisting in a program which a group of mothers helped put together, with the endorsement of the school board. "The weekends are the time when Earl and I can let go and have some fun."

VICKY: Mike's date for the evening. Twenty-four years old. She works as a legal secretary. She also attends night classes at a nearby university where she isn't working toward any degree but taking courses which are interesting and challenging. Wherever she goes, Vicky keeps a small notebook close to her. She writes poetry. It can be in a crowded department store, on the beach, or waiting in line to see a movie. Almost before the notebook is out of her totebag, the pencil is building verse. Vicky is five-foot-four with sandy brown hair, worn pulled back in a bun. Her blue eyes have a smile to them when she talks. She is as lithe and vibrant as if she were still in her teens. Everything about her reflects sensuality. Vicky wore a long "granny dress' with mutton sleeves. Only lacing kept the low, decolletage front together There was a remarkable shyness about her, considering how she responded when she finally opened up.

Jealousy, Sex, and Strangers— A Female View

The interviewer started off by raising questions about how women select men at a party and how they feel when they see their husbands having sex with other women.

SUSAN: Frankly, it gives me pleasure seeing my husband having pleasure.

INTERVIEWER: *What about the fear of losing him to another woman?*

SUSAN: I had that fear only before we were married. I didn't know what he was doing when he wasn't with me.

BARBARA: (Smiling) But now you do.

SUSAN: All the time. (The group laughs) We've been married for ten years. I feel secure that our relationship is rather permanent. The only time he has had sex with a woman when I wasn't around was when I insisted that he should. I was in my ninth month, and I'm sorry, but there was just no way. I don't care what some of those books say. They're all written by doctors who haven't carried a baby full term. (General laughter)

INT.: *Did your husband raise the question?*

SUSAN: By that time I think my poor husband had serious doubts whether he could raise anything any longer.

GINA: You have to know Earl. When he gets nervous, he's something.

SUSAN: I just told him, "Earl, please go out. Do something. Call Fred and see if you can go to the party Friday night alone. I'm sure the other people will understand." So he did. He enjoyed himself and came home at a reasonable hour. In fact, as I recall, he called me a half hour before he left the party to see how I was getting along.

BARBARA: (Addressing interviewer) The only real threat to a swinging marriage comes if a husband develops a romance with a nonswinging woman . . . If he meets a girl, and I

250

don't care how attractive she is, at a swinging party and goes to bed with her, that kills any chance for romance.

INT.: (Puzzled) *Are you saying that instant sex kills the chance of love?*

BARBARA: "Instant sex," to use your phrase, in a swinging scene with mutual approval is entirely different from "love." To fall in love, there has to be a buildup. Dates. Doing lots of other things together. You develop a series of feelings that add to the physical act of sex. Anyway, that's what I call love. And the threat of that, to my husband, doesn't exist when we swing.

INT.: *I take it you also aren't very bothered when Larry* (Barbara's husband) *is having sex with another woman.*

BARBARA: Well, I'm busy, too, you know.

INT.: *Is it mainly a matter of distance—the fact that you're separated?*

GINA: I don't think so. Angelo and I often have sex with other people in the same room. We like to be close to each other, to reach over and touch hands. It's a very beautiful feeling and, as far as jealousy is concerned, I think it's just the opposite for both of us. After we've had a pleasant evening with others, we're happy to be back together. We love one another.

BARBARA: I think with married swingers, there's not much of a jealousy factor after they get into the act, except when there's trouble in the marriage to begin with. Isn't jealousy really a fear of losing something or someone that is of value to you? (She pauses, remembering something, and cups her hand over her mouth) Hmm, I don't think I should tell this. Will Larry ask to hear these tapes?

INT.: *He may.*

BARBARA: Oh boy. (Shrugs her shoulders) He won't get mad . . . (almost in a whisper) . . . I think. It involves a mutual friend of ours. She's a swinger like us. Married. She had a feeling that one of her husband's secretaries was making a play for him. She never confronted him with it, but she had a feeling . . . Well, he was supposed to go on a convention and he wanted to take his wife along . . . She decided to fake an illness and encouraged her husband to go on the trip with his secretary who was supposed to be at the conference anyway. I presume they both went to bed at least once before the convention was over.

INT.: *To sleep?*

BARBARA: Bed-sex, not bed-sleep. You know what I mean. As it turned out, the episode soured my friend's husband's "sneak-it-on-the-side" syndrome, which most normal males go through. He happily went back to his swinging wife and I'll bet she is better in bed than his silly, high-schoolish secretary any time.

INT.: *Are you recommending this as a therapeutic answer to the "other woman?"*

BARBARA: No. I think it's rather risky unless you feel pretty good about the sex you're having with your husband. That would be the deciding factor for me, anyway.

VICKY: About that "other woman": I have a great deal of confidence in myself. I'm single, but when I have something going with a man there is no woman who can take him away from me. It's impossible unless I want it to happen.

INT.: *Are you suggesting you have a special kind of sexual power?*

VICKY: Yes.

INT.: *How do you married women feel about this sexual power?*

SUSAN: I have it. (She gives the rest of the group a mischievous "should I or shouldn't I say it" look.) I can walk into any room full of men—and flex a lot of muscles. (Laughter) I can. (She lowers her head in a little girl look.) I do feel that the woman is the center of all sexuality. There is no end to the number of orgasms I can have when I'm in the mood . . . (Then, reflectively) The main thing for the woman is not to abuse that God-given privilege. I look upon it as a gift that should be shared with my husband and any other man I like.

GINA: You put that very well, Susie. It works, too. For instance, if Angelo is resting, but Susie's motor is running, maybe Barbara's husband, Larry, who's been idling in neutral is ready to go again . . . I don't know about Vicky and other single girls, but most of my married friends need other men to help them along. Then they can come, come, come.

SUSAN: And the men whose penises are soft and sleepy can help by giving us oral sex and massages.

INT.: *It seems that it's "in" to talk about the multiorgasmic woman. Is this a revolution or what?*

GINA: The most appropriate word is "return," a reawakening. Biologically speaking, women have always had these capacities but, culturally, the powers-that-be have draped us with blankets to hide our sexuality even from ourselves.

INT.: *Was this repression of feminine sexual impulses a cultural conditioning?*

GINA: In some cultures it was physical. I've been working on a paper for a seminar on Eastern religions and came across some chapters in "The Devil Drives," one of the biographies of Sir Richard Burton, where he discussed what Eastern men used to do to their harem women. They had them circumcised! Their clitorises were severed, much as a baby boy's tip is cut soon after birth.

SUSAN: (Making a pained face) Really? How awful for a woman to go through something like that!

BARBARA: That's barbaric!

GINA: Among the Moslems, it's still a practice today. The ritual is supposed to have been invented by Sarah who mutilated Hagar for jealousy and was afterward ordered by Allah to have herself circumcised. The Moslims defend it as the proper equivalent of male circumcision because supposedly it evens the sensitivity of the genitals by reducing it equally in both sexes. And because the uncircumcised woman has more orgasms and frequent coitus would injure her health!

VICKY: (Exclaiming) You've got to be kidding!

VICKY: So you're saying, Gina, that putting the wraps on a woman's sex was a way of preserving the male's ego.

GINA: Exactly. In some cultures, they try to solve the problem with a knife. Western societies have disguised the knife and called it a "taboo" instead. But the pain inflicted on women has been just as damaging. (She turns and soberly stares at the interviewer.)

INT.: *Don't look at me as if I'm responsible, just because I'm a man.*

SUSAN: Shame on you for thinking that swinging women are that chauvinistic!

BARBARA: Next thing you know, you're going to call us a group of nymphomaniacs.

INT.: *That's a good question. What* does *constitute nymphomania?*

GINA: Certainly not a continuity of orgasmic satisfaction.

INT.: *Well, if you need all those men to satisfy you, are you really satisfied?*

VICKY: You really have some weird ideas! I think you're just plain envious. I pity people like you.

INT.: *Why?*

VICKY: You don't know what you're missing.

SUSAN: (Coquettishly) I know—*you.*

VICKY: Well, maybe you're right. I can make love all day and all night.

INT.: *That doesn't leave much room for anything else.*

BARBARA: I'm sure she takes coffee breaks.

VICKY: I have a refrigerator in my bedroom.

INT.: *Is this lovemaking? It sounds more like a marathon without much feeling.*

VICKY: Pardon me, but it isn't. When I'm making love with someone, I make love, and for that moment, I am *in* love.

GINA: (Interrupting) I don't know how you're using that word . . .

VICKY: Please let me finish. It's far more meaningful than what you ladies do—walking into a bedroom with any Tom, Dick or Harry.

SUSAN: (Begins to bristle) Your grammar's a little off. More often than not, we walk into a bedroom with Tom, Dick *and* Harry.

BARBARA: (Looks at interviewer and gestures toward Vicky) *She* doesn't sound like a swinger.

GINA: Is she a spy?

SUSAN: (To interviewer) Come on, now, is Vicky a plant?

INT.: (Laughing) *Will the real Vicky please stand up?*

VICKY: I'm one of Mike's (the bachelor) many girlfriends, and he is one of my many boyfriends.

SUSAN: Well, surely he's taken you to swinging parties.

VICKY: (Shaking her head) He's wanted to, but I've refused to go. I don't consider myself a real swinger. I enjoy sexual experiences with several people at a time—men and women—but they've been in very intimate surroundings and the people have all been close to me. I just won't walk into a room and have sex with anyone. I'm sorry—I couldn't do it.

INT.: *Why not?*

VICKY: Because I couldn't.

BARBARA: You're not answering his question.

VICKY: For one thing, I detest the idea of undressing in front of people I don't know. There! Are you satisfied?

INT.: *At what point can you make that adjustment?*

VICKY: When the vibes are right. When we're communicating, having a mental rapport.

INT.: *Do you have to know that person?*

VICKY: No.

INT.: *Can a stranger qualify?*

VICKY: If that feeling of rapport is there.

INT.: *Anywhere?*

VICKY: Yes, even walking down the street. I can meet somebody and have these feelings without having to go to a swinging party for the explicit purpose of having sex. This business of walking around naked like a slave at an auction—forget it.

BARBARA: That's not at all what it's like!

VICKY: I've heard from Mike what it's like. It's organized sex. And I think you plan it to death. I can feel sexy anyplace, even in church.

INT.: *You met somebody in church?*

VICKY: Yes. When the minister was giving his sermon, I noticed a man seated next to me. We had instant rapport. After the minister gave the closing prayer, I got up, walked over to the man, we smiled, and we walked out together.

SUSAN: I've heard of religious experiences before, but this—

VICKY: Let me tell you—it was beautiful! I had a beautiful thing going with him.

INT.: *How often do these beautiful, accidental things happen to you?*

VICKY: Quite often. Sex is a part of the whole me. I use it, especially if I'm tense or frustrated.

INT.: *How?*

VICKY: Masturbating. I think a woman should play with herself.

SUSAN: Or use a vibrator.

VICKY: Those things are not all that fantastic.

BARBARA: Unless you're a woman with terrible problems, eventually, if the batteries last, a vibrator can give you absolutely marvelous orgasms.

VICKY: (Shrugging) Why go to all that trouble? I just use my fingers.

SUSAN: That can be limiting, don't you think?

VICKY: No, no. I even do it in my car, driving down the freeway when the traffic is bumper to bumper and I'm getting all upset about it. One hand stays on the steering wheel and the other hand goes on me.

INT.: (Looks at Vicky for a long moment, then says slowly:) *Tell me, Vicky, were you always like this?*

VICKY: (Smiling) You're just envious.

INT.: *I don't know about that, but I'm skeptical.*

VICKY: Look, when I'm in the right mood, I can have an orgasm just by talking to someone on the telephone—or even shaking hands . . .

Swinging Women's Inhibitions—Do's, Don'ts and Maybe's

Vicky went for a coffee break and didn't return during this portion of the taping. The interviewer began by asking several questions about feminine sexual hangups and how they are handled in the groupsex scene.

GINA: I've seen women at their first swinging party sit in a corner, fully or semidressed, all evening long, terrified. They usually have a negative self-image because they're not gifted with perfect features.

SUSAN: But what a joy when they find out how a woman can make up for nature's flaws in so many other ways.

INT.: *Well, how?*

BARBABA: If you were at a swinging party and Susie walked by in the raw, you'd follow her . . . (Laughter) And you know why? Because she knows how to use her voice. That's how my husband was first attracted to her. A kind of inviting innocence. I remember Larry telling me when he first met Susie how he couldn't take his eyes off her face.

SUSAN: He made me feel so good the way he looked at me. But you're right about voices, especially with those of us who are shy.

GINA: Watch out for the shy ones. I remember one tiny, demure little girl who struck Angelo's fancy one night. We were in the same room. I was surprised when Angelo brought her in, because most of the evening she'd been sitting in the shadows, hardly breathing . . . Well, after Angelo began cuddling her, she started carrying on. And I mean just that. Actually yelling out in joy, so loud that everyone in the room ended up stopping their own activities to watch. This little church mouse was incredibly verbal once Angelo got her going. And animated, too. The way she wiggled her body around! I tell you, it was something to see. She and my husband had a perfectly marvelous time.

INT.: *I keep hearing about fantastic sexual experiences. Don't swinging women ever have bad trips?*

GINA: Of course. It's a matter of mood and circumstances. I've gone to parties where something or someone created a distasteful atmosphere that ruined the entire evening . . .

BARBARA: One thing I simply can't stand is when a man tries to paw me. I don't like it when he equates virility with roughness. If he wants to play rough, let him tackle football players, not me.

SUSAN: Some strangers are very pushy: the inexperienced, uptight newcomers. They want to get that girl—that extra scalp. It's a game of "body count" for them. But the more they press, the more they're rebuffed and that can cause ugly scenes. I especially remember a party where a wife was having a better time than her husband. This fellow started drinking and sulking. Then he stormed through the bedrooms until he found

257

his wife and created quite a row. He actually got her hysterical. He demanded that she get dressed right away and go home with him. And he was very abusive with his language.

INT.: *What happened?*

SUSAN: Some of the other men tried to calm him down, but it didn't work. Even after they left there was a pall on the evening.

GINA: Those occurrences happen more often than not at orgies where there is less control over who brings whom. Angelo and I find those scenes distasteful.

BARBARA: I'd go a little further than that. Orgies—where most of the freaks and the people on hard drugs hang out—give swinging a bad name.

INT.: *What about the risk of pregnancy? And venereal disease? Does that concern you?*

SUSAN: Of course it does. But you make a value judgment somewhere along the line about the pros and cons of swinging. Life is awfully risky anyway—whether it's crossing a street or plugging in an electric toaster. I think that, philosophically, it's a matter of weighing alternatives. Are you willing to run a minimal risk for maximum pleasure? I am. And many of my friends are, too.

Swinging and Friendships

The interviewer asked about what seems to be one of the most important aspects of swinging—the search for "new people," new friendships that lead to nonswinging relationships.

BARBARA: There is definitely a need among swingers to meet new partners, new faces. When you first begin swinging, I think it's particularly important. After all, you're looking for a variety of sexual experiences. There is a sexual adventure in going to bed with relative strangers. Now you'll find out: what are they like? How will they love?

GINA: I think this need is even greater for a swinging man.

SUSAN: Yes. For some reason the man is more curious. In the end, it may be more of an intellectual curiosity with him than anything else, but it does exist. I know it does with *my* husband. (In a mock reprimanding manner) He's *always* looking.

BARBARA: Yes—for you!

(Laughter)

GINA: You must realize, though, that going to a swinging party isn't all sex, sex, sex. We go there to meet new friends.

INT.: *Exactly what do you mean by "new friends?"*

GINA: People you want to be with, not just for sex but for their minds as well. We go to concerts together. We go on weekend skiing trips, where there's no swinging at all, not even subtle attempts to get things going.

INT.: *Are these friendships different from those with nonswingers?*

GINA: Yes, I think they are. We feel more compatible with swinging friends, more open and honest, because of our past sexual relationships with them. Talking about *anything* becomes easier.

VICKY: You can find that in nonswinging people, too, Gina. I mean, just because you start off saying hello in bed and wind up close friends doesn't take the relationship necessarily into the open.

SUSAN: Well, we think it does.

VICKY: I think it doesn't.

SUSAN: I think you should come to one of our swinging parties.

BARBARA: (Laughing) I think she shouldn't!

VICKY: I'll think about it.

(Laughter)

INT.: *What happens to the sexual aspect of these relationships when people become close friends?*

GINA: It wanes.

INT.: *Why?*

SUSAN: You probably get to know them too well.

INT.: *So you swing in smaller, more select, groups with your friends . . .*

SUSAN: Yes, but then it becomes almost like a marriage . . . Earl feels he should swing with the girl; I feel I should swing with her husband. It gets to a point where you resent it if you do and you resent it if you don't. That's why swinging with just two or three couples is often too confining.

BARBARA: It becomes nothing at all. We're not together just to have sex. (Pause) Did *I* just say that?

SUSAN: Sometimes the husband decides, "Let's stop for a while." Sometimes it's the wife's decision.

INT.: *More often than not?*

SUSAN: It depends. Larry will probably disagree when he hears this, but, from my own personal experience, whenever I've wanted to cool it for a while, Larry's done his best to change my mind.

INT.: *What happens then?*

SUSAN: If I insist, he ends up going along with me.

GINA: You drop out. Some couples can swing four or five nights a week. I can't. I tend to become a little satiated with sex. My body needs a rest sometimes.

BARBARA: But wouldn't you say, Gina, that those people who go to one party after another are the exception rather than the rule?

GINA: Oh yes. Definitely.

INT.: *What are some other reasons that lead swinging women to drop out?*

SUSAN: Too many parties can become boring and redundant. It's just like doing too much of anything: if you work too hard or too many hours, if you go to plays or movies too often, if you play golf or tennis too much.

INT.: *How long does a dropping out period last?*

GINA: For some, maybe a few weeks; for others, a month; for still others, many months.

INT.: *And then?*

BARBARA: You're back in the mood and sometimes you feel like you're beginning for the first time again. There's the desire. The need. The fun of it.

INT.: *Does swinging become the most important part of your life once you've gotten back into it again?*

BARBARA: Do you see me running out of the room, looking for Susan's husband?

(Laughter)

SUSAN: I dare you.

(More laughter)

BARBARA: No, seriously . . . (To interviewer:) You act as if once we get into sex, that's all we do.

VICKY: Well, I think he's right.

SUSAN: Look, Miss Sex-on-the-Freeway, we have more things going on for us than you have with your sexual smorgasbörd.

INT.: *You must admit that people who don't swing think . . .*

SUSAN: What—that we're all sex machines?

INT.: *Yes.*

SUSAN: You have it in reverse! We're not preoccupied with sex. It's there always, when we want it.

GINA: Look, you straight people fight for it, you cheat for it, you conspire for it—everything: scheme, beg, sometimes even kill for it. Swinging is quite a nonviolent form of sexual recreation, enjoyment and pleasure. You know we can take it or leave it.

INT.: *How does it affect the time you allow for other things?*

GINA: Let me tell you what I do. Besides raising our two beautiful children, besides taking care of this house by myself, I'm also involved with Angelo in helping to research and put together a collection of essays. We're going to have this published in paperback and get it used as a textbook for both the primary and secondary grades. This takes a lot of time, but I love the work and I feel it's a valuable contribution. My gosh, I'm not in bed every minute of my life!

SUSAN: I think swinging actually frees us to do these things . . . I work at a hospital in our community with other trained volunteers . . . I think the difficulty for me still is taking the patients' problems back home with me. I can't help but become emotionally involved when I see a man in his early thirties being rushed in after suffering a heart attack. I can't help but think, my God, what if that happened to Earl! They're so young, with so much of a future to look forward to. And look what happens!

BARBARA: I keep telling my husband to slow down. But he never will. He seems to thrive on pressure. That's probably why I like to get out and do things.

261

INT.: *All this and heaven, too—in bed.* (He shakes his head) *They won't believe this.*

BARBARA: In Peoria?

INT.: *Anywhere.*

GINA: They'll think it's a great, big put-on.

INT.: *Exactly.*

SUSAN: (Laughing. Then, to interviewer:) Well, you just tell it the way it is.

INT.: *Speaking about "the way it is": Many of the swingers we've talked to are afraid to tell their children "the way it is." How do you feel about that?*

BARBARA: Some swinging parents tell their kids; others don't. I feel it's an individual decision.

INT.: *Have you told your children yet?*

BARBARA: No.

INT.: *Why not?*

BARBARA: Because I feel they're not ready to be told yet.

INT.: *What are your reservations about telling them?*

BARBARA: (Thinking for a moment) You see, their concept of love is seeing mommy and daddy together. What happens when they know that mommy and daddy are together with other people, displaying a kind of intimacy that the children have only seen with Larry and myself? I'm not talking about intercourse, but kissing and hugging. An additional sexual relationship outside of the home simply can't be understood by our children yet. It's not in their world of perception.

GINA: I don't know, Barbara. Kids nowadays are so aware, and they're so far ahead of us when we were at the same age, that I really don't see why it's so bad if you tell them that you and Larry swing. I think it's better for the children to know. My own kids had questions. And they worried about it for a while. But they also know that Angelo and I love each other and love them dearly, and would never do anything to hurt them. As long as the love in our home is there all the time, I can't think of how it will shake their own world.

SUSAN: I haven't told my kids yet, although Earl and I have talked about it. I think we will, though. And I have a feeling it'll be soon.

262

INT.: *So that judgment seems to be quite individual.*

GINA: Yes, I think it is.

BARBABA: I would agree.

INT.: *What about other ethical judgments? For instance, about infidelity?*

GINA: Obviously, we view it differently.

SUSAN: I love my husband. I love him a lot. We both know we like extramarital relations . . . But not behind each other's backs.

GINA: There's a graduate student who works in our office. He makes no bones about it: he'd like very much to go to bed with me. I find him physically attractive, but I just won't do it.

INT.: *Why not?*

GINA: Because I feel I'd be cheating on my husband . . . It was my ethic as a single woman, and it's my ethic now: never cheat on a man.

BARBARA: If I met someone outside of the swinging scene who wants to have sex with me and I share that feeling with him, then I suggest he try swinging, either with his wife or, if he isn't married, with a girlfriend.

INT.: *Isn't swinging a form of cheating?*

GINA: No! The husband and wife are doing it together . . . out in the open. There's nothing deceitful or dishonest about it.

INT.: *If it's such a good thing, why are most swingers so secretive?*

SUSAN: I don't think most of them are and when they *are*, I think mainly it's out of concern that they may be criticized or ostracized in their community. Certainly, I'm concerned about that, more so for my children and relatives than for myself.

BARBARA: Larry and I do feel that we are distinctly part of a minority. Sometimes people are downright nasty when they discover that their friends or neighbors are doing things that threaten their own life-style. So why look for trouble? Why create problems?

VICKY: Well, it doesn't bother me! I tell people how I feel about sex and what I do.

GINA: You're not married, Vicky. You don't have children and the responsibilities that go with that . . . I've made it a point

263

from the very beginning to tell people that Angelo and I are nudists. They've come to accept nudism. But swinging is still too new. Maybe in time I'll tell them.

INT.: *Do you feel that sexual freedom for the woman affects her femininity?*

SUSAN: (Laughing) Just what do you mean by femininity?

INT.: *I'm talking about romanticism, innocence.*

BARBARA: That's ridiculous!

GINA: I think a woman becomes much more alluring, more real and more natural when she's enjoying her sexual capacities, giving as well as receiving.

26

JUDY:

What Makes a Woman a Good Lover

Swingers agree that there are ways to learn what makes a good lover. So we were looking for a man and a woman who could articulate clearly and honestly whatever it is that makes swingers feel competent and confident about sex—in terms applicable to nonswingers as well.

We talked about our search to the participants of our symposiums and the couples gave it some thought. Finally, Angelo and Gina came up with two names—Judy, who is married; and Phil, a doctor, who is a bachelor. Most of the couples either knew Judy and Phil or had heard good things about them. Not only about their sexual prowess but that they were also nice people. Kind people.

Judy is in her early thirties and the mother of three children. She was waiting for me (Paul Rubenstein) outside, at the wrought-iron front gate, as I pulled up to the curb. It had been a long drive because that morning I had driven several hundred miles to meet interviewees.

Judy was not a perfect 36-24-36. She said: "I could stand to take off a few pounds. I've tried this plan, that plan, Dr. this, Dr. that. I lose, but three days later it comes back."

She wore long, bell-bottom flairs, a pullover sweater with a V neck—and no bra. I couldn't help but notice, and I guess I blushed a little. Judy smiled. "It was my husband's idea," she said. And paused. "Actually it was mine, but I let him think it was his. I just wanted to see how it felt. Like a man who wants to grow a beard, I'm a woman who wanted to be unbra'd for a change." She shrugged.

She led me toward the front door. Their home was a comfortable ranch style, L-shaped house on a hill, overlooking the mountains.

I guess I was breathing rather hard, walking up.

"Let me give you a hand with your briefcase, at least," Judy said.

I laughed to myself. I must have looked like a Fuller Brush man or an encyclopedia salesman, carrying my attaché case in one hand and lugging a tape recorder in the other, and it was a long walk.

Judy explained that they bought the home because of all its land: three acres. The home itself had eight rooms, including the recreation room adjacent to the large, Early-American-style kitchen.

Things inside looked neat and relaxed. A few of the kids' toys were still out. The morning newspaper was still on a coffee table in the living room. No plastic covers on any of the chairs, either.

I must have been exhausted because when I sat down, I sank into the chair, sighing. Judy cocked her head sympathetically and smiled. "I bet I know what you'd like to do right now. How about a nice, cool shower to freshen up a bit. We have a guest room with a shower."

I felt a little uneasy. My wife is very understanding, but I imagined her saying to me later, "How did the interviews go today, darling?"

"Oh, fine. Everything was fine. I even took a shower at my last stop."

How could a shower affect my faithfulness?

"Where's the guest room?"

The room was done like a captain's cabin with navigational dials and gauges hung on the wood-paneled walls. There were charts, framed and hung. A steering wheel, still on its mount, was fastened to the middle of the floor. It had been taken from an old

Missouri steamer. Judy bought it as a surprise for her husband's thirty-fourth birthday at an auction.

Two bunk beds were in one corner, along with plenty of plaid-colored blankets and overstuffed pillows. But Judy showed me to a larger bathroom near the master bedroom. There were plenty of towels, even a razor and shaving cream. Next door was a sauna and a small tub with a whirlpool machine.

Judy smiled and quietly closed the door behind her.

As I walked gingerly into the shower I noticed a mural: five squares across and five squares down, each depicting a man and a woman, representing twenty-five different positions for intercourse. I nearly scalded myself with hot water before I was able to shake off my preoccupation with the pictures.

When I walked into the living room where Judy was waiting, I said "That's one of the most interesting bathrooms I've ever taken a shower in."

Judy laughed. "Did you memorize the wall?"

"Don't those people ever get tired?"

"Never." She smiled.

Judy helped me to plug in the tape recorder—her perfume reminded me of carnations—and the first question I asked was . . .

INTERVIEWER: *You know how to make a man feel welcome, don't you?*

JUDY: (Smiling) If you like him, show it. Making him feel comfortable is one way . . . That's far more rewarding than those silly games some women play with their men.

INT.: *Don't you ever play games?*

JUDY: Sometimes. If I do, then it's a game played with awareness. I'm aware that a man likes to feel appreciated. He likes to know that a woman cares for him, enough to make him feel special . . . When you walked in, you looked tired. No, "beat" is the word. This project is important to you. I'm sure you want to do the best job you can. So I took the initiative and suggested the shower. I knew you felt a little uneasy about it; that's why I didn't hover around. I may never see you again after this. But right now I'm with *you*. And that's the way I feel in any game I play—interviews, sex, whatever.

INT.: *Does your sexual honesty affect your nonswinging relationships?*

JUDY: I want to tell you about a nonswinging girlfriend of mine. We're the same age. She's beautiful. Absolutely. One day we got together for lunch and Lorraine poured her heart out about her sex life. For a moment I looked at her and thought she was crazy. Of all people, why is she telling this to *me*? Then she proceeds to confess that she's jealous of me. Me? Yes, because I was always having fun. I always seemed to look satisfied. I this, I that. She broke down and sobbed. I finally got it out of her why: she simply couldn't perform in bed. She went to a psychologist. She went on a vacation. She went to visit her mother. She bought a new car. She did everything to escape from trying to cope with her problem. I call this playing the game backward. Reversing gears. Starting with the hungup feeling you have, about sex or any other relationship, and letting that control your activity, as opposed to starting with a clean slate, knowing who you are and then being able to play the game of awareness with whomever you want.

INT.: *Are you denying the fact that many people can get help from professional sources?*

JUDY: Of course, they can—if they want to. But self-help, I feel, is still best. That means you have to dislike yourself enough to want to change your own image. I had to do that, or I would have lost my husband. I did and it started with sex. Now I *do* feel very confident when it comes to sex. But I'm no expert. I just work at it. Do you know what I mean?

INT.: *Not exactly.*

JUDY: Well, take Lorraine. She was beautiful and she thought that was all she had to be. The doors would open, especially bedroom doors. Well, they did, but what happened inside? Her fear of sharing, her tightness, turned men off. I think being beautiful is all right if you are, but it's really a matter of what a man considers beauty to be. Let me ask *you* something. Have you ever met a woman who turned you on just by the way she did something when she was close to you—like while you were dancing?

INT.: (After a pause) *Yes . . .*

JUDY: Was she attractive?

INT.: *She was average looking, but she was warm to be near. I remember when we danced, her body kind of melted into mine.*

JUDY: (After an exclamation) She moved with you, didn't she?

INT.: *Right.*

JUDY: (Nodding) *She* had a sexual awareness of her body and her personality and knew how to use both of them subtly. She had sexuousness.

INT.: *You may have coined a new word: "sexuousness."*

JUDY: I like that . . . Well, I, too, let the man feel he is leading. I'll let you in on a little secret. Most of the time *I* am. But the man doesn't know. Most women should do this. Either consciously or subconsciously. By the way, how was she holding you?

INT.: *Not tightly, but I was aware of it, aware of her.*

JUDY: Good. Dancing shouldn't be a wrestling match. I probably hold a man the same way she does: just enough pressure to let him know I'm with him, so he doesn't think he has a dish rag in his arms. I like resting my fingers just barely on his neck, almost the way you'd cup a baby's head if you were holding it in your arms. If I want to, I may rub his ears or his neck a little bit with my fingers. Even when the music stops, the closeness shouldn't.

INT.: *How do you manage that?*

JUDY: (Almost in a whisper) I place my hand very softly on his stomach and move away like this. (She gets up) Here, let me show you. (She does) This is a way of showing a man you enjoyed him. These are the subtleties I use, my friends use. And they work. (She pauses and smiles) By the way, I don't mean to sound curious, but I am. That girl you danced with, did you two end up in bed?

INT.: *No.*

JUDY: Really? What happened?

INT.: I'm married.

JUDY: (Laughing) Well, at least you're honest . . .

INT.: (Smiling) *Are your subtleties a conscious effort on your part?*

JUDY: Conscious, yes. Devious, no. And one thing that can turn a man off fast is coming on too strong. That can be very

269

threatening. He starts worrying, "How can I compete with that? She may expect too much of me." When sex becomes competitive, an issue of conquest, somebody is bound to lose. It's self-defeating. If I'm going to make love to a man, I must show him I want it as much as he does.

INT.: *Do you put yourself in a special frame of mind, a mood?*

JUDY: Yes, and it starts before the night begins. I can be shopping or attending a PTA meeting . . .

INT.: *PTA?*

JUDY: (Nodding) Anywhere you are. It's a matter of setting good thoughts in motion.

INT.: *Good thoughts?*

JUDY: How my lover will be in bed. What he'll do. What juicy little things I have in mind. I may want to try out something new on my husband. No grand design. No road map with little symbols or a blueprint or a clock on the wall to look up to and say, "Now it's time to turn over. Now it's time to put my mouth here and take it away from there. Time's up. Switch." That's what makes sex mechanical.

INT.: *How do you know what to do?*

JUDY: You don't. You play it by ear. Your goal is to please your man. Or men. (She laughs) The moment he or they step through that doorway.

INT.: *For the sake of simplicity, let's assume this is a one-to-one relationship.*

JUDY: Sure. Now, where was I?

INT.: *He had just put his foot through the doorway.*

JUDY: Yes . . . And if he likes a "hello" kiss, then give him one; one that says not only "hello" but that guarantees he'll stay a while. If he seems tired, I encourage him to rest. I might massage his back. I'd say to women: don't do it just for two minutes; stretch it out. Every man loves his back rubbed. Don't sit on the side of the couch—straddle him. Help him take his shirt off. Keep some massage liquid in the house. Squeeze a few drops in your hand and rub it around the palms of your hand before you spread it on his back. This way, you warm the liquid up a bit before it touches him. Then swirl your hands, starting from his shoulders and go all the way down to the lower part of his back—and down farther if you want.

270

INT.: *Suppose this is the first time you've been out with this man.*

JUDY: Make him feel that it *isn't*. That's the best advice I can give to any woman seeing a date for the first time. Listen to him. If he talks about what happened at the office, be sympathetic, be understanding. If he asks for advice, give it to him—if you think that what you say might be of help. If not, then tell him, "I honestly don't know." More important than anything else, I try to look and feel as fresh and vibrant as I can before I see my man. Sometimes that means taking a shower or a bath, depending on my mood. There are a lot of bath oils and bubble baths on the market. And scented douches, too. Nowadays it's almost like going into an ice cream parlor— you have such a choice of flavors and scents . . . And, of course, there are perfumes. I prefer the fresh-smelling scents and I make sure that they're nonallergenic. I remember I once tried a perfume which the ad said "would get the man." I got him all right! I never saw someone sneeze so hard and so much in my life. The poor guy's nose became so stuffed up and so swollen that he couldn't smell anything. Your hair is another touchy subject. And I mean just that. If you style it, let it be a come-on, not a haystack full of needles. By that I mean—no pins. I had a friend who once got her hair done in a bouffant, something like that. Anyway it was sticky. Matted down. Matted up. Twirled. Swirled. And she still had to keep it together with pins. The man she was with that night met a fate worse than death. She was giving him head. He got so excited that his penis slipped out of her mouth and got caught in her hair . . . I don't have to tell you the rest. That ended their night and sent him to the doctor . . . I stay away from any kind of jewelry that could cause problems, and I keep my hair long and loose.

INT.: *Why?*

JUDY: Some men like to be tickled with my hair ends.

INT.: *Really?*

JUDY: Really . . . Across their necks, underarms, all over the genital area. It's a soft, delicate sensation. (She gets up from her chair and rests on her knees and the palms of her hands.) You can either face him or turn yourself around with your head the other way. I lower my head like this, and then slowly whirl my hair around in a sweeping action. Depending on

271

which way I'm facing him, I can start that movement from his neck and then work myself all the way down. Again, it depends on the man. Some men like women with short hair. I know long hair does sometimes get in the way but, for me, anyway, it's worth it . . . (She gets up and returns to the chair.) Oh, also, *don't* wear things that change your form. You are what you are. Learn to make the most of it. Sexiness has almost nothing to do with bodily dimensions. It's really a feeling, a radiation between people. I know from talking to a number of thin women, for example, they have so many things working for them in bed that the men don't get a chance to think about squeezing what isn't there. (Judy then started showing me some of her "sexercises." She even got me into the act by demonstrating one that a man and woman can do together. First, you both sit down on the floor. Arch your legs upward, and place them as close as possible to the sides of the partner. Move as close together as possible, but do not use your hands to pull yourself toward each other. Then Judy clasped her hands behind my back, told me to clasp my hands behind her back. Then at the same time, we were supposed to raise ourselves up to a standing position. I realized why she was smiling so much after I tried. We didn't—quite—make it—off—the—ground and it took a few minutes to get our legs untangled.)

JUDY: Did you feel anything?

INT.: *Oh, yes.*

JUDY: Try it with your wife sometimes. You wind up in all kinds of positions. Oh gosh, there are lots of ways for a woman to become sexually activated once she gets to know her body. She can touch it. Feel it. It's a healthy kind of narcissism. Get to know your breasts. Your vaginal area. What's on top and what's inside. Learn to work the sexual muscles: the pelvic muscles, the anal muscles. Squeezing-in exercises are a great way. Lie on a bed, arch your legs into one of those yummy positions you use in intercourse and begin to contract anal muscles. With a little practice each day, you can learn how literally to hold a man's penis inside you by muscle contraction alone. No hands. No legs, Only contracting. A number of books on natural childbirth describe these muscle

272

contraction and expansion exercises, but you don't have to be pregnant to use them . . . Muscle contractions can really send a man into orbit. He doesn't have to move up or down or in and out. Once he's inside you, let your muscles take over. And if you really know the man well, you can make a little game out of it. See how long it takes him before he can get out. I can assure you he'll take his time finding out . . . Far Eastern women have been practicing this art for a long time. If it works for them, there's no reason why it can't work for Americans. I know. I do it all the time, especially after we've both reached a number of orgasms. My man's tired out now and wants some assistance from me. So I bring my muscles into play. It's easy with a little practice. Really. You've got to know your body. If you won't, don't expect your man to.

INT.: *How do you start this process of "getting to know yourself?"*

JUDY: For me, it was by masturbating. I do it a lot. It isn't any substitute for the joys of actual intercourse with a man, but it does keep my body at a high key of sexual awareness. And there is another thing I've discovered about places to masturbate. Forget the old-fashioned notion about doing it only in the bedroom or bathroom . . . Not long ago, I was with a group of close friends and we got on the subject of how many ordinary household gadgets can be brought into play. One of the girls told me that she just pulls down the shades in the kitchen, plugs in her blender, making sure the top is secure, turns it on, and lets it vibrate all over her. Or she puts it between her legs. Another woman told us she goes into the living room, puts a record on her stereo, one with a lot of drum beats, bass rhythm—hard rock. Then she straddles one of the speakers, being careful not to break it, and turns up the volume. From what she tells me, those vibrations are really something else. Another girl uses an electric toothbrush —either the vibrating, rotating tip, or she turns it the other way around, letting the handle do the vibrating. Obviously, you shouldn't put the tip inside you, but you can guide it around softly on the outside. Let's see . . . what are some of the other things? Oh yes, my own suggestion is an ordinary football. I found this especially useful when I first got involved in oral genital sex. Some women feel either embarrassed

273

or uncomfortable at first, about receiving a man down there. Sometimes it can be cumbersome. Sometimes you're physically uncomfortable if you don't know what to do with your legs. Should they be spread out or closed against the man's face? What if he prefers to lie on his side as he gives you head? His neck can become tired. He needs some support and you have to learn how to use your calves and thighs to help anchor him and to alleviate some of the pressure of his weight. One day, my husband and I were watching the Los Angeles Rams play the Green Bay Packers. And there was that convex, warm brown leather football. (At this point, the interviewer shakes his head, unable to control a rather incredulous look.) I know what you're thinking. But don't be so small-minded. I got one of my jars of skin cream out, spread some on the football, wrapped my legs around it, closed my eyes and let my imagination go to work for me, too. I rolled over to the side, brought my legs up, still pressed to the football, turned and twisted every way I could. It was very stimulating . . . Any woman with imagination and a little ingenuity can come up with even better ideas than these. Just look around your house. You'll be surprised and pleased with what you'll be able to discover and use . . . Oh yes, I almost forgot —my favorite.

INT.: *You mean there's something better than a football?*

JUDY: Don't be facetious. This one requires two balloons and an unpeeled banana.

INT.: (Starts laughing) *You've got to be kidding.*

JUDY: Stop putting me down. You don't even know what I'm talking about.

INT.: *I'm afraid to ask.*

JUDY: That's because you're inhibited . . . Where was I? Oh yes, first you moisten your lips and your tongue. Then slowly blow up one balloon. Squeeze it. Stop for a moment. Feel it. Rub your fingers lightly over it. Darn—I wish I had a balloon.

INT.: *That's okay. You're doing fine.*

JUDY: After it's blown up, rub your nose and lips against it, around, caress it. Put the balloon to the side of your face. Then repeat the same steps with the second balloon. Blow a little. Stop a little. Squeeze. Rub, Caress, After you've blown up the two balloons, place them next to each other. Try lying on your back with the balloons resting just over your face. Wiggle your nose between the crack. After a while (Judy's voice almost sounds as if she is telling a nursery rhyme) unpeel the banana. Slowly. Fit the banana in between the two balloons. Squeeze the balloons, keeping the banana in place. Hold them in front of you. Then, with your two hands squeezing the balloons and with the banana sticking out, start kissing the banana. Then let your tongue move up and down the stem, then start nibbling a little with your lips. Pinch it. Then slowly open your lips, breathe a little air out. You can pucker your lips if you want. Slip the banana in as far as you can. See if you can tickle the roof of your mouth with it. (She shrugs gleefully.) Then use your imagination.

INT.: *You're very inventive.*

JUDY: It's fun. You're being too serious about it. A man's sexual needs vary quite a bit. Often he can't, for one reason or another, quite articulate just what he wants done to him in bed. Either he's afraid to ask or his feelings are sealed off by a wall of inhibitions. Maybe it's because of the way he's been brought up. Or some bad sexual scenes. How many married men do you know who are afraid to ask their wives to do something different in bed out of fear that their wives will be insulted, will label it bad or dirty. Lots of wives have been programmed in that Victorian way. It's a problem both men and women have to work out together. Certainly among swinging women, and believe me it works for nonswinging women as well, once a woman discovers her femininity, she'll also know her sexuality. She'll learn ways to stretch out the experience. The first time she and her husband or boyfriend enjoy sex need only be the beginning of a wonderful evening, not the end of it.

INT.: *If you're speaking about people with Victorian hangups, isn't a change easier said than done?*

JUDY: It's never done if it isn't said and tried and tried again. Like with me. I don't think there's one man I've been to bed with who didn't like oral sex. I consider that request not only normal but one that *should* be an important and ful-filling part of any sexual encounter. Oral sex isn't dirty. It helps the man and the woman along. It varies sexual experiences. There is simply something about a woman's mouth caressing a man's penis that's a turn-on. For both of them. The warmth of it inside her mouth. The moisture of her tongue and lips. The visual appeal of the woman seeing the penis. Treating it as something special. Watching the man's erection build. Feeling it throb in her mouth. The same thing with a man. Watching the woman's vagina. Seeing the secretion. The smells, the natural odors. The first time I had oral sex with a man, it was kind of clumsy. I was unsure of myself. So? I learned by my mistakes. I learned not to start with the obvious. Build the experience. Give yourself and your man time to enjoy the mounting. For me, the first thing I like is to take a bath or shower together with my man. Then I help him towel off. To finish up, we go into the bedroom, I have him lie down and start blowing him dry. Just blowing. All over. And then I start caressing his toes.

INT.: *Did I hear you correctly?*

JUDY: (Nodding) One of my swinging friends, Lillian, introduced me to that delightful bit of foreplay. A lot of nerve endings are in your feet. You'd be surprised what a charge a man can get when you start sucking on his toes, one at a time, as if they're five different sized penises. It's part of the build-up and it's a lot of fun, too. Especially when you look at him while you're doing it. Let your eyes tell him what you're planning to do next. That's another important thing I've learned in sexual communication. Always remember that the person you're with is special. Keep kissing *him*, not an image out of some other time. And the best way to keep things in the here-and-now is to look at each other, to smile, to laugh, to touch . . . When you finally do move gently up to his penis, don't attack it as if it's an enemy. Treat it the way you should every other part of his body, with the same tender, loving care. You'll learn that certain areas of his penis are more excitable than others. Half the fun is discovering these places. Work with your tongue and lips until you find good spots. Ask him what's best. Give him the same stroke with your mouth that you'd like him to use with you when it's his turn. Think of his penis as a straw to suck on. Or a

276

lollipop. In fact, using a lollipop or an ice-cream cone to practice on works. I've done it. Believe me, it's helpful. Vary the strokes of your tongue. Rotate from the base of the penis to the top. Licking and kissing the head of the penis and then working down to his testicles can be incredible . . . And then there is that ring just below the head, where the stem begins. All you have to do is look at it and he'll start raising an erection. Well, that's not *all* you have to do, but you know what I mean.

INT.: *Yes.*

JUDY: I'm a nibbler, too. I don't bite him or hurt him, but I like to use my lips to pinch a little . . . Here's another thing. Sometimes, I'll dart my tongue in and out, going from the top of his penis down the stem to his testicles, and then circle around, under them, and then make a soft landing on the skin which leads to the anal opening. A woman friend of mine calls that "going into the hangar." And, if you want, depending on you, spend a little time with his rectum . . . Let your mind and your taste buds dictate what is most pleasing for your man . . . Then he'll be ready to give you a superscrumtious time. Help him along. Tell him what you like. Don't be a lazy bug in bed. Turn over when he wants you to. Lift things up and give him plenty of room. Guide his hands, his head, his penis, if you have to. Don't lie flat on your back. Try arching yourself upward, with only your shoulders on the pillow, so you can wrap your legs around his neck, smother him with your thighs and let his ears feel how hot you are. Another friend, Gladys, told me of a position which is guaranteed. First, help him to sustain a hardy erection. Then sit on top of him, help him insert his penis into you, and then turn 180 degrees one way and then reverse the circle. He'll do anything you ask, he'll be so turned on. He'll also be reaching areas inside you that will lead to so many delicious orgasms. But when you feel one coming, make sure you stop turning or you may spin round so fast you won't be able to stop! Always keep in mind that a woman can have as many orgasms as she wants. But don't let this sexual power go to your head. Because the *man* you're with is the one who'll give you these plateaus of sexual excitement. Whatever you do—*don't com-*

plain that he's not doing it right. Instead, tell him what you like. Tell him gently, with a smile. Don't dare use tired, old clichés like, "Oh, honey, not that . . ." or "You're hurting me" or put a grimace on your face which sets up all sorts of negative vibes. Those things aren't part of feminine sexuality. And while we're at it, forget about the children. So many of my nonswinging, frustrated women friends can't understand why their husbands go soft right after they hear something like, "Darling, was someone at the door? Do you thing it's the kids?" What these women are really saying is that they'd like someone to be at the door. Also, don't say to him, "Please, you're too heavy on me." Or, "Are you okay?" Because in the heat of passion he may get worried and say, "Yes, I'm okay. What's the matter? Are you all right? Is everything okay? Something's bothering you. I know it. Tell me. What is it?" Incidentally, hypochondriacs are dreadful bed partners. That's why they end up sleeping alone . . . Think of sex as something to be created, to be molded, and you'll always have as much as you want. And when you think you've finished with your man for the evening, stop a while. Then tell him softly, "Let's do it one more time." And the last time, let it be all his, not yours. (Judy pauses and reflects for a moment.) What more can I say? No, wait! There's one thing more. I've never refused my husband when he has wanted sex except when I've been very sick or have my period. Even with my period, I've given him oral sex. So it wasn't reciprocal that time—that didn't bother me. And I've never given up on him if he's had a difficult time raising an erection. I've always helped. I've always been patient. I've never mocked him or held him up to ridicule. Not often, anyway. I don't want to sound like a saint. I'm not. I've learned a lot because I've had a loving husband and a lot of swinging friends who've also cared.

27

PHIL:

What Makes a Man a Good Lover

We met Phil on a Sunday afternoon at the hospital in California, where he was a resident physician in his last year of training.

The description Judy had given us of him was almost picture perfect: broad shoulders, a pleasant smile. His black eyes stare quietly at you. His hair is long, shaped naturally: curly, dark brown, with traces of premature gray. He has dimples: "My mother told me those were the two places God touched me. Maybe she was right."

A warm, friendly voice puts anyone at ease on first meeting Phil. He said, "I don't know about this great lover image some of my friends have been telling you about—"

"Judy has told us a lot."

"I guess I'm going to have to say all the right things . . ."

He showed us around the hospital, and no matter where we walked, doctors, nurses, patients stopped him, said hello and seemed to want to take up all his time. No one was brushed off.

As we took the elevator up, Phil said, "You know, I've spent

279

the last ten years in college, medical school, interning, residency. I may not be forty until I practice. I wish they wouldn't use the word 'practice.' Somehow it sounds like I don't know what I'm doing yet. By this time I better . . ."

His little "hole in the wall" was on the fifth floor. "It's my hiding place, more often than not my sleeping place, kitchen, library—"

PHIL: Please excuse the way my office looks. I'm working on a paper I have to deliver before a group of colleagues and I've gotten so I leave all my research books open. There's just no time to file anything.

INTERVIEWER: *That's all right. It looks like my office. What's your paper about?*

PHIL: A disease that affects small children . . . sometimes I feel like refining someone else's technique rather than creating something on my own. I admire you. When you're still a resident and you see hundreds of patients a day, there isn't much time for innovations.

INT.: *But you think about them.*

PHIL: Constantly, but there are always people higher up, doctors who won't accept a new idea. I don't now whether they're scared or dumb (shrugging his shoulders).

INT.: *Would you ever consider giving up medicine?*

PHIL: Give it up? Never. I may be the guy who'll come up with the discovery of all discoveries.

INT.: *At least you haven't given up on women.*

PHIL: (Smiling) That's something else again. That's where you can learn to be an expert without risking a fatality, even if you fail at first.

INT.: *I wonder. Some men feel they die in bed all the time.*

PHIL: (Laughing) Yes, but there's always a way to revive them.

INT.: *Always?*

PHIL: Sure, if there's a friendship working when a man and a woman want their relationship to get somewhere.

INT.: *Do you find such friendships in swinging?*

PHIL: To a point, sure, although you obviously have more time to spend with a girl in a nonswinging relationship. I also date a lot of girls who aren't swingers.

INT.: *Is there a carry-over of your attitudes?*

PHIL: From swinging to nonswinging?

INT.: *Yes.*

PHILS Of course. A swinging woman loves to be pleasured. But a woman is a woman whether she swings or not. So whatever works in a swinging situation also works outside swinging. The man is still out to give the woman what she wants. And that takes a little soul-searching because now we're talking about the male ego.

INT.: *We can't deny that we have one.*

PHIL: Right, but we can admit that what we think is masculine sometimes turns out to boring for a woman and sometimes downright obnoxious. A girl doesn't like to be pawed. Nor does she like a man to act like a child who's desperate for attention. If he begs and he's lucky, he may get a crumb and no more. The same is true of men who complain, "Please, you've got to help me." Or, "I can't move!" Chances are a woman will tell him he'd better help himself if he's in that much trouble. And too many times a man resorts to telling a girl "I love you," and she responds with "and I love you too," and you both know damned well you don't mean it. So what's the point in saying? Because that's going to lead you to the bedroom? That's silly. But if you *show* the woman she means something to you—that's different. Now you're developing levels of meaning. A feeling of romance. A caring for the woman.

INT.: *With everyone you date?*

PHIL: Everyone of them, yes sir. She may like flowers or crazy things like a lollipop. It shows her that you care if you take time to buy her that silly gift, and it really isn't silly to her. I remember dating a girl once and noticing that a button on her coat sleeve was missing. One day when I was shopping for myself at a department store, I stopped at the notions department, found a matching button and bought it. The next time I saw her I gave it to her, gift wrapped in a huge box with a big red ribbon and bow on it. When she opened it she became teary-eyed. How did I remember? She said it was one of the "nicest, sweetest things" anyone had ever done. It showed her that I was paying enough attention to her. A lot of guys settle for buying the most convenient thing. That's really wasting money. It's not saying anything.

INT.: *But how do you find time for all this?*

PHIL: Loving takes time. It's not a quick exercise.

INT.: *Or the minute waltz?*

PHIL: (Laughing) No, not that either. You've got to plan. If I've gone out with a girl before, some of my free moments are spent thinking about what we've done before and what we'll be doing together the night we go out.

INT.: *And if you're taking out a girl for the first time?*

PHIL: Then I try to find out as much as I can before we see each other. I'm a listener. What she has to tell me over the phone can't be any less important than what I have to say. There's no room for ego in any romance. The first phone call can be important. If you know some of her friends, then you can ask them about her, as long as you don't do it in a sly way. You can even ask her mother about her. I have a friend who does that. He calls the girl when he knows she won't be home but her mother will. And he talks to the mother even though he's never met her before either. By the time he's finished talking to her he often knows the daughter's whole history— or just about.

INT.: *What if the father answers?*

PHIL: (Laughing) Then say you have the wrong number. The biggest problem is when a girl is sharing an apartment with a roommate. Then you have to make absolutely sure not to give the impression that you might like the rommate instead. No matter how tempting that might be . . . Getting back to your question about finding enough time: my hours are the kind that never really end. When it's impossible to plan for the week ahead, I won't. My free weekends mean a great deal to me, so I don't want to waste them by poor planning. I set a date for a time I know I can meet. For me, seven p.m. is ridiculous. I know I won't be ready. I don't want to feel panicked when I walk out my door. An extra hour or two with the girl isn't worth it because I know I'll look beat and

I'll probably act sour. So I do give myself plenty of time. And that includes time to exercise a little when I get home, to work off some nervous energy, then a shower, and then a nap. . . . Quickie naps are easy to learn. One thing I do is close my eyes and imagine I'm staring at a white sheet. I fall asleep almost immediately and an hour is all I need. (The phone rings. Phil is needed downstairs.) You're going to have to excuse me for a few minutes. One of the interns on my staff is celebrating his birthday, and some of the residents and nurses are throwing a surprise party for him in the X-Ray room. That's the only place we've got to do this. Why don't you take one of those naps I was telling you about? The cot over here looks hard but it usually does the trick.

(Two hours later Phil walks in, some strain around his eyes, his brow furrowed.)

INT.: *Was the party too much for you?*

PHIL: We had a minor emergency just before we blew out the candles. A young boy was brought in who just had the wind knocked out of him in a football game. Nothing serious, but we had to use the X-Ray room to take a few pictures. The boy got a piece of cake and then we sent him on his way. Now, where were we?

INT.: *Talking about women.*

PHIL: That's picking me up already.

INT.: *Do you have any special places you like to take a girl?*

PHIL: (Smiling) My place. No, it depends on the girl. If she's a music buff—classical, rock, whatever—I'll take her to a concert. There are small night clubs for rock music. Sometimes we spend a whole day together water skiing, boating. In the winter months, it's skiing. I've found some nice, out-of-the-way places to eat an hour's drive from the city where it's quiet, not too many people, candlelight, no one's in a hurry to give you your check and push you out the door.

INT.: *But what if you both want to stay in for an evening, either your place or hers?*

PHIL: Okay, then I say it. I don't try to be coy. I don't hint around. I never treat staying at my place as something naughty. It's an apartment with a kitchen and a living room, and a bathroom. Yes, and a bedroom. Am I going to pretend that my date has never seen a man's bedroom before? Let's not be ridiculous. One of the biggest mistakes a guy makes is being naïve or foolish enough to think a girl he's going to take out is still a virgin. Chances are she's not. Chances are you're not either. So you're both equals. If she leads you to believe that she's a virgin, it's probably because you've made her feel like a virgin by acting silly about spending the night together. And of course there are preliminaries leading up to making love—but not games that belong in high school or in college. Remember, she's a woman, not a toy or a machine or your possession either. Love her. Make her feel she's wanted. Let's be honest. A woman can perform far longer than a man any night. She has a natural gift for having one orgasm after the next for an extended period of time until she becomes exhausted. I see this regularly at swinging parties and a man can interpret this in a number of ways. It can scare him because he knows the woman is sexually superior in bed, or he can view this as a great opportunity really to turn the woman on. If he does, *she's* going to respond to him in a like way. But to have this happen means the man must work at it. He's willing to lock in and discover those things that excite her and the first few moments are the most important. Just hold her against your body and squeeze her. Take your time. Kiss her. I mean all over. Don't be afraid: her breasts, her vaginal area, her legs, her arms, her back, her neck, her ears—everywhere. Let your lips taste her skin. Let your face feel the warmth of her body. Let your nose smell her fragrance. Let her come a few times before you do. She secretes and your mouth tastes it. Then kiss her on her lips. Show her this is clean and enjoyable. And whenever she comes, don't let up. Keep her going with your fingers. Or your lips and tongue. Tell her how great she's doing. Talk to her . . . (Phil pauses and looks out the window.) Look at that building: it's going to be one of those plush high-rise apartments. Every day for the last six months I've watched them working on it, floor by floor. First the foundation, then the superstructure, then the bricks. Pretty soon people will be moving in and smelling the freshness of a newly completed building. There's life to that piece of concrete. If we can treat inanimate objects with care and a feeling of pride and accomplishment, think what we can do with people!

INT.: *I understand what you mean.*

PHIL: I'm not saying that everything I've told you is perfect or will work all the time. How can I best say it? I dig women. No, that's not good enough . . . every time I'm with a girl I'm learning something new. I'm convinced that by giving to her first, I'll nearly always be satisfied myself, too. There's no substitute for a beautiful sexual relationship. There's no substitute for a turned-on woman. Anything that blocks it from happening is all in the mind. If the man is willing to pleasure her first—and I can't help repeating myself—and if he's willing to take the time, he'll enjoy himself more and longer. He'll want to come more than once, too, and he won't get tired. That feeling vanishes when you experience what a girl can do for you once you've got her going. There's plenty of time to reach climaxes together. The feeling of being inside her, feeling her capture you, it's fantastic! But everything builds in stages until you are ready for the final moment. Then both of you can wrap yourselves up in each other and close your eyes, sink into that beautiful dream together, waking up, doing it again, swimming in her warmth, reaching the core of her life. Sex has a lot of lyricism to it, like a fine work of art; always with more meaning than the time before.

28

Summing Up

A five-part documentary that was aired in 1970 over a local television channel in Los Angeles reflects the prevailing attitude on swinging. Most of the experts, including a psychiatrist and a minister, echoed the familiar cliché that group sex is a "no-no," a threat to the family unit that has been the cornerstone of Western culture.

We share the concern over the fate of the family unit, but we believe that it is principally threatened by the high rate of unhappiness and divorce generated in Victorian prudishness and the Puritan ethic. We also agree with Edward M. Brecher who wrote about groupsex in his historical study, *The Sex Researchers*:

> At long last, scientists could directly observe how human beings behave after they have shed their inhibitions and taboos. I wish I could report that departments of psychiatry, psychology, human biology, anthropology, sociology, and other medical and social sciences in our leading universities and medical research centers

286

promptly realized the significance of this rich new research opportunity, and sent fully qualified multidisciplinary teams out into the field to make studies in depth, financed by generous grants from the National Institutes of Health and the major foundations. But that, alas, is not what happened . . .

Until it does happen we will remain trapped by our own mythology, especially by the myth celebrated in the charming witticism:

"Hoggamous, higgamous, men are polygamous.
Higgamous, hoggamous, women monogamous."

Libraries are bursting with literature on male sexual prowess while the poor woman is said not to be too interested in physical, animalistic sex. Supposedly, she is innately romantic, prefers to be monogamous, raising children, caring for the home, the animals, ever the mother, the mistress, the wife. The information that has come to light in our sampling (and which concurs with similar conclusions reached by Dr. Gilbert Bartell, the [James R.] Smiths, and other researchers) strongly indicates that this is not the case. Once the woman, often a late starter, gets into the swinging scene, she seems to participate more fully and adjust more rapidly than her man. Dr. Bartell and the Smiths conclude that multiorgasmic intercourse with many men in one prolonged sexual experience is a rare occurrence. In this respect, our research differs sharply with these studies. In our sampling, almost fifty-four percent of the single and married women have, on several occasions, experienced this euphoric multiorgasmic release with a sequence of several men for prolonged periods of time.

"What this does is destroy the 'stud' theory of sex," says Rabbi Allen Secher: "Roles become reversed, and it is now the female who becomes the center of attraction, the primary agent, the reigning queen."

Dr. Robert R. Bell, a noted sociologist and sex researcher at Temple University who studied married swingers in the Philadelphia area, offers an interesting parallel: "The wife frequently enters marriage with some inhibitions and anxieties as to her sexual participation," he writes. "But as the newness of (her) sexual availability wears off, her husband's interests often decrease. At the same time, the wife's inhibitions are often removed and her sexual interests become greater."[1]

And why not? In a monograph entitled "The Evolution and Nature of Female Sexuality in Relation to Psychoanalytic Theory," published in 1966 in the *Journal of the American Psychoanalytic Association*, Dr. Mary Jane Sherfey wrote:

> . . . *The human female is in fact not sexually inadequate or inferior* . . . The more orgasms a woman has, the stronger they become; the more orgasms she has, the more she *can* have. To all intents and purposes, *the human female is sexually insatiable in the presence of the highest degrees of sexual satiation* . . .

In support of this unorthodox view, Dr. Sherfey cited considerable scientific documentation, especially from the authoritative findings of Dr. William H. Masters and Virginia E. Johnson. In their book *Human Sexual Response*, these researchers reported:

> If a female who is capable of having regular orgasms is properly stimulated within a short period after her first climax, she will in most instances be capable of having a second, third, fourth, and even a fifth and sixth orgasm before she is fully satiated. As contrasted with the male's usual inability to have more than one orgasm in a short period, many females, especially when clitorally stimulated, can regularly have five or six full orgasms within a matter of minutes . . . mechanical stimulation, as with the electric vibrator, is less tiring and induces a woman to go on to long stimulative sessions of an hour or more during which she may have from 20 to 50 consecutive orgasms. She will stop only when totally exhausted. Such sessions [occur] as often as 2–3 times a week.

There are recorded cases of a dozen or more men having intercourse with one woman in rapid succession. Since the writers on this subject are invariably men, they interpret such events as prostitution or mass rape—the "gang bang" so familiar in porno-

---

[1] Bell, Robert R., "Swinging—The Sexual Exchange of Marriage Partners." Paper presented before the Society for the Study of Social Problems. Washington, D.C., August 1970.

graphic writing and adolescent folklore. Dr. Sherfey suggests an
alternative explanation:

> Throughout historic times and even today it could well
> be that women have indulged in the so-called "orgiastic
> parties," having relations with one man after another,
> for precisely the purpose of gratifying this capacity for
> numerous, successive orgasms with intravaginal coi-
> tion. . . . I urge the reexamination of the vague and
> controversial concepts of nymphomania and promis-
> cuity without frigidity . . . It could well be that the
> "oversexed" is actually exhibiting a normal sexuality—
> although, because of it, her integration into society may
> leave much to be desired . . .
>
> All relevant data from the 12000 B.C. to 8000 B.C.
> period indicate that precivilized woman enjoyed full
> sexual freedom and was often totally incapable of con-
> trolling her sexual drive. Therefore, I propose that one
> of the reasons for the long delay between the earliest
> development of agriculture (c. 12000 B.C.) and the rise
> of urban life and the beginning of recorded knowledge
> (c. 8000–5000 B.C.) was the ungovernable cyclic sexual
> drive of women. Not until these drives were gradually
> brought under control by rigidly enforced social codes
> could family life become the stabilizing and creative
> crucible from which modern civilized man could emerge.[2]

It would appear, then, that women's new awareness of their
sexual capacity is not a revolution but a reawakening. And our
sampling suggests that unlimited multiorgasmic response with an
uninterrupted series of males does not appear to jeopardize family
life and child care. Many of the women who participate in these
extended sexual encounters, with their husbands in attendance,
leave telephone numbers with their babysitters so that they can
be summoned in case of need, just as they would if they were
attending a bridge party or a movie.

Testimony in this regard comes from one of the participants
in the Smith's field study, which was quoted in Edward Brecher's
book, *The Sex Researchers*:

[2] *op. cit.*

289

I was one of the two males who on this occasion spent the night with R. in her home. R. is one of the two most multiorgasmic women I have ever met. Sexual activity occupied approximately the first four hours of the night, and was renewed in the morning. . . . While no one kept count, I would estimate that she experienced between 100 and 200 orgasms during the four-hour period. . . . About an hour and a half after the evening session began, R. suddenly catapulted herself out of bed, bolted out of the room, and disappeared without warning or explanation. The other male and I were utterly baffled . . . After a discreet interval, I followed her out of the room. To my amazement, I found her three bedrooms away, comforting her three-year-old son who had awakened and cried out in the night.

Neither the other male nor I had heard anything at all . . . But R. at the height of a period of sexual arousal as extreme as any I have ever seen in a woman, heard the cry three bedrooms away through two closed doors, and responded to it instantaneously in the orthodox maternal way.[3]

Another surprising revelation from our sampling is that men seem to accept this reality of feminine sexual stamina and adjust to it in a variety of ways. One of the most popular responses has been the encouragement of a considerable amount of oral sex with women pleasuring other women. Almost ninety-eight percent of the swingers we interviewed insisted they do not consider this activity to be lesbianism.

Surveys by the late Dr. Alfred C. Kinsey indicate that in the nonswinging world about four percent of the American males indulge in acts of homosexuality with other men, but no more than one percent of American females indulge in such acts with other females. In the swinging scene, according to our sampling, there is an astonishing reversal: there are hardly any male-to-male homesexual encounters, but a high ratio of women pleasuring women. Most of our women informants who indulge (and

[3] Brecher, Edward M., *The Sex Researchers*. Boston: Little, Brown & Co., 1969, p. 196.

over forty percent do) state that they find it stimulating and enjoyable and that their men encourage it.

Other researchers find female-with-female relationships even more common. In a study of fifty New York City swingers, most of them single, two anthropologists, George C. and Nena O'Neill, placed the incidence at sixty percent. They commented: "Apparently the lack of strong taboos concerning female homosexuality, the experimental nature of the group behavior, group acceptance and sanction and, perhaps most important of all, the active encouragement of the males, contribute to the high incidence of female-female contact."[4]

Many of the men indicate that viewing a woman having oral sex with another woman turns them on, and an almost equal number emphasize that it is also a great relief because it relieves them from having to keep up with the women. A vast majority of the men—almost sixty-five percent—appear not to be threatened at all by this kind of activity. Furthermore men seem to be very much in charge at swinging parties and, from what we can gather, in their homes and at work as well.

What are the implications, if any, for nonswinging men? Dr. Rollo May, in his book *Love and Will*, expresses deep concern about the response of nonswinging men to the liberated female's sexuality. Dr. May is worried because sex has become so available that the only way to preserve any inner center, he feels is to learn to have intercourse without commitment. Indeed, men appear to be withdrawing from sex. Other authorities also not that the male is becoming more impotent or at least reluctant to face up to a woman's new-found sexual awareness.

Theologian Harvey Cox explains this trend as man's repressed fear of involvement with women. Dr. May sees it as evidence that the new egalitarianism of the sexes threatens men. Drs. Benjamin Spock and Margaret Mead seem to concur with Dr. May, indicating that many men are, indeed, finding it more and more difficult to say yes.

Is the swinging man reacting with more maturity and making a healthier adjustment to these biological realities? Does group-

4 O'Neill, George C. and Nena, "Patterns in Group Sexual Activity." *Journal of Sex Research*, Vol. 6, no. 2, pp. 101–12. May 1970.

sex offer viable alternatives for other people, married or single? In light of the serious sexual distress that exists in America, academicians and scholars could well afford—as Edward Brecher observed—to examine the groupsex phenomenon with the care that they applied in the past to other less threatening sexual activities. Groupsex is going on and increasing whether society approves or not. Whether this is a sign of decline for Western civilization or, as some swingers feel, an attempt to readjust sexual realities to biological instincts, is open to debate. Certainly, a high percentage of the swinging people in our sampling seem to feel that for them this sexual reawakening has redeeming values.

Perhaps the most positive contribution of groupsex phenomenon to the nonswinging world is as a preview of things to come. Here men and women appear to be achieving startling changes in their sexual identities; the men seem to be able to handle women's richer sexual capacities and stronger needs without much visible threat to their masculinity. The women do not appear to destroy the family unit in the pursuit and the achievement of their needs. The men continue to maintain dominance as economic providers—be they the hunters of game as in the days of the caveman, or the providers of more precious skins, such as mink or sable.

There is also much evidence that the woman, awakening to her own sexuality, is not desirous of maligning her mate's masculinity. The opposite seems to be the case. When sex is enjoyed, it becomes less threatening, more casual, and more energy is left for a more fulfilling exploration of other life priorities.

Perhaps most significant of all is the consensus, from our sampling at least, that for the people who continue to swing over a long period of time, *sex becomes less and less important—the emphasis clearly turns from quantity to quality.*

And what about the children of swinging parents? Their newfound knowledge does not appear to encourage wild, orgiastic experiments. They seem, rather, to prefer one-to-one relationships with deep caring, without rigid structure, without a guarantee that it will always have to be this way. They appear to favor a modified form of monogamy, and a healthier, more balanced man/woman relationship, based on a more realistic understanding of sex.

The eminent psychoanalyst, Dr. Martin Grotjahn, comments on this development in his perceptive essay, "Laughter and Sex": "They (boys and girls) have already accepted and established a far-reaching equality between the sexes. Boys no longer wish to deny some so-called 'feminine' trends in themselves and girls do not want to deny some so-called 'masculine' trends in themselves, such as intelligence, courage, acceptance of sex, freedom of movement and expression, and the right to spontaneous response . . ."[5]

Perhaps these trends herald new modes of family living, uniting people in a much less restrictive family unit.

What will happen as sexual freedom increases even further? Dr. Bell, the Temple University sociologist, speculates:

Many in the younger generation are growing up with a philosophy that sex can be recreational and privately decided upon. It is logical to predict that, as they marry, more and more will have "swinging" experiences. In fact, it is striking that many "swingers" today are in their early twenties. . . . The swinging phenomenon appears inevitable in a society where moral norms are rapidly losing their strength and where values centered on individual moral decisions are becoming increasingly powerful, especially among the younger generation.[6]

Can people who have been inculcated with Puritan values shed their conditioning so dramatically in a short period of time? If they do, what are the emotional consequences? Is it possible to stretch the accordion of feeling, to equate love-sex and sex-sex without condemning all sex to pure hedonism? Much more research is needed to answer these and other questions that are being raised by groupsex practices. Meanwhile in the present social crisis, with so many people searching for identity, it seems to us that if we are to make this search a rewarding one, it would be valuable to accept some of the realities of groupsex—not necessarily as a desirable change but as a change that is, at the very least, real.

[5] Dr. Martin Grotjahn, "Laughter and Sex." From *A Celebration of Laughter* (Werner M. Mendel, Ed.) Los Angeles: Mara Books 1970.
[6] Robert R. Bell, *op. cit.*

Glossary

Bisexual: Men and women acting out sexual desires for persons of the opposite and same sex.

Breaking In: A term applied by experienced swingers when they invite couples who have never swung. "Breaking in" means providing encouragement and answers to questions of interested newcomers.

Closet Swingers: Men and women who go to extremes to hide the fact that they are swingers. In some smaller locales, closet swingers may turn out to be next-door neighbors.

Couples: Husbands and wives or single men and women living together.

Cunnilingus: Oral stimulation of the vaginal area.

Fellatio: Oral stimulation of the penis.

French Culture: Cunnilingus and fellatio.

Gay: Homosexual or lesbian.

Giving Head: Oral sexual activities performed by men or women.

Greek Culture: Anal intercourse.

Groupsex: Consenting adult couple engaging in sexual activities with more than one other person.

Hard-Core Swingers: Swingers who participate in groupsex encounters over extended periods, sometimes beginning on a Friday night and lasting until the following Monday morning. They may also participate in weekend orgies plus up to four nights of swinging during the week.

Head-Jockey: A man who prefers oral sex to straight intercourse.

Host and Hostess: The husband and wife or the unmarried couple whose house or apartment provides the setting for a swinging party.

Informal Swingers: Swinging marrieds and singles who engage in weekend swinging in small numbers and consider the establishing of friendships to be an important part of their groupsex behavior.

Intimate Parties: Informal groupsex get-togethers limited to no more than eight couples.

Kinky Sex: Abnormal sexual behavior considered taboo by a majority of swingers, such as sado-masochism, bondage and discipline, bestiality.

Modern Marrieds: Swinging married couples.

Multiple Orgasms: A series of orgasms experienced by a woman, one after another.

New Faces: The term applied by experienced swingers to new swingers.

Orgasm: Vaginal or penile climax.

Roman Culture: Orgies.

Straight People: The term applied by swingers to the nonswinging population, but not necessarily synonomous with "square" or prudish.

Swinging: See "Groupsex."

Swinging Clubs: Places where swingers meet, including certain bars, nightclubs or private establishments. Activities are usually restricted to making contacts for future swinging sessions.

Swinging Magazines: Magazines designed primarily for swingers. They feature classified advertisements of swingers seeking new sexual contacts as well as stories related to swinging.

Swinging Resorts: Rural retreats where swinging and sexual awareness are allowed to flourish. Some swinging resorts also provide sensitivity training. The majority encourage nudism. Some sponsor family weekends where husbands, wives and children spend two-day vacations. When children are present, swinging is either suspended or takes place in an area far removed from the youngsters. All these retreats charge a membership fee, usually on an annual basis.

Threesomes, Foursomes, Fivesomes, Sixsomes and Moresomes: The number of people performing sexual activities as a unit, although not all participants are necessarily active at the same time or as one group. For example, two or more men may pleasure one or more women simultaneously.

Wife-Swapping: Exchange of spouses between two married couples. Usually limited to pairing off in separate bedrooms with no other couples involved.

Women On Women: Swinging women who find pleasure in giving sexual stimulation to other women but do not consider this a lesbian or even bisexual act.

Bibliography

ABSE, D.W., NASH, E.M., JESSNER, N.L., eds., *Sexual Disorder and Marriage: In Marriage Counseling in Medical Practice.* Chapel Hill: University of North Carolina Press, 1964.

ACKERMAN, N.W., *The Psychodynamics of Family Life: Diagnosis and Treatment of Family Relationships.* New York: Basic Books, 1958.

ALEXANDER, F., "Psychoanalysis and Psychotherapy." *J. Amer. Psychoanal. Association,* 1954.

ARMSTRONG, E.B., "The Possibility of Sexual Happiness in Old Age." *Advances in Sex Research,* BEIGEL, H.G., ed. New York: Hoeber-Harper, 1963.

ATHANASIOU, R., SHAVER, P., AND TRAVIS, C., "Sex: Once Again a Function of Religion." *Psychology Today,* July 1970.

AVERY, P. AND E., *Some Notes on Wife Swapping, Sex in America* GRUNWALD, H., ed. New York: Bantam, 1964.

BABCHUK, N., AND BATES, A. "The Primary Relations of Middle Class Couples: A Study in Male Dominance." *American Sociological Review,* June 1963.

BAILEY, D.S., *The Mystery of Love and Marriage: A Study in the Theology of Sexual Relations.* New York: Harper, 1962.

297

BAILEY, D.S., *Sexual Relations in Christian Thought*. New York: Harper, 1959.

BAILEY, D.S., *Common Sense About Sexual Ethics: A Christian View*. New York: Macmillan, 1962.

BARKER, W.J., "Female Sexuality." *J. Amer. Psychoanal. Association*, 1968.

BARNETT, H.G., *Innovation: The Basis of Cultural Change*. New York: McGraw-Hill, 1953.

BARTELL, G.D., *Group Sex: A Scientist's Eyewitness Report on the American Way of Swinging*. New York: Peter H. Wyden, Inc., 1971.

BARTELL, G.D., "Group Sex Among the Mid-Americans." *J. Sex Research*, May 1970.

BARUCH, D.W., AND MILLER, H., *Sex in Marriage*. New York: Hoeber-Harper, 1962.

BASSETT, M., *A New Sex Ethics and Marriage Structure*. New York: Philosophical Library, 1961.

BEACH, F.A., *Hormones and Behavior*. New York: Harper, 1948.

BEAUVOIR, S.DE., *The Second Sex*. New York: Alfred A. Knopf, 1955.

BECKER, H., AND HILL, R., *Family, Marriage and Parenthood*. Boston: Heath, 1948.

BELL, R.R., *Pre-Marital Sex in a Changing Society*. New Jersey: Prentice-Hall, 1966.

BELL, R.R., "Swinging—The Sexual Exchange of Marriage Partners." Presented: Society for the Study of Social Problems, Washington, D. C., August 1970.

BENEDEK, T., "Benedek's discussion of M.J. Sherfey's paper on Female Sexuality." *J. Amer. Psychoanal. Association*, 1968.

BERGLER, E., "The Problem of Frigidity." *Psychiatric Quarterly*, 1944.

BERGLER, E., "Frigidity in the Female: Misconceptious and Facts." *Marriage Hygiene*, 1947.

BIRD, J.W., *The Freedom of Sexual Love*. New York: Doubleday, 1967.

BLISS, E.L., ed., *Roots of Behavior*. New York: Harper, 1962.

BOHM, E., "Jealousy." (A. Ellis and A. Abarbanel, Eds.), *Encyclopedia of Sexual Behavior,"* Vol. 1, New York: Hawthorne, 1969.

BONAPARTE, M., *Female Sexuality*. New York: International Universities Press, 1953.

BOSLEY, H.A., "You Shall Not Commit Adultery." *Readers Digest*, October 1967.

BRECHER, R., AND BRECHER, E., eds. *An Analysis of Human Sexual Response*. Boston: Little, Brown, 1966.

BRECHER, E.M., *A New Way to Help Troubled Marriages. Redbook,* March 1968.

BRECHER, E.M., *The Sex Researchers.* Boston: Little, Brown, 1969.

BREEDLOVE, W. AND J., *Swap Clubs.* Los Angeles: Sherbourne Press, 1964.

BROTHERS, J., *Woman.* New York: Doubleday, 1961.

BROWN, D.G., "Female Orgasm and Sexual Inadequacy." In *An Analysis of Human Sexual Response,* Brecher, E. and R., eds. Boston: Little, Brown, 1966.

BUCK, P.S., "Changing Relationships Between Men and Women." In *American Woman: The Changing Image,* Cassara, B., ed. Boston: Beacon Press, 1962.

CALDERONE, M.S., *Release from Sexual Tensions.* New York: Random House, 1960.

CALHOUN, ARTHUR W., *A Social History of the American Family.* Vol. 1. New York: Barnes & Noble, 1960.

CAPRIO, F.S., *The Sexually Adequate Male.* New York: Grune & Stratton, 1950.

CAPRIO, F.S., *The Sexually Adequate Female.* New York: Citadel Press, 1953.

CAPRIO, F.S., *Variation in Sexual Behavior.* New York: Grove Press, 1955.

CLARK, A., AND WALLIN, P., "Women's Sexual Responsiveness and The Duration and Quality of Their Marriages." *Amer. J. Sociol.,* September 1965.

CLARK, L., "Sexual Adjustment in Marriage." Abarbanel, A. and Ellis, A., eds. *Encyclopedia of Sexual Behavior.* New York: Hawthorne Books, 1961.

CLEAVER, E.C., *Soul On Ice.* New York: Dell, 1968.

COHEN, A.K., "The Study of Social Organization and Deviant Behavior." Merton, R.K., et al, eds. *Sociology Today.* New York: Basic Books, 1959.

COHEN, A.K., *Deviance and Control.* New Jersey: Prentice-Hall, 1966.

COLE, W.G., *Sex in Christianity and Psychoanalysis.* New York: Oxford University Press, 1955.

COLE, W.G., *Sex and Love in the Bible.* New York: Association Press, 1959.

COLTON, H., "Adults Need Sex Education Too." Los Angeles: *Family Forum,* 1970.

COMFORT, A., *Sex in Society.* New York: Citadel Press, 1966.

CUBER, J.F., AND HARROF., P.B., *Sex and the Significant Americans:*

299

A Study of Sexual Behavior Among the Affluent. Baltimore:
Penguin Books, 1965.

DAVIS, K., *Sexual Behavior.* Merton, R.K., and Nisbet, R.A., eds.
In *The Contemporary Social Problems.* New York: Harcourt,
Brace, & World, 1966.

DAVIS, M., *The Sexual Responsibility of Women.* New York: Dial
Press, 1956.

DAVIS, M., *Sexual Responsibility in Marriage.* New York: Dial Press,
1963.

DENFELD, D., AND GORDON, M., "The Sociology of Mate Swapping."
J. of Sex Research, May 1970.

DEUTSCH, H., *The Psychology of Women.* Vols. 1, 2. New York:
Grune & Stratton, 1945.

DEVEREUX, G., "The Significance of the External Female Genitalia
and of Female Orgasm for the Male." *J. Amer. Psychoanal. Association,* 1958.

DICKINSON, R.L., *Atlas of Human Sex Anatomy.* Baltimore: Williams
& Wilkins, 1949.

DICKINSON, R.L., AND BEAM, L., *A Thousand Marriages.* Baltimore:
Williams & Wilkins, 1931.

DICKINSON, R.L., AND BEAM, L., *The Single Woman.* Baltimore:
Williams & Wilkins, 1934.

ELLIS, A., *Wife Swapping.* Chicago: New Classics House, 1965.

ELLIS, A., ed., *Sex Life of the American Woman and the Kinsey Report.* New York: Greenberg, 1954.

ELLIS, A., *The Art and Science of Love.* New York: Lyle Stuart,
1960.

ELLIS, A., *The American Sexual Tragedy.* New York: Lyle Stuart,
1962.

ELLIS, A., *Sex Without Guilt.* New York: Lyle Stuart, 1966.

ERIKSON, K.T., *Wayward Puritans.* New York: John Wiley, 1966.

FARBER, B., *Family: Organization and Interaction.* San Francisco:
Chandler, 1964.

FENICHEL, O., "Problems of Psychoanalytic Technique." *Psychoanalytic Quarterly,* 1941.

FERGUSON, C., *The Male Attitude.* Boston: Little, Brown, 1966.

FORD, C.S., AND BEACH, F.A., *Patterns of Sexual Behavior.* New York:
Harper, 1951.

FREUD, S., *Three Essays on the Theory of Sexuality (1905).* Standard
Edition. London: Hogarth Press, 1953.

FREUD, S., "Three Contributions to the Theory of Sex." In *The Basic*

Writings of Sigmund Freud (Brill, A.A., ed., trans.). New York: Modern Library, 1938.

FREUD, S., *Sexuality and the Psychology of Love.* New York: Collier, 1963.

FRIEDAN, B., *The Feminine Mystique.* New York: W.W. Norton, 1963.

FROMM, E., *The Art of Loving.* New York: Harper, 1956.

FROMM, E., *Escape from Freedom.* New York: Avon, 1965.

GAGNON, J.H., "Sexuality and Sexual Learning in the Child." Psychiatry, 1965.

GAGNON, J.H., "Sexual Behavior Deviation: Social Aspects." *Annals of the American Academy of Political and Social Science,* March 1968.

GEBHARD, P.H., "Human Sex Behavior Research." In *Perspectives in Production and Sexual Behavior.* Diamond, M., ed. Bloomington: Indiana University Press, 1968.

GOODE, W.J., *World Revolution and Family Patterns.* New York: Free Press of Glencoe, 1963.

GOODE, W.J., *The Family.* New Jersey: Prentice-Hall, 1964.

GORDIS, R., *Sex and the Family in the Jewish Tradition.* New York: The Burning Bush Press, 1967.

GRIMM, R., *Love and Sexuality*, Mace, D.R., trans. New York: Association Press, 1964.

GROTJAHN, MARTIN, *Beyond Laughter.* New York: McGraw-Hill Book Company, Inc., 1957.

GROTJAHN, MARTIN, "Laughter and Sex." From *A Celebration of Laughter*, Mendel, Werner M., ed. Los Angeles: Mara Books, 1970.

GROTJAHN, M., "Problems and Techniques of Supervision." *Psychiatry*, 1955.

GROTJAHN, M., *Psychoanalysis and the Family Neurosis.* New York: Norton, 1960.

GRUNWALD, H.A., *Sex in America.* New York: Bantam, 1964.

HACKER, H.M., "The New Burdens of Masculinity." *Marriage and Family Living,* August 1957.

HEIMAN, M., "Female Sexuality: Introduction." *J. Amer. Psychoanal. Association,* July 1968.

HEIMAN, M., "Heiman's Discussion of Sherfey's Paper on Female Sexuality." *J. Amer. Psychoanal. Association,* 1968.

HEIMAN, M., "Sexual Response in Women: A Correlation of Physiological Findings With Psychoanalytic Concepts." *J. Amer. Psychoanal. Association,* 1963.

301

HILL, R., "The American Family of the Future." *J. of Marriage and the Family,* February 1964.

HOLLENDER, M.H., "Women's Fantasies During Sexual Intercourse." *Arch. Gen. Psych.,* 1963.

HOOKER, E., "Sexual Behavior: Homosexuality." *International Encyclopedia of the Social Sciences,* Vol. 14. Macmillan and the Free Press, 1968.

HORNEY, R., AND KELMAN, H. (ed.), *Feminine Psychology.* New York: W.W. Norton, 1967.

HUNT, M., *Her Infinite Variety: The American Woman as a Lover, Mate, and Rival.* New York: Harper, 1962.

ILFELD, F., AND LAUER, R., *Social Nudism in America.* New Haven: College and University Press, 1964.

"J", *The Sensuous Woman.* New York: Lyle Stuart, 1970.

KAPLAN, B., ed., *Studying Personality Cross-Culturally.* New York: Harper, 1961.

KARDINER, A., *Sex and Morality.* Indianapolis: Bobbs-Merrill, 1954.

KEIL, N., *The Universal Experience of Adolescence.* New York: International Universities Press, 1964; Boston: Beacon Press, paperback ed.

KESTENBERG, J.S., *On The Development of Maternal Feelings in Early Childhood.* Psychoanal. Stud. Child, 1956.

KESTENBERG, J.S., "Outside and Inside, Male and Female." *J. Amer. Psychoanal. Association,* July 1968.

KESTENBERG, J.S., "Vicissitudes of Female Sexuality." *J. Amer. Psychoanal. Association,* 1956.

KESTENBERG, J.S., "Kestenberg's Discussion of Sherfey's Paper on Female Sexuality." *J. Amer. Psychoanal. Association,* 1968.

KESTENBERG, J.S., "Phases of Adolescence, Part III, With Suggestions For a Correlation of Psychic and Hormonal Organizations. Part III Puberty Growth, Differentiation, and Consolidation." *J. Amer. Academy of Child Psychiatry,* Vol. 7, no. 1, January 1968.

KINSEY, A.C., POMEROY, W.B., AND MARTIN, C.E., *Sexual Behavior in the Human Male.* Philadelphia: W.B. Saunders, 1948.

KINSEY, A.C., POMEROY, W.B., MARTIN, C.E., AND GEBHARD, P.H., "Concepts of Normality and Abnormality in Sexual Behavior." In *Psychosexual Development in Health and Disease,* Hoch, P., and Zubin, J., eds. New York: Grune & Stratton, 1949.

KINSEY, A.C., POMEROY, W.B., MARTIN, C.E. AND GEBHARD, P.H., *Sexual Behavior in the Human Female.* Philadelphia: W.B. Saunders, 1953.

KIRKENDALL, L.A., "Sex Drive." In *The Encyclopedia of Sexual Be-*

havior. Ellis, A., and Abarbanel, A., eds. New York. Hawthorne, 1961.

KIRKENDALL, L.A., *Pre-Marital Intercourse in Interpersonal Relations.* New York: Julian Press, 1961.

KNIGHT, A., AND ALPERT, H., "The History of Sex, Part 17: The Stag Film." *Playboy,* November 1967.

KRONHAUSEN, P. AND E., *The Sexually Responsive Woman.* New York: Grove Press, 1964.

LEWISOHN, R., *A History of Sexual Customs.* New York: Harper, 1958.

LICHTENSTEIN, H., "Identity and Sexuality: A Study of Their Interrelationship in Man." *J. Amer. Psychoanal. Association,* 1961.

LIEF, H.I., AND REED, D.M., "Normal Psychosexual Functioning." In *Comprehensive Textbook of Psychiatry.* Freedman, A.M., and Kaplan, H.I., eds. Baltimore: Williams & Wilkins, 1967.

LINDSEY, B.B., AND EVANS, W., *The Companionate Marriage.* New York: Dell, 1965.

LOCKE, H.J., *Predicting Adjustment in Marriage.* New York: Holt, Rinehart & Winston, 1951.

Look magazine. Special Issue: "The American Family." January 26, 1971.

LUNDBERG, F., AND FARNHAM, M., *Modern Women: The Lost Sex.* New York: Harper, 1947.

"M", *The Sensuous Man.* New York: Lyle Stuart, 1971.

MARMOR, J., "Some Considerations Concerning Orgasm in the Female." *Psychosomatic Medicine,* 1964.

MCGARY, J.L., *Human Sexuality.* Princeton: Van Nostrand, 1967.

MASLOW, A., "Self-Esteem, Dominance Feeling, and Sexuality in Women." *J. Soc. Psychol.,* 1942.

MASLOW, A., *Motivation and Personality.* New York: Harper, 1954.

MASLOW, A., "Self-Actualizing People: A Study of Psychological Health." In *Self: Explorations in Personal Growth.* Moustakas, C.E., ed. New York: Harper, 1956.

MASTERS, W.H., AND JOHNSON, V., *Human Sexual Inadequacy.* Boston: Little, Brown, 1970.

MASTERS, W.H., "Sex Life of the Aging Female." In *Sex in Our Culture.* Groves, G., and Stone, A., eds. New York: Emerson Books, 1955.

MASTERS, W.H., AND JOHNSON, V.E., "Sexual Response. Part II. Anatomy and Physiology." In *Human Reproduction and Sexual Behavior,* Lloyd, C.W., ed. Philadelphia: Lea & Febiger, 1964.

MASTERS, W.H., AND JOHNSON, V.E., "The Sexual Response Cycles of the Human Male and Female: Comparative Anatomy and Physiology." In *Sex and Behavior*, Beach, F.A., ed. New York: John Wiley, 1965.

MASTERS, W.H., AND JOHNSON, V.E., "Counseling With Sexually Incompatible Marriage Partners." In *Counseling in Marital and Sexual Problems: A Physician's Handbook*, Klemer, R.H., ed. Baltimore: Williams & Wilkins, 1965.

MASTERS, W.H., AND JOHNSON, V.E., "The Sexual Response Cycle of the Human Female. I. Gross Anatomic Considerations. In *Sex Research: New Developments*, Money, J., ed. New York: Holt, Rinehart & Winston, 1965.

MASTERS, W.H., AND JOHNSON, V.E., *Human Sexual Response.* Boston: Little, Brown, 1966.

MASTERS, W.H., AND JOHNSON, V.E., "Human Sexual Inadequacy and Some Parameters of Therapy." In *Perspectives in Reproduction and Sexual Behavior*, Diamond, M., ed. Bloomington: Indiana University Press, 1968.

MEAD, B.T., "Sexual Problems." *Medical Times*, 1962.

MEAD, M., *Male and Female: A Study of the Sexes in a Changing World*. New York: Dell, 1949.

MENDEL, WERNER, M., *A Celebration of Laughter*. Los Angeles: Mara Books, Inc., 1970.

MENNIGER, K.A., "Impotence and Frigidity." *Bulletin Menninger Clinic*, 1937.

MERTON, R.K., "Social Problems and Sociological Theory." In *Contemporary Social Problems*, Merton, R.K., and Nisbet, R.A., New York: Harcourt, Brace & World, 1966.

MONEY, J., ed. *Sex Research: New Developments*. New York: Holt, Rinehart & Winston, 1965.

MONTAGU, A., *Sex, Man & Society*. New York: G.P. Putnam, 1969.

MOORE, B.E.. "Panel Report: Frigidity in Women." *J. Amer. Psychoanal. Association*, 1961.

MUSSEN, P.A., GONGER, J.J., and KAGAN, J., *Child Development and Personality*. 2nd Ed. New York: Harper, 1963.

O'NEILL, G.C., AND N., "Patterns in Group Sexual Activity." *J. Sex Research*, May 1970.

ORR, D.W., "Anthropological and Historical Notes on the Female Sexual Role." *J. Amer. Psychoanal. Association*, July 1968.

PACKARD, V., *The Sexual Wilderness: The Contemporary Upheaval in Male-Female Relationships*. New York: David McKay, 1968.

Playboy: From Playboy/The Sexual Revolution. Playboy Interview: Masters and Johnson. Chicago: Playboy Press, 1970.

POMEROY, W.B., *Boys and Sex.* New York: Delacorte Press, 1968.

POMEROY, W.B., *Girls and Sex.* New York: Delacorte Press, 1969.

RABIN, A., "Kibbutz Children—Research Findings to Date." From *Children,* September-October 1958.

RADO, S., "An Adaptational View of Sexual Behavior." In *Psychoanalysis of Behavior.* New York: Grune & Stratton, 1956.

RAINER, J. AND J., *Sexual Pleasure in Marriage.* New York: Julian Messner, 1959.

REIK, T., *Psychology of Sex Relations.* New York: Rinehart, 1945.

REISS, I.L., *The Social Context of Premarital Sexual Permissiveness.* New York: Holt, Rinehart & Winston, 1967.

REISS, I.L., *Pre-Marital Sexual Standards in America.* New York: Free Press of Glencoe, 1960.

REUBEN, D., *Everything You Always Wanted to Know About Sex—But Were Afraid to Ask.* New York: David McKay, 1969.

RHEINGOLD, J.C., *The Fear of Being a Woman: A Theory of Maternal Destructiveness.* New York: Grune & Stratton, 1964.

RUTLEDGE, A.L., "Sexual Failure in the Male." *Sexology* Magazine, 1963.

SCHIMEL, J.L., "The Psychopathology of Egalitarianism in Sexual Relations." *Psychiatry,* 1962.

SCHEEHY, G., STEINEM, G., AND HAMILL, P., "Love In The Age of Options." *New York* Magazine, February 16, 1970.

SHERFEY, M.J., "The Evolution and Nature of Female Sexuality in Relation to Psychoanalytic Theory." *J. Amer. Psychoanal. Association,* Vol. 14, January 1966.

SMITH, J. AND L.G., "Co-Marital Sex and the Sexual Freedom Movement." *J. of Sex Research,* Vol. 6, May 1970.

STOKES, W.R., *Married Love in Today's World.* New York: Citadel Press, 1962.

SYMONDS, C., "Pilot Study of the Peripheral Behavior of Sexual Mate Swappers." Unpublished Master's Thesis, University of California, Riverside, 1968.

THEOBOLD, R., *An Alternative Future for America.* (Edited by Kendall College) Chicago: Swallow Press, 1968.

THOMASON, B., "Marital Sexual Behavior and Total Marital Adjustment: A Research Report." In *Sexual Behavior in American Society,* Himelhoch, J., and Fava, S., eds. New York: W.W. Norton, 1950.

THOMPSON, C., *Psychoanalysis: Evolution and Development.* New York: Hermitage, 1950.

Time Magazine. "Repairing the Conjugal Bed," May 25, 1970.

Time Magazine. "The U.S. Family: 'Help!' The American Family: Future Uncertain," December 28, 1970.

VAN DE VELDE, T.H., *Sex Hostility in Marriage: Its Origin, Prevention, and Treatment,* Marr, H., trans. New York: Covici-Friede Publishers, 1931.

VAN DE VELDE, T.H., *Ideal Marriage: Its Physiology and Technique,* Browne, S., trans. New York: Random House, 1965.

VATSAYANA, *Kama Sutra,* Burton, R., and Arbuthnot, F.F., trans. London: Luxor Press, 1967.

VOLLNER, H., "Jealousy and Children." *Amer. J. of Ortho. Psychiatry,* 1946.

WALKER, K., AND FLETCHER, P., *Sex and Society.* Baltimore: Penguin, 1955.

WALLACE, A.F.G., *Culture and Personality.* New York: Random House, 1968.

WALLIN, P., "A Study of Orgasm as a Condition of Women's Enjoyment of Intercourse." *J. Soc. Psychol.* Vol. 51, 1960.

WARREN, J.T., *The Second Sexual Revolution.* New York: Lancer, 1966.

WATTS, A.W., *Nature, Man and Woman.* New York: Pantheon, 1958.

WRIGHT, H., *Sex and Society.* A New Code of Sexual Behavior. Seattle: University of Washington Press, 1969.